Advance Praise for *Why Men Earn More*:

"*Why Men Earn More* is **more than a book—it is news.** News not just about pay, but about the underlying relationship between the sexes. A brilliant, lucid and persuasive book that will change both personal lives and government policy."
—Nathaniel Branden, author, *Self-Esteem at Work*

"Filled with fascinating data and unique ideas, *Why Men Earn More* is written with an unflinching honesty that reflects a deep respect for women. It is a book every woman must read who wants to earn more, or to understand the psychology of the workplace or of men. Brilliant, compassionate and wise."
—Barbara Stanny, author, *Secrets of Six-Figure Women*:
Surprising Strategies to Up Your Earnings and Change Your Life
and *Prince Charming Isn't Coming: How Women Get
Smart About Money*

"Highly original, pioneering research offering both sexes creative opportunities for much wiser life and work choices."
—T George Harris, former editor of *Harvard Business Review*
and editor-in-chief of *Psychology Today*

"This is a fast-moving, entertaining and fact-filled book that explores clearly a great question of our time."
—Brian Tracy, author, *Time Power* and *TurboCoach*

"Once again Warren Farrell has shed light on an important and often misunderstood issue. This light empowers the reader to use the new insights to make better choices to create the life and results they truly desire."

—Jack Canfield, co-creator,
Chicken Soup for the Soul at Work
and *The Success Principles*

"I have five granddaughters; please send me five copies."
—Raymond M. Alden, former president,
United Telecom, precursor of Sprint

"As usual, Warren replaces mythology with cool, clear reasoning. On this journey into workplace/gender issues, he speaks his truths clearly and with compassion. Who wouldn't gain from this book?"
—Susan Deitz, syndicated columnist; author,
*Single File: How to Live Happily Forever After
With or Without Prince Charming*

"*Why Men Earn More* is nothing less than a guidebook for a woman to dramatically increase her salary by making smarter choices in the workplace, combined with an understanding of what trade-offs might be involved. Lying to women about why they are earning less is one of the most disempowering acts imaginable, and Warren Farrell, by bringing a good dose of truth into the conversation, has written a remarkably liberating book for both men and women."
—Ken Wilber, author, *A Brief History of Everything*

"Warren Farrell presents us with astonishing facts in this well-documented book! It will dispel so many hurtful myths that keep women stuck in the powerlessness of a victim mentality. An important read for both women and men alike."
—Susan Jeffers, Ph.D., author, *Feel the Fear and Do It
Anyway* and *Embracing Uncertainty*

"Every woman should read *Why Men Earn More* to get ideas as to how to raise her own pay. Every man should read it to ease his conscience. And both should read it to increase their respect and appreciation for each other."
—Jennifer Roback Morse, Ph.D., research fellow,
Hoover Institution, Stanford University

Why Men Earn More

The Startling Truth Behind the Pay Gap— and What Women Can Do About It

Warren Farrell, Ph.D.

◢AMACOM

American Management Association
New York • Atlanta • Brussels • Chicago • Mexico City • San Francisco
Shanghai • Tokyo • Toronto • Washington, D.C.

To Dad, Mom, Lee, Gail, Wayne, and Liz

Special discounts on bulk quantities of AMACOM books are available to corporations, professional associations, and other organizations. For details, contact Special Sales Department, AMACOM, a division of American Management Association, 1601 Broadway, New York, NY 10019. Tel.: 212-903-8316. Fax: 212-903-8083.
Web site: www. amacombooks.org

This publication is designed to provide accurate and authoritative information in regard to the subject matter covered. It is sold with the understanding that the publisher is not engaged in rendering legal, accounting, or other professional service. If legal advice or other expert assistance is required, the services of a competent professional person should be sought.

Library of Congress Cataloging-in-Publication Data

Farrell, Warren.
   Why men earn more : the startling truth behind the pay gap—and what women can do about it / Warren Farrell.
       p.   cm.
   Includes bibliographical references and index.
   ISBN 0-8144-7210-9
   1. Pay equity.   2. Women—Employment.   3. Equal pay for equal work.   I. Title.

HD6061.F37   2005
331.2'153—dc22

2004022209

CREDITS: Cartoon on p. 21: Non Sequitur © 1998 Wiley Miller. Dist. By Universal Press Syndicate. Reprinted with permission. All rights reserved. IBM ad on p. 26: Originally appeared in *Ms.* October, 1985, pp. 48–49. Cartoon on p. 26: Cathy © 1984 Cathy Guisewite. Reprinted with permission of Universal Press Syndicate. All rights reserved. Cartoon on p. 107: Cathy © 2004 Cathy Guisewite. Reprinted with permission of Universal Press Syndicate. All rights reserved. Cartoons on pp. 122 and 204: Reprinted with special permission of King Features Syndicate. Photo on p. 195: Reprinted with permission. Cartoon on p. 216: Reprinted with special permission of King Features Syndicate.

Printing number

10 9 8 7 6 5 4 3 2 1

Table of Contents

PART TWO
Women in the Workplace

Acknowledgments

Writing a book that questions prevailing beliefs is lonely. But such a book is not written in a vacuum—its spirit is seeded by parents, nourished by family, sustained by friends, and invested in by a publisher.

I witness the seeds of this book's spirit as I listen to my dad continue to question prevailing beliefs, even at 94 years of age. Or recall my mother or sister not just posing questions, but finding usable answers to prevailing beliefs about health.

The part of my family that nourishes me includes watching my dad and stepmom, Lee, support each other through cancer and heart attacks even as my dad prepares for the next ski season. Their commitment inspires mine toward my beloved wife, Liz Dowling, who in turn sustains me with both her giving and caring energy and the home we create with her teenaged daughters and my stepdaughters, Erin and Alex.

No friend has supported this book as much as Greg Dennis, who first enhanced my life by introducing me to Liz, and then enhanced the manuscript by editing it. The contributions of other friends include clippings and commentary supplied every day for years by Steve de Luca, which have provided many of this book's examples; Leslie Ellen Ray volunteered the author's photograph; and excellent editorial suggestions were received by Marty Nemko, Steve Collins, Jennifer Roback-Morse, and Dianne Sukiennik.

Why Men Earn More would be a much weaker book without the two summers spent by Harvard graduate student Yonatan Gelblum gathering raw data and scholarly journals, doing calculations, and discussing interpretations. One summer he literally moved in with us!

Joyce McHugh supplied thoughtful comments in her role as assistant even in the manuscript's primitive stages about a decade ago, and more recently as a friend. Other assistants who added significantly at points during this decade are Eric Pihl, Erika Packard, Sonya Rowe, Michael Estes, Daryoush Parsia, Wenessa Clarke, Sophia Ruiz, and Alexa Deere.

I was seldom more inspired writing this book than after I completed each interview with the successful women whose names you will soon discover, more than a couple of whom were referred by Marshall Goldsmith.

I am especially happy with the extraordinary efforts of the team guided and given the freedom to be creative by Hank Kennedy, president of AMACOM: from my delightful editor, Ellen Kadin, who shepherded this book through every stage, to my developmental editor, Charles Levine. Both editors immersed themselves in every sentence and footnote—to the great benefit of the book. Andy Ambraziejus led us toward the finish line with the skill of a horse whisperer jockey at the Kentucky Derby. I am grateful to the proactive and competent publicity work of Irene Majuk, Mary Lengle, and Heidi Krupp; the contributions of Jenny Wesselmann and Cathleen Ouderkirk; and the support of Jacquie Flynn, Brett Wean, and Rosemary Carlough. This team, along with AMACOM's decision to invite me to speak with their sales staff, their sales staff's enthusiasm in presenting to distributors, and AMACOM making *Why Men Earn More* their lead book in the 2004–2005 catalog, has led to one happy author.

Foreword

It should come as no surprise that the lesson learned at an early age is that females deal with people better. The myth still prevails that men are rational, women intuitive. Anatomy creates destiny: Women are well qualified for the jobs that pay less.

As an employment lawyer for the past 30 years, I represent corporate executives who bring discrimination cases. For the men, the issue is most often the failure of corporate America to accommodate their requests for flextime, parental leave, and other issues related to full participation in family life.

For the women, the issue is most often the glass ceiling (or stone wall) they encounter when they seek to be promoted. They have great performance reviews and terrific statistics; they work all the time; yet less qualified men are making the leap to the higher-paying positions.

One reason is that women are frequently not on the correct track at the company. The top vice presidents are usually selected from manufacturing, sales, or operations, and the talented women are working in human resources. It is a challenge to convince them, and the CEO, that women "want to play with the big boys." Women start out in human resources because they are "good with people." I suggest they are good with people as they move over to fast-track sales or operations.

To further understand equality issues, read this latest work by Warren Farrell. He reviews and explicates the facts and figures—and more important, the history and philosophy—of the varying expectations and gender role stereotypes that influence everything we do, including at the workplace. He shows that men are not involved in a nefarious plot to keep the female wage down there at $32,000, but rather, as Betty Friedan taught us four decades ago, they are fellow victims in the sex role wars. It was Friedan's brilliant realization that feminism was best not only for women, but also for children and men, that made NOW the success it has been.

As Farrell described in an earlier book, *Father and Child Reunion*, the recent generation of men is more involved than were their fathers. Children of both genders can then observe sex roles that are broad, not stifling. The task is to convince mothers, fathers, judges, and employers, that parental leave, parental time off, and flextime are as much the right and the responsibility of male parents as of female parents.

We discussed this vision of the future at NOW meetings as early as 1967. Since 1974, feminist attorneys have been urging *parental leave* (rather than *maternity leave*) for clients. We know that what brings equality to women also brings equality to men.

Am I hopeful? A pithy answer to why men earn more is that men were there, in the workplace, earlier. They know more about navigating, because they were there first. As we are convincing all who will listen that women can do what men do, we must continue to press for the concept that men can do what women do.

As Warren Farrell expresses it: "Our daughters deserve that." So do our sons.

We have been working for gender equality for a short time, given the span of human history. Eventually, it will even up. I am very hopeful.

Karen DeCrow
President, National Organization for Women, 1974–1977

A Personal Introduction: How the Journey Began

My motivations for writing this book include the very personal. My wife and I are raising two teenage girls, Erin and Alex. They are technically her daughters and my stepdaughters, but, as their challenges become ours, they've gotten into my blood and certainly into my heart. At ages 17 and 18, they are entering the world of work. It is my hope this book helps them balance the need for money with the need for fulfillment—to not just make a better living, but to create a better life.

My journey with Alex and Erin started some 11 years ago. My tennis partner, Greg, told me his business partner, Liz, had just completed a divorce. He didn't want to play cupid, but . . .

Liz is now my wife. At the time, Liz was living in a small rental fixer-upper with Alex and Erin. She was juggling her child-raising with starting her own little public relations business from a desk in her home. Working until midnight was not unusual. While some of Liz's women friends shopped 'til they dropped, Liz juggled 'til she plopped.

Over the course of the next four years, Liz's dedication had gradually paid off. Her business was booming, she was winning clients away from major PR firms . . . she had become a success story. That was the upside. On the downside, her blood pressure was dangerously high, and more than once she fell asleep beginning a sentence about work and woke up ending the sentence.

Now, as we sat down to "enjoy" breakfast, her eyes were already commuting to work. . . .

"What's happening, honey?"

"Oh, sorry. . . . It's Kristin. She's been seeing how well I've been doing and wants more money."

"You've already increased her salary a few times, haven't you?"

"Yes, but her landlord has a buyer for the home she's living in. She's been given her 30-days' notice, and equivalent rentals are about twice the price. She's panicking."

"It's getting close to Christmas. Do you have another raise planned for her?"

"Yes, and, as you know, I've given her an incentive for each media placement, so she makes about twice what she used to make."

"Is there any way for her to make more money than she does?"

"Yes, she could work more hours a week, but I had to persuade her to work more than 30 hours a week because she wants to have time for her son, time to exercise, do yoga, meditate, and, as she puts it, 'keep her life in balance.' "

"Sounds like she's making a healthy choice, but if you're paying people to do yoga, let me know, I'll quit my writing and work for you! Seriously, what's her perspective on this?"

"Well, she feels her contributions are every bit as valuable as mine; that as a result of her keeping her life in balance, she brings the very best of herself to work; that she's very bright, works hard, has good ideas, a positive attitude, and that, therefore, there shouldn't be such a big gap between her pay and mine."

"How do you feel about that?"

"Well, on the one hand, I think everything she says about herself is true. She's very good, she's gotten much better, she has good ideas, her confidence is building, and I'd sure hate to lose her. Besides, I don't want her to have to live in a place she can't stand. I know that she doesn't have much money, that she doesn't get child support, and that her parents don't help her. I consider her a friend—I hate it when she hurts."

"But something is still bugging you. When I looked up from the melon, your eyes had some hurt in them, almost like you didn't feel you were being understood."

"Yeah, that's true. I guess I feel that I have basically the same qualities I had three years ago as a worker, but the reason I'm making more now is because I took the risk of working for myself without any security or benefits, without any guarantee of an income, or without any guarantee that my 50- to 60-hour weeks would have any payoff."

"Also, you're much more a prisoner of your work," I added. "When there's a deadline, you work the extra hours no matter what you feel like doing. And for the first few years we knew each other, you were generating business everywhere you went. A party, even a Thanksgiving dinner at friends', was potential business. And even now, you rarely check out psychologically."

"True. And you know how I hate traveling, especially going to Minneapolis in midweek, having to rearrange everything with the kids, leave them, return jet-lag tired, and then deal with the results of their neglect, including my guilt."

"What I hear you saying, then, is that you want Kristin to know that there's something more to getting paid and more than being a good worker who follows directions well, or even who executes creatively. Is your dilemma that you want to let her know the money you make comes because of sacrifices she's not willing to make because she's choosing to live a healthier, more-balanced life, yet you're afraid to tell her that because you don't want her to feel you don't value her contribution?"

"Yes. And there's one other thing. I want her to appreciate that one thing I do with my extra money is to create a security blanket for her—so that if we suddenly lose two of our clients and therefore most of our income, I can draw on savings and not have to let her go."

"So you need a security blanket to give her a security blanket? And you want her to know there are no free security blankets?"

"Right," Liz laughed.

"I hope you also want enough money so you can begin to cut back on work, meditate, do yoga, and balance your life the way Kristin balances hers (hint, hint!)."

Shortly after this discussion with Liz, I was talking with some people after giving a workshop. A tall, silver-haired man hovered in the background. His patience was studied, as if calculating the costs and benefits of waiting. When the group dissipated, he stepped forward cautiously.

"Listen, I've got a problem. In the past few years, our company has been sued for sex discrimination three times."

"You must be pretty involved with your company."

"How's that?"

"You use 'I' and 'our company' interchangeably."

"Oh," he laughed, a tad embarrassed. "Well, the lawsuits are wreaking havoc on the company and me. They're forcing us to put into legal fees what we should be putting into products and into raises for people who are working, not suing.

"And the other thing is, it's destroying morale. And not just among the men. After I gave a speech about the importance of hiring women, even one of my women managers said, 'I like what you're saying about hiring women, but the higher up in the company I go, the more afraid I am to hire a woman for the company, 'cause all three of the lawsuits we've received have been from women. I'm afraid of being the one to hire somebody who will sue the company.'"

I switched to a softer, more of a tell-me-in-confidence tone. "Tell me . . . off the record. Are you paying women less than men?"

He thought long enough to make me assume the answer was "yes." Then he surprised me. "No. In reality, no. But sometimes it appears that we do."

"How so?"

"Sometimes we promote a woman faster than we would a man, giving her the same job title as a man, but she has fewer years with the company."

"So you pay her less?"

"Yes. We'd pay anyone with fewer years less, but we move good women more quickly than we move good men, which is really discrimination against men, but it ends up looking like discrimination against women when we pay them less for less seniority."

"Sort of ironic, huh?"

"Yeah. In fact, it's worse than that. Last year, I asked who was willing to relocate to bail out two of our problem branches: one in Alaska and one in Kansas. No one volunteered. So I offered extra pay. Then one of the men says, 'Maybe. I'll have to check with my family.' I ask if there are any women who want to go. The reaction is, 'Are you kidding? To Alaska?' Well, one single woman did perk up a bit, about there being a lot of single guys there, but then she unperked when she recalled that the cost of living is higher there. So I offered even more money to go to Alaska."

I laugh, "I can see it coming. She still says no; he says yes, but now you've got a guy with the same job title earning much more than his female colleague."

"Yep, nail on the head. It looks like clear-cut discrimination, until you realize that anyone with more years would have higher pay, and that anyone who took that job in Alaska would have higher pay."

"So you want to be fair—even acknowledged for bending over backwards to promote women—but when you're fair, the men get higher pay because they make more sacrifices, and even when you promote women faster, the men sometimes still get higher pay because they have more years of experience."

"Yes," he said. "And the HR people look at the raw data of men getting more pay and falsely conclude women are subject to discrimination. I feel this myself until I look more closely! Anyway, the result of no one understanding this is a lawsuit, an aggrieved woman, damaged morale, and even women managers who are afraid to hire women! Why don't you write a book called What to Do before You Sue?"

I smile. From the impatience in the night custodian's eyes, our delay isn't giving him higher pay. As we're "swept away," I promise to give his situation some thought. That conversation was about 15 years ago. I've given it some thought.

Both Liz and the male executive valued their female employees. Both credited their competence, intelligence, and effectiveness. Both respected their decisions to keep their work lives and personal lives in balance—in fact, Liz was envious of it. Yet both Liz and the corporate executive were grasping for a way to tell their women employees what they could do to receive higher pay.

Helping women achieve higher pay is a core goal of this book. But an even more important goal is helping women understand the trade-offs involved—and to determine whether higher pay is worth the trade-offs. In my research, I have uncovered 25 differences in the way women and men behave in the workplace. Taken together, **these 25 differences lead to men receiving higher pay and women having better lives,** or at least more balanced lives.

Why Men Earn More gives both sexes many ways to both earn

more money and have even better lives. For example, both men and women pharmacists average higher pay than doctors, and have both more control over their schedules and less pressure in their lives.

Similarly, most hazardous professions, such as the armed services, give a woman the same pay and benefits as a man for only a fraction of the hazards risked by her male counterpart. On the surface, this appears to benefit only women. But as men see what women do to remain safer in hazardous professions, it creates options for a man's safety as well.

Most of the 25 ways to higher pay offer every family new options.[1] For example, we discover in the chapter "Doing Time" that a person working 45 hours per week averages 44% more income than someone working 40 hours per week. That's 44% more income for 13% more time. The implications? If you're a woman interested in both a high-powered career and healthy children, you'll discover when it benefits the children for Dad to be a full-time dad while you are the family's "financial womb."

In brief, *Why Men Earn More* helps men, women, and families discover which choices lead to higher pay, which lead to better lives, and which lead to both higher pay and better lives. Part Two looks at the contributions women are making to the workplace, how women's and men's differences can best support each other, and the continuing role of discrimination against women. The most original portion of Part Two is the chapters on the best-kept secrets about discrimination in favor of women (and against men), and the "Genetic Celebrity Pay Gap."

Woven throughout *Why Men Earn More* is also this hard news: *The Startling Truth Behind the Pay Gap* (the remainder of the subtitle, in case you've forgotten!). As we look closely at men's and women's workplace decisions, it helps us see the gap in pay in a different light—why, for example, the gap in pay is much greater between never-married versus married men (62 cents to the dollar) than it is between women and men (80 cents to the dollar).[2]

The startling truth behind the pay gap was discovered in the same journey that uncovered the 25 ways to bridge the gap. It's a journey that started one day when I was on the board of directors of the National Organization for Women (NOW) in New York City . . .

What Happened on the Way to the Gap in Pay?

During the three years I spent on the board of the National Organization for Women in New York City (from 1970 to 1973), my colleagues and I often wore a "59¢" pin to call attention to what we considered to be the pay gap at the time between women and men, and thus to recruit new members to fight against the embedded societal discrimination against women we felt this gap symbolized.

I accepted the 59 cents statistic so blindly that it took me two years to ask myself this question: **"If an employer had to pay a man one dollar for the same work a woman could do for 59 cents, why would anyone hire a man?"**

Put another way, "Wouldn't any employer who hired men for $1.00 soon be put out of business by someone who hired only women for 59 cents?" Few consumers would pay a dollar for the same product they could buy for 59 cents. In fact, the employer would go out of business hiring men at any level if women could do the same work for 59 cents.[3]

I opened my mind to the possibility that, while business executives certainly did discriminate, business has a built-in system of punishments for those who do. The punishment is called "losing money." The penalty for repeat offenders is called "going out of business."

When I spoke with CEOs of large companies or even small business owners like Liz and her partner Greg (a.k.a. Cupid), they all felt they hired women in the hopes they would become successful. A successful woman is called a return on their investment. Their women employees' successes helped their own dreams come true. As one CEO told me, "My female employees' success is my job tenure." Men executives do not see themselves as threatened by successful women, but as being in search of successful women. They feel threatened by unsuccessful women. Ditto for men.

This made a few other things make sense. I knew Jewish and Japanese workers were subjected to discrimination, yet they earned more to the dollar than Caucasians.[4] Employers who survived seemed to conquer prejudice for profit. Well, maybe not conquer prejudice, but at least put prejudice about an employee's background in one corner, if the employee put profits in their corner. Those who allowed their prejudice to rule them paid, in effect, "the discrimination tax."

Well, at least that was the possibility to which I was trying to open my mind. However, if paying women unequally didn't make economic sense, what then explained the gap in pay, which—while decreasing from 59 cents to the dollar to its 2004 gap of 80 cents to the dollar—was still huge?[5] If men are being paid even a penny more than women for the same work, then that suggests an attitude of disrespect for women; and it would undermine the economy by paying men more for work that could be done for less. It certainly doesn't make sense to outsource if we aren't effectively using our own resources.

My colleagues in NOW had an answer: "Male bosses are blinded to the positive contributions women make to productivity so they don't realize they are hurting themselves." That was among the kinder answers. And it was a possibility. So I checked it out. What happened when women didn't have men bosses, or even women bosses who might be "adapting the rules of the patriarchy in order to become a boss"? I sought to discover what women who were their own bosses earned in comparison to men who were their own bosses.

I was at first shocked by the findings. When there was no boss to "hold women back," women who owned their own businesses netted, at the time (1970s through 1990s) between 29% and 35% of what men netted; today, women who own their own businesses net only 49% of their male counterparts' net earnings.[6] This made me ask, "**If male bosses are to blame, why are women netting less than men when they are their own bosses?**"

As I explored businesses owned by women versus men, I discovered that nowhere is the male-female difference in priorities clearer than in the difference between these businesses. I discovered how running one's own business tended either to follow what I came to call "the high-pay formula" in exchange for lifestyle trade-offs or to follow "the low-pay formula" in exchange for lifestyle payoffs.

I began to scout around. I discovered that the U.S. Bureau of Labor Statistics found as long ago as the early 1980s that companies paid men and women equal money when their titles were the same, their responsibilities the same, and their responsibilities were of equal size—for example, both regional buyers for Nordstrom's, not one a local and one a regional buyer.[7] But although this was published in the official publication of the U.S. Bureau of Labor Statistics, I had never read of the study in a single paper or heard of it in the media. To my surprise (in those years of my innocence), once gender equality was found, the gender comparison was not only ignored but never updated.

At the same time, a longitudinal survey found that when women and men started at the same time as engineers; worked in the same settings; with equal professional experience, training, family status, and absences; the women engineers received the same pay.[8] It too was neither publicized nor updated. I began to see that we study what gets funded, and what gets funded depends a lot on what's likely to be found.

"Is it possible," I asked, "that men and women have different work goals and treat work differently?" If so, would pinpointing these differences be more helpful to women than assuming men bosses didn't value them?

As I freed my mind to consider alternative perspectives, I vaguely recalled a statistic in Jessie Bernard's *The Future of Marriage,* one of the favorite books among the early feminists.[9] I had half-registered this statistic at the time, but probably discarded it from full consideration because it created too much cognitive dissonance with my assumptions of discrimination against women. I pulled it off the shelf for a second read.

Yes, there it was, in an appendix: Census Bureau figures show that even during the 1950s (which Alex studies in ancient history class!) there was less than a 2% pay gap between never-married women and men; and never-married white women between 45 and 54 earned 106% of what their never-married white male counterparts made.[10]

I thought about these findings in relation to affirmative action.

Obviously, this was prior to affirmative action. In fact, this pay equality had occurred even prior to the Equal Pay Act of 1963. And prior to the current feminist movement.

I was sure this example, though, was an aberration. I began checking. Of course, almost all studies showed men earned more, but as soon as I checked on unmarried women who had worked every year since leaving school, I found that they too earned slightly more than their male counterparts, and that was as far back as 1966.[11] And in 1969, even as I was claiming discrimination against women professors while doing my doctorate at NYU, **nationwide, women professors who had never been married and never published earned 145% the income of their counterpart male colleagues.**[12] This is not a typo: The women earned 45% more than the men.

A feminist colleague objected with a half-smile, "Never-married women are winners; never-married men are losers." She clarified, "I mean never-married men are not as educated, are less likely to work hard. That's why women don't marry them. Never-married women can take care of themselves, so they don't get married."

I checked. Sure enough, never-married women were more educated.[13] So I checked the latest data among educated men and women working full-time. The results? **The men earn only 85% of what the women earn;** put another way, the women earn 117% of what the men earn, as Figure 1 on the next page illustrates.[14]

If all these findings had a common theme, it was "It's marriage and children, stupid!" Well, with each chapter of *Why Men Earn More*, we'll see more about how our paycheck is influenced by our family role, and how we can use this information to tailor our family's need for our income versus our time.

When I shared these findings with some of my colleagues, the response (aside from having fewer colleagues!) from a couple of them was, "Not so fast . . . it's really the part-time women who are subject to discrimination." Maybe. So I checked that out, too.

To get 2004 data on part-time workers required obtaining unpublished Census Bureau data. I was surprised at what it revealed: **A part-time working woman makes $1.10 for every dollar made by her male counterpart.**[15] (Men and women who work part-time both average 20 hours a week.[16])

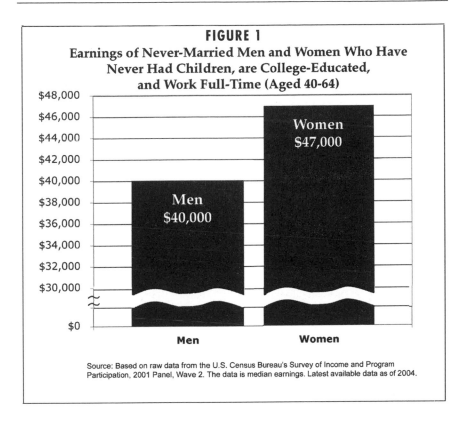

FIGURE 1

Earnings of Never-Married Men and Women Who Have Never Had Children, are College-Educated, and Work Full-Time (Aged 40-64)

Source: Based on raw data from the U.S. Census Bureau's Survey of Income and Program Participation, 2001 Panel, Wave 2. The data is median earnings. Latest available data as of 2004.

How the Focus on Discrimination Against Women Is Now Undermining Women

Now I was more curious: If gender discrimination might not account for the pay gap between the genders, what might?

As soon as I asked "what might?" I took my binoculars away from "the assumption of discrimination" and freed myself to discover whether a man earns more because on average his contribution to raising children is more likely to be raising money, which makes him more willing to work late whenever needed, more willing to take on less-desirable assignments, travel more, or move to out-of-the-way locations. Thus began the discovery of 25 reasons men do earn more, as well as the search for what each way was worth, the trade-offs, and which trade-offs the women I interviewed felt were worth it. The search led to *Why Men Earn More*.

The years of research for *Why Men Earn More* made it increasingly clear that the focus on discrimination against women—a focus that used to help women—is now undermining women. Here's an example. When we focus our binoculars on discrimination among doctors, we see only that young, men physicians earn 41% more than young, women physicians.[17] We will see how this focus leads a woman to miss opportunities to increase her earnings by about 54%. Our focus on discrimination against women during the past 30 years has blinded us to such opportunities for women.

Still, I couldn't help but wonder how this could be true if virtually everyone saw it differently. Had I used the 59 cent statistic as proof of discrimination, just as everyone in the fourteenth century used a glance at the horizon as "proof" the world is flat?

Making full use of the 25 ways to higher pay—the same 25 reasons men earn more—requires absorbing some basic principles, the first of which is "the pay paradox."

Power and Pay: The Pay Paradox

I define power as "control over one's life." If we become a doctor to get the approval of our parents, we don't have power, we have a problem: dependency on approval. Private power that does not include public power is meaningful; public power that does not include private power is meaningless. Let's apply this to earning power . . .

We often hear that men earn more money and therefore have more power. No. Pay is not about power. **Pay is about giving up power to get the power of pay.** Sometimes it is about giving up what we'd love to do to gain the power to send our daughter to a better doctor.

Here's the pay paradox that *Why Men Earn More* explains: Men earn more money, therefore men have more power; and men earn more money, therefore men have less power (earning more money as an obligation, not an option). The opposite is true for women: Women earn less money, therefore women have less power; and women earn less money, therefore women have more power (the option to raise children, or to not take a hazardous job). Obviously, these are only general patterns—the same general patterns that produce the gap in pay.

This paradox is woven into each of the 25 ways to increase pay. That is, each way can either increase or decrease power. If we become successful at work and a failure at home, we have both increased and decreased our power. We're in *Who's Who In The World* and *Who's Nobody At Home.*

Low pay makes us feel powerless unless we are conscious of the decisions we make to accept low pay as a trade-off for the slice of life we receive in return. Then we feel powerful and happy, rather than angry because we feel like victims of discrimination.

If earning money feels like power, then each of the 25 ways to high pay will feel empowering—they're all ways to earn more money. But if having control over your life feels like power, then picking and choosing the nuggets that can be tailored to this stage of your life and your personality will be empowering.

How to Do What You Love and Still Be in Demand

In *Why Men Earn More* we discover the economic price women pay when they seek the careers that are more fulfilling, flexible, and safe.

Here's the rub. Careers that are fulfilling, flexible, and safe usually pay less. The pay can be lower because more people compete to be fulfilled, causing the supply to exceed the demand for the most fulfilling jobs. Thus a librarian with a master's degree may be upset if she is paid little more than a garbage collector who dropped out of high school. But a person wishing to be a librarian finds herself competing with more people, since more people enjoy reading books than smelling garbage. Similarly, an art historian with a Ph.D. earns less on the unemployment line than a coal miner in the mine, because more people prefer discussing art than contracting black lung disease. The librarian and art historian work in safe environments; the garbage collector and coal miner do not. Since fewer people have a death wish, we pay people more to do work they aren't dying to do: I call this "the death professions bonus."

How can we do what we love and still be in demand? The first principle involves checking out whether someone else's idea of bad news is your idea of good news.

For most people, the bad news is that the highway to high pay is often a toll road.[18] The good news is that what is a toll to one person may be nirvana to another. I would personally hate to work as a cook in a hot kitchen; for Erin, my stepdaughter, that's nirvana. Similarly, most people would prefer to work indoors rather than being in what I call an "exposure profession"—exposed to the wind, rain, sleet, and snow. However, many park rangers choose their jobs exactly because they will be outdoors.

So one use of *Why Men Earn More* is to select opportunities that suit you and create higher pay because they don't appeal to others.

A second, more fascinating principle (in my opinion) is seeking what you love to do in a field that represents what you hate to do. Let's say you'd love to be a therapist, but in your town they're a dime a dozen. You'll be able to discover where therapists are most needed by looking at professions whose training is the opposite of that of a therapist—for example, the military.

You check out the military because you know that to prepare people to die, the military cannot afford to attract large numbers of people who will be in touch with their feelings and sensitivities. The motto of military training is, "When the going gets tough, the tough get going," not "When the going gets tough, the tough call a therapist." So the military cannot easily draw people from within its ranks to become therapists.

Exactly for this reason, there's a vacuum in the military to fulfill the needs a therapist fulfills. Military men and women have families, and families need feelings. Stuffing feelings leads to volcanoes of anger, lost tempers, and domestic violence. Thus the need for a therapist. The lost tempers and domestic violence may lead to divorces, causing mother-dominated families, and sensitive sons who feel rejected by a military dad who sees his son's sensitivity as failure. Thus the need for a therapist.

Once this principle—seeking what you love to do in a field that represents what you hate—is understood, it can be used by virtually any personality and tailored to your stage of life. Thus, if you've been a soldier rather than a therapist, but are tired, wounded, or no longer wish to risk your life, look to the places where you despise what is going on. For example, you may be repulsed by the school system, or by families where you feel the parents have put their needs first and gotten divorced. You are saddened by underachieving children brought up without good discipline, boundaries, or values.

Your military background, then, gives you an understanding of the need for boundary enforcement, discipline, and the value of pushing a child to do what she or he didn't think could be done and was too lazy to try. You hate the words "self-esteem," even as you sense that a child who is encouraged in this way ultimately feels a lot better about her- or himself.

By using the principle of seeking what you love to do in a field that represents what you hate, you'll discover how much you are needed, for example, to run a school system or to teach in a boarding school, often with children who have discipline problems. These children, often from parents unable to enforce boundaries with consequences, are in need of leaders who learned to always have a consequence for any violated boundary.

The Challenge of *Why Men Earn More*

Every complex problem has a simple solution—usually the wrong one. Whether it's one-week diets or men-on-white-horses, the promise of magic keeps hope alive, but its failure to work leaves a vacuum we are seduced to fill by the Sirens of simple solutions. And, because simple solutions sell well, the Sirens are well employed.

Why Men Earn More challenges those Sirens. Despite this book's being a source of female empowerment, if you are a woman, you might nevertheless feel torn between logical agreement and emotional resistance. Why? **It seems like a simpler solution to blame men for the pay gap than to engineer your own bridge to higher pay.**

Here's the underlying seduction: We all feel we should be valued more than we are: 83% of workers feel they perform above average![19] Which means that when a peer gets promoted first, almost 83% of the workers are left feeling like victims. But when a man rationalizes, "I lost the promotion because I'm not as good an ass-kisser as Harvey," his rationalizing is apparent. Men who claim to be victims are called whiners and thought of by both sexes as wimps and losers. This keeps their mouths shut.

Currently, women at least feel validated when they see headlines about the multi-million-dollar class action lawsuits filed by the working-class women of Wal-Mart (1.5 million) or the millionaire women of Wall Street. This makes women feel, "It's obvious, discrimination is everywhere; men just don't know how to value women." When a woman sees women win money by filing lawsuits, she sees a different reality for herself than a man sees for himself: She often sees victim status creating victim power; he sees victim status creating loser status.

If *Why Men Earn More* requires putting the assumption of victim status "on hold," it also encourages the reader to take it "off hold" if, after checking out the 25 ways, the conclusion is "discrimination." At that point the case for being a victim is viable.

This book may also come easier to men than women because of boys' early associations with hard data. Lots of boys spend much of their youth debating which team and which player would do best. The game and players varied, but one thing was constant: The excitement of sports gave many boys an incentive to learn how statistics could be used to assess productivity. First, statistics are used to define productivity ("Which is better—a 0.333 batting average or a 3.33 ERA?"); second, a boy learned dozens of statistics are needed to get a fair assessment of which teams and players were the most productive; and third, perhaps most important, statistics don't explain everything and everything is debatable. Fortunately, he didn't know he was learning any of this!

As this boy grows up and he hears that men and women with the same number of years of experience at the same job should earn the same money, this doesn't compute for him. For him, only productivity is marketable for pay. He "gets it" that productivity may not be limited to competence and goal scoring alone, but also to abilities like drawing paying crowds.

If men know these things, why don't they speak up? In part, because these differences are so subtly woven into the web of male socialization and biology that most men just weave their web almost as a spider would, not being able to clearly explain how or why—it's just what they do. But understanding the emotional connection for men between money and love is crucial for any woman who cares to understand men.

Historically, just as women raised children, men raised money. The fathers' Catch-22 was to receive the love of his family by being away from the love of his family (killing animals, killing the enemy, or making a killing on Wall Street). Paradoxically, he was earning money to earn love. Or even more paradoxically, making a killing to love.

The traditional male journey—the journey to become a hero—involves slaying dragons, or overcoming obstacles. Each of these "ways to higher pay" can be seen as an obstacle which must be overcome, a dragon which must be slain, to achieve higher pay.

A hero had to risk death. He learned the ultimate irony: that he would be more valued the more he was willing to make himself disposable. Today, this translates into men's greater willingness to take on hazardous jobs to provide for their families, resulting in a workplace in which 92% of deaths occur to men.[20]

This is why these ways to higher pay are ingrained in male socialization. But they are also ingrained in male genes. When a woman finds herself more attracted to the officer and gentleman than to the private and gentleman, or more attracted to the surgeon than the man nurse, and thus marries and has children with the officer or surgeon, she is also making a choice of the genes her children will become.

But *Why Men Earn More* offers 25 workplace decisions to take us beyond both our genes and socialization. These are not personality characteristics. The highly paid women I interviewed for this book had many personality characteristics, such as drive and toughness, and many skills, such as negotiating, that characterize highly paid people of both sexes. This book has focused less on these personality characteristics, which are hard to change, than on 25 behaviors that almost anyone can change (without 20 years of therapy or a lobotomy!).

Today, a middle- or upper-middle-class boy often gets socialized differently than in the past. He is encouraged to "do what you love"—to be a human being rather than just a human doing. This is wonderful, but if he marries and his wife wants the option of spending more time with the children, she may feel she can exercise that option only if he accelerates his breadwinning capability. Now he's in conflict between loving what he does and what he does to receive love.

This book will help men with this "fulfillment socialization" to choose among these trade-offs as much as it will help women.

The Uses of *Why Men Earn More* for Employers (and the Government)

This is a book to empower employees, help companies both profit and prevent lawsuits, and help the government prevent discrimination. Here's why that's a precarious combination . . .

Employers today often feel they are in a precarious relationship with their female employees. Will the woman submitting her employment file today be filing a lawsuit tomorrow? Why, when the gap in male and female pay is at its least, are women's lawsuits against companies the most?

When there was no societal permission for divorce, husbands supplied women's income for a lifetime, so a woman who wanted more income had only her husband to turn to. When divorces became more common, women were thrust into a world as foreign to them as diapers at 3 a.m. were to their husbands. The government eased the transition for women, in some ways becoming a substitute husband.

Instead of men and unions fighting the company, women and the government began fighting the company. Men had always known how to fight men, but they had learned to protect women. Now they found themselves protecting women from sex discrimination and sexual harassment, while protecting themselves from lawsuits for sex discrimination and sexual harassment. They were valuing women as a resource, but weighing that value against demands for maternity leaves and flextime; for telecommuting, job sharing, health and dental insurance; for child care facilities and insurance for the child care. At the same time, they knew that if they supplied these options for women, they would have to supply them for men, and soon outsourcing would look very appealing.

Within the company, the human resources division was often organizing both personnel data and programs to combat everything from sex discrimination to sexual harassment, often making it easier for the government to organize its case on behalf of the woman against the company. That's why, taken together, employers today often feel in a precarious relationship with their women employees.

When the government is telling companies to both promote women more quickly and pay women more, companies often feel in a Catch-22: forced to pay women with less experience the same as men with more experience. When the company is sued, and realizes that any policies that benefit women will never compete with the headlines created by a lunch meeting at Hooters or by the attitudes of some genuinely sexist bosses, it faces reality: Its day in court is not worth months of humiliating headlines that undermine company morale, engender gossip, give incentives for other employees to consider their experiences from a perspective of being victimized, and scare future employees from even applying.

How does a company respond? The way anyone in that situation would—by becoming passive-aggressive: paying lip-service to the value of women, but being protective and cautious about women, thereby undermining women's real value.

The goal of *Why Men Earn More* is to give women ways of earning more rather than suing more, and to give companies ways of teaching women how to earn more, and give the government ways of separating real discrimination from its appearance, thus erasing the need for companies to become passive-aggressive and undermine women.

Why Men Earn More gives human resource divisions of larger companies 25 guidelines for measuring contributions, thus shifting the HR paradigm from a starting assumption of "the higher the percentage of men, the greater the discrimination against women," to a starting point of 25 measurements of who is making which contributions to the company that the company needs when the company needs it. Thus the employer who promotes according to performance, rather than the employer who tries to equalize the sexes' pay without regard to performance, is seen as the true champion of equality.

Is this idealistic? Quite the opposite. A company creates opportunities for women because women create opportunities for the company. A company that thinks like that is a company that you want to be with, because they'll be profitable enough to keep promoting you. Any company that just thinks about "opportunities for women" is being patronizing: You can detect a company's genuine respect for women when they follow three steps in sequence:

1. They are enthusiastic about opportunities created by women;
2. They are sensitive to how they need to respond to take advantage of those opportunities; and
3. They are fascinated to see how those adaptations can also be used by men.

These 25 measurements will ultimately enable the HR divisions to be more viable. We tend to do what we measure. I believe these 25 ways will assist the transition of HR divisions from being advocates for women and minorities to mediators focusing equally on the rights of everyone. The outcome? More communication, less litigation. Communication creates understanding, and understanding creates compassion. Few people sue someone for whom they feel compassion. And few people sue someone from whom they feel compassion.

The Methods, the Data, and the Caveats

One caveat to what you read in this book: I always try to get the most up-to-date data—often raw and unpublished data. But some data collection is funded more than others. At this moment in history, gender-specific research is funded with a consciousness toward making women in the workplace look equally engaged but unequally paid. So studies that might predictably uncover why women earn less—by choosing more fulfilling, flexible, and people-oriented fields; working fewer hours; working in less hazardous jobs; working indoors; moving less quickly to less desirable locations; taking more family leaves; working in subfields that pay less—are studies less often funded or updated. Perhaps, as this book makes clear the degree to which women and men, employers and employees, and the government and corporations are all in the same boat, it will help make it politically possible to fund the updating of such research. Perhaps.

A second caveat: Since this book is about pay, "work" refers to paid work, not work at home: Women's and men's contributions inside the home are a topic in another book of mine (*Women Can't Hear What Men Don't Say*).

Third caveat: There are many ways to increase pay that *Why Men Earn More* does not address. I do not address the power of body language, attitudes, dress, and good communication skills. I ignore many methods of motivation, like reading biographies, and many ways of enhancing strategic thinking, such as playing chess. Not only are these ways already covered by other books, but most are skills men need to learn from women at least as much as vice versa—therefore they don't tell us why *men* earn more.

The society that teaches a woman to focus on ways of earning rather than discrimination is a society that pioneers the next evolutionary transition for women: a transition from female "victim power" to female earning power. Female victim power is engendered by new affirmative action–type programs and enforcements that expand as her victim status expands. Women's earning power is expanded by tailoring to her personal life the 25 ways to higher pay. May this book allow many Alexes and Erins to have more earning power.

Warren Farrell
Carlsbad, California
www.warrenfarrell.com

PART ONE

Twenty-Five Ways to Increase Your Pay

CHAPTER 1

Field of Dreams

Choose the Right Field and
Higher Pay Will Come

What We Miss When We Follow Our Bliss

Self-help books for those who believe "You can have it all" often advise, "Follow your bliss, and money will follow."[1]

Following one's bliss is generally a great idea for personal health, but rarely as good for one's financial health. Or, at least, not good enough to finance a family. Virtually every artist, writer, and actor is following a dream; but "starving artist" is a cliché for a reason. Therefore, in a family with children, if one parent is following bliss, the partner of the blissful often needs to accumulate the money. The partner of the blissful is usually the one less filled with bliss and more filled with stress. Example? I write this as the blissful; it can be more stressful on my wife.

With the collapse of the stock markets, many who considered "You can have it all" their birthright were either converting to Prozac or morphing into another reality: "trade-offs." The reality of trade-offs is more like, "When you follow your bliss, it's money you'll miss." Unless . . .

Act One of the trade-offs play is the balancing act. For example, if you are entering your field of dreams (your personal Champs

Élysées, if you will), and you wish to survive financially, expect to balance the bliss with the stress of working longer hours, living in a city (or commuting to one so your family can smell the suburban roses), or spending weekends traveling on business while the rest of your family snaps pictures of their Kodak moments.

You soon realize that the "best" artists are not necessarily the best at art, but the artists most willing to make trade-offs to be the best blend of artist and businessperson. I recall admiring an artist's gorgeous paintings and asking him what the hardest part of being an artist was. His answer? "Translating the admiring comments of people like you into dollars. When I can't do that, I frame the prints of artists who can. Both are stressful." Blissful, meet stressful.

The good news is that one person's sacrifice—such as working longer than 9 to 5—is another's source of meaning: creating challenge, income, identity, social exchanges, and the basis for respect in a professional community.

The challenge of creating a high-pay formula is finding what you enjoy that generates high pay. It is discovering what's a plus to you that might be a trade-off to someone else.

If you have already chosen a field, are the first three chapters relevant to you? Absolutely. In six ways:

First, you'll see how you can double your earnings by changing your subfield. For example, a nurse anesthetist can earn more than the average doctor.

Second, maybe that night you quit work early, you got pregnant. How much money do you lose if you take care of your children full-time, versus part-time, versus stay-at-work full-time while your husband cares for the children? The answers are surprising. See the section "Updating" in Chapter 3 and Chapter 4, "Doing Time."

Third, within any given career, priorities shift. Remember that night you stopped work early and your wife got pregnant? Priority shift coming up: You *were* writing books reflecting your heart; what arc the trade-offs in writing copy for Hewlett-Packard?

Fourth, if you've already chosen a field, these first three chapters will help you see when the field you've chosen is transforming or disappearing right before your eyes, and how to find the career opportunities that are being upsized as others are being downsized. For example, if you're in computers, you might not be inclined to look at the steel industry since, until recently, strong muscles were more important than strong minds. Now, though, the steel industry is filled with opportunities in computers ranging from robotics technology to determining the best markets for 700 different types of steel.

Fifth, if you've already chosen a field but can't find a job because your field is so fulfilling that it's flooded, these chapters will show you how to locate hard-to-find opportunities in a fulfilling field. If you've read the Introduction, you have already been introduced to locating hard-to-find opportunities.

Finally, use these chapters to help your children make their wisest choices. Of course, the best way to do that is to be a role model of an explorer who adapts to change rather than fears it.

Playing the Field

Although almost every career track has hidden opportunities, before we look at each tree, let's get perspective on the forest.

When the *Jobs Rated Almanac* rates 250 jobs based on a combination of factors such as income, work environment, employment outlook, physical demands, security, and stress, here are its top 25:[2]

Best Jobs and Ranking

1. Biologist
2. Actuary
3. Financial planner
4. Computer systems analyst
5. Accountant
6. Software engineer
7. Meteorologist
8. Paralegal assistant
9. Statistician
10. Astronomer
11. Mathematician
12. Parole officer
13. Hospital administrator
14. Architectural drafter
15. Physiologist
16. Dietician
17. Web site manager
18. Physicist
19. Audiologist
20. Agency director (nonprofit)
21. Industrial designer
22. Chemist
23. Medical laboratory technician
24. Archeologist
25. Economist

Here are the *Almanac*'s 25 worst jobs:[3]

Worst Jobs and Ranking	% Male[4]
226. Stationary engineer (for diesel engines, etc.)	98%
227. Sheet metal worker	96%
228. Carpenter	99%
229. Drill-press operator	n/a
230. Mail carrier	68%
231. Dishwasher	82%
232. Garbage collector	93%
233. Meter reader	88%
234. Dairy farmer	n/a
235. Boilermaker	100%
236. Firefighter	97%
237. Butcher	73%
238. Welder	n/a
239. Dancer	20%
240. Roustabout (oil field laborer)	100%
241. Stevedore (loads ships)	93%
242. Roofer	99%
243. Farmer	n/a
244. Construction worker (laborer)	97%
245. Taxi driver	88%
246. Seaman	82%
247. Ironworker	100%
248. Cowboy	n/a
249. Fisherman	90%
250. Lumberjack	98%

Average 92% Male

One good piece of news for women from the *Almanac*'s worst-job list: We often hear that women are segregated into lower-paying jobs. A quick look at the worst-job list reveals that 20 of the 21 worst jobs for which gender breakdowns are available are male-dominated jobs.[5] What is probably true is that **women are more likely to take lower-paid jobs precisely to avoid these worst jobs.**

Most of these worst jobs have little going for them—not fulfill-ment, security, or pay, but lots of stress and physical demands. They are dominated by men because they pay *something*, and if the alter-native is not feeding your family, something is better than nothing.

There's one exception I would take to the worst-job ranking. As a college student I spent each holiday season working as a mail carrier (number 230). Though it was in New Jersey's cold, slush, and snow, I found it a pleasant job. Today, with mail trucks replacing backs-and-legs as the basic equipment, and women now earning about $40,000 a year plus government benefits, it has become in my opinion a good job opportunity.[6]

Let's switch gears. If we're going to play the field, let's start with some playing.

Pretend you are a finalist competing to be on *Jeopardy*. The first finalist to do the following perfectly wins: Rank these six professions according to which pays the most—aircraft pilot, chemical engineer, college teacher, financial manager, pharmacist, physician. Hint: Watch out for pharmacist.

Check your ranking against Table 1.

I warned you about pharmacist, didn't I? Who would have thought they earn more than physicians? We hear parents proudly proclaim, "My child, the doctor," not "My child, the pharmacist." And the phar-macist has better hours and lower malpractice insurance to boot.

Notice, though, that most of those 20 occupations require advanced degrees. Suppose you don't have—or want to have—an advanced degree? And you hate carrying mail, but love *L.A. Law?*

TABLE 1   The 20 Occupations That Pay the Most[7]

(Ranked by Median Income)

Position	Income	Men's Income	Women's Income	Women's Pay as % of Men's	% Women in the Field
Lawyers	$81,120	$84,188	$73,476	87%	32%
Chief executives	$81,016	$90,272	$64,636	72%	23%
Engineering managers	$77,168	$76,752	$82,784	108%	10%
Pharmacists	$76,804	$79,716	$70,928	89%	47%
Physicians and surgeons	$73,060	$87,204	$51,428	59%	31%
Computer and information systems managers	$72,852	$74,724	$66,560	89%	30%
Aerospace engineers	$70,824	$70,356	$78,416	111%	9%
Aircraft pilots and flight engineers	$70,200	$70,720	$21,268	30%	4%
Electrical and electronics engineers	$69,264	$70,096	$55,756	80%	7%
Chemical engineers	$65,000	$67,028	$52,260	78%	20%
Computer software engineers	$64,584	$69,472	$52,260	75%	22%
Mechanical engineers	$60,736	$61,048	$52,260	86%	4%
Civil engineers	$59,800	$60,528	$49,400	82%	10%
General and operations managers	$59,072	$60,840	$50,232	83%	26%
Marketing and sales managers	$58,604	$66,092	$47,008	71%	38%
Management analysts	$57,980	$65,884	$50,804	77%	45%
Judges, magistrates, and other judicial workers	$57,720	$83,772	$43,888	100%	54%
Purchasing managers	$57,616	$67,444	$43,888	65%	39%
Personal financial advisers	$56,888	$64,584	$41,600	64%	30%
Computer hardware engineers	$56,316	$59,124	$42,744	72%	11%

Consider being a detective or criminal investigator—they average about $50,000.[8]

Table 2 lists the 15 occupations with the highest starting salaries that require only a bachelor's degree. Fortunately, their salaries are in the ballpark of the salaries of those with more advanced degrees.

TABLE 2   The 15 Occupations with Highest Starting Salaries
for People Receiving a Bachelor's Degree[9]

(Ranked by Average Starting Offer)

Occupation	Average Offer	Men's Offer	Women's Offer	Women's Offer as % of Men's	% Women in Field
Pharmacist	$83,642	N/A	N/A	N/A	N/A
Bioengineering	$52,700	$52,500	$52,750	100%	80%
Hardware design & development	$52,659	$53,691	$49,963	93%	38%
Software design & development	$51,762	$52,074	$49,363	95%	21%
Investment banking (mergers and acquisitions)	$50,640	$48,667	$56,667	116%	14%
Power systems engineering	$50,510	$50,575	$50,214	99%	18%
Production engineering	$50,036	$50,130	$51,841	103%	27%
Research & development engineering	$48,386	$48,309	$49,088	102%	34%
Manufacturing/industrial engineering	$47,974	$47,734	$48,182	101%	39%
National security	$47,817	$47,962	$47,222	98%	38%
Occupational therapy	$47,750	N/A	$47,750	N/A	100%
Other engineering	$47,657	$46,939	$49,239	105%	26%
Systems/programming engineering	$47,230	$47,674	$44,963	94%	32%
Industrial hygiene/occupational safety engineering	$47,040	$48,300	$45,780	95%	50%
Project engineering	$46,241	$45,863	$47,887	104%	14%

That's the good news. The bad news is that as of 2005, a bachelor of science degree is no longer enough to be a pharmacist. It now requires six years after high school, and your degree will be a Pharm.D. This is still an excellent trade-off, since it will doubtless create a hierarchy within the pharmacy profession, and the people with the six-year degrees will be more valued than people with only a bachelor's degree. In either case, the profession is undervalued for its high pay, despite having many of the characteristics, such as flexibility and a good working environment, that often lead to low pay.

As we discover the characteristics of fields to which women tend to be drawn, we'll see they include physical safety, little financial risk, no exposure to inclement weather, pleasant working conditions, short commutes, and no midnight-to-8 a.m. shifts. Problem is, these positive conditions often create a low-pay formula since most people prefer these conditions. (It's the supply and demand thing—in case you missed the Introduction.) Therefore, fields with these positive conditions that nevertheless pay a lot are a find. Note that most of these fields do contain many of these conditions, but two of these top fields attract very few women. See if you can spot them in Table 2.

They are software and hardware design and development. Throughout this book, the myriad of ways in which a woman who masters computers can use that expertise to master her life will become apparent. Ditto for mastering a technical field; power systems engineering and project engineering, for example, pay well but attract few women.

Now, see if you can notice some differences between the fields that pay the most (Tables 1 and 2), and those that pay the least (Table 3).

Most apparent is the bias among the highest-paid workers toward engineering, computers, and the hard sciences, while **the lowest-paid are doing work that almost any adult can do—therefore there is no end to the supply of available people.**

The subtitle of this book implies the empowerment of women. So here's a table that will blow your mind (Table 4). There are more than 80 fields in which women earn more than men, but some are too small to be statistically significant, and who wants to read that much? Let's look at just the larger fields, and only the ones in which women earn at least 5% more than men—not just for starting salaries, but on average. That would be 39 fields. That's right, almost 40 fields in which women earn at least 5% more. See if you can guess *any* three. No cheating.

TABLE 3   20 Lowest-Paying Fields[10]

(Ranked by Median Incomes)

Position	Income	Men's	Women's	Women's as % of Men's	% Women in the Field
Counter attendants, cafeteria, food concession, and coffee shop	$14,352	$14,872	$14,092	98%	64%
Dishwashers	$14,976	$15,080	$14,716	98%	18%
Combined food preparation and serving workers, including fast food	$16,432	$15,964	$16,588	104%	77%
Cashiers	$16,588	$17,628	$16,380	93%	75%
Food preparation workers	$16,640	$17,368	$16,120	93%	50%
Hosts and hostesses, restaurant, lounge, and coffee shop	$16,692	$20,748	$16,120	78%	78%
Maids and housekeeping cleaners	$16,796	$19,292	$16,484	85%	85%
Pressers, textile, garment, and related materials	$16,796	$21,632	$16,172	75%	75%
Child care workers	$17,160	$19,188	$16,952	88%	95%
Dining room and cafeteria attendants and bartender helpers	$17,212	$18,356	$15,912	87%	43%
Cooks	$17,368	$18,096	$16,484	91%	39%
Waiters and waitresses	$17,420	$20,020	$16,536	83%	68%
Sewing machine operators	$17,888	$20,228	$16,952	84%	76%
Laundry and dry-cleaning workers	$18,096	$19,552	$17,056	87%	63%
Packers and packagers, hand	$18,096	$17,940	$18,200	101%	62%
Food preparation and serving related occupations	$18,148	$19,396	$16,952	87%	49%
Teacher assistants	$18,252	$21,944	$17,888	82%	91%
Personal and home care aides	$18,252	$21,736	$17,784	82%	88%
Farming, fishing, and forestry occupations	$19,188	$19,968	$16,536	83%	20%
Service station attendants	$19,188	$19,292	$18,876	98%	12%

TABLE 4   39 Fields in Which Women Earn at Least 5% More Than Men[11]

(Ranked by Women's Median Pay)

Field	Women's	Men's	Women's Pay as % of Men's	Women's Addit'l Pay
Sales engineers[12]	$89,908	$62,660	143%	$27,2
Engineering managers	$82,784	$76,752	108%	$6,03
Aerospace engineers	$78,416	$70,356	111%	$8,06
Financial analysts	$69,004	$58,604	118%	$10,4
Radiation therapists	$59,124	$53,300	111%	$5,82
Statisticians	$49,140	$36,296	135%	$12,8
Tool and die makers	$46,228	$40,144	115%	$6,08
Other education, training, and library workers	$46,176	$42,120	110%	$4,05
Speech-language pathologists	$45,136	$35,048	129%	$10,0
Legislators	$43,316	$32,656	133%	$10,6
Other transportation workers	$43,160	$33,124	130%	$10,0
Advertising and promotions managers	$42,068	$40,144	105%	$1,92
Agricultural and food scientists	$41,704	$39,156	107%	$2,54
Telecommunications line installers and repairers	$40,716	$36,348	112%	$4,36
Automotive service technicians and mechanics	$40,664	$31,460	129%	$9,20
Precision instrument and equipment repairers	$40,612	$37,648	108%	$2,96
Meter readers, utilities	$36,348	$31,668	115%	$4,68
Motion picture projectionists	$35,412	$27,924	127%	$7,48
Surveying and mapping technicians	$34,840	$32,864	106%	$1,97
Supervisors, protective service workers, all other	$34,684	$32,656	106%	$2,02
Library technicians	$33,384	$29,328	114%	$4,05
Biological technicians	$32,292	$26,364	122%	$5,92
Automotive body and related repairers	$30,888	$28,132	110%	$2,75
Human resources assistants, except payroll and timekeeping	$30,420	$28,028	109%	$2,39
Funeral service workers	$30,108	$24,492	123%	$5,61

TABLE 4   (Continued)

(Ranked by Women's Median Pay)

Field	Women's	Men's	Women's as % of Men's	Women's Addit'l Pay
Rolling machine setters, operators, and tenders, metal and plastic	$29,692	$25,064	118%	$4,62
Information and record clerks, all other	$29,484	$26,312	112%	$3,17
Aircraft structure, surfaces, rigging, and systems assemblers	$28,652	$26,676	107%	$1,97
Food batchmakers	$27,872	$23,400	119%	$4,47
Helpers, construction trades	$26,936	$21,736	124%	$5,20
Baggage porters, bellhops, and concierges	$26,468	$21,684	122%	$4,78
Residential advisers	$24,492	$23,036	106%	$1,45
Gaming services workers	$24,076	$22,308	108%	$1,76
Library assistants, clerical	$23,608	$18,512	128%	$5,09
Motor vehicle operators, all other	$22,412	$18,252	123%	$4,16
Telephone operators	$22,152	$18,356	121%	$3,79
Personal care and service workers, all other	$19,864	$17,160	116%	$2,70
Lifeguards and other protective service workers	$19,188	$18,356	105%	$832
Crossing guards	$18,824	$16,640	113%	$2,18

Note that when women's pay is significantly greater than men's, it can be in male-dominated fields, female-dominated fields, or well-integrated fields. In fact, of the 15 top-paying fields in which women out-earn men, 9 are male-dominated. Obviously, male dominance does not necessarily mean making rules to benefit men at the expense of women. These greater incomes for women will seem much more surprising as we tap into the 25 work choices they tend to make that normally lead to workers earning less income.

As usual, engineering contains women's most underutilized opportunities, with women sales engineers earning about $90,000 per year (143% of what men sales engineers make). The highest-paying of these fields to which women are attracted is radiation therapist. As for financial analyst, well, many women go into accounting, so if you have a propensity for numbers why not make $70,000 a year as a financial analyst?

I mentioned that these 39 fields are only the *larger* ones that pay women more than men. For a more select group of women who want to earn more than a quarter million a year, who like working in a female-dominated field, have a creative mind, and don't mind a grueling pace, my favorite recommendation is from a *Working Women* survey, finding that chief executives of advertising agencies who are women average $275,000.[13] (And by the way, these women exceed their male counterparts by more than $20,000 per year.)

What can a woman major in if she wishes to be in a field in which her starting pay will be higher than her male counterpart's? Here are 29 such majors (Table 5). One caveat about this table: The field of psychology is listed with poor starting pay. It becomes a high-pay field, though, for many people with marriage and family therapy degrees who go into private practice and who are talented, as well as for people with Ph.D.'s in clinical psychology, even if they are less talented. And don't forget to compute what majoring in computers can afford you—not just "things" but the flexibility to work for others or for yourself, part-time or overtime, to become a geek or subsidize vacations, or even to subsidize writing a book.

When we look at the actual occupations in which women with bachelor's degrees receive starting salaries that are higher than men's, perhaps the biggest "find" for women is investment banking (Table 6). Usually thought of as an "old boy" field that discriminates against women, it turns out to be one more male-dominated field that in fact

TABLE 5   29 College Majors That Lead to Women with Bachelor's Degrees Being Offered Higher Starting Salaries Than Men[14]

Major	Women's Average Starting Salary	Men's Average Starting Salary	Women's Pay Advantage	Women's Pay as % of Men's	% Degrees Granted to Women
Petroleum engineering	$61,540	$57,156	$4,384	108%	22%
Chemical engineering	$52,857	$51,921	$936	102%	39%
Computer engineering	$51,763	$51,622	$141	100%	19%
Electrical/electronics & communications engineering	$50,099	$49,753	$346	101%	20%
Mechanical engineering	$49,379	$48,070	$1,309	103%	19%
Aerospace/aeronautical/ astronautical engineering	$49,326	$48,571	$755	102%	44%
Metallurgical engineering (incl. ceramic science/eng.)	$48,945	$46,100	$2,845	106%	30%
Computer programming	$48,943	$41,750	$7,193	117%	50%
Computer science	$47,337	$47,245	$92	100%	19%
Engineering technology	$47,000	$43,846	$3,154	107%	8%
Physics	$46,290	$39,772	$6,518	116%	43%
Agricultural engineering	$44,333	$40,399	$3,934	110%	10%
Computer systems analysis	$44,214	$38,722	$5,492	114%	44%
Construction science/mgmt.	$43,598	$41,893	$1,705	104%	9%
Business systems networking/ telecommunications	$43,438	$41,284	$2,154	105%	45%
Architectural engineering	$42,880	$40,426	$2,454	106%	17%
Civil engineering	$41,832	$41,385	$447	101%	24%
Logistics/materials mgmt.	$39,407	$38,032	$1,375	104%	44%
Information sciences & systems	$38,057	$37,350	$707	102%	29%
Chemistry	$37,391	$36,289	$1,102	103%	69%
Agricultural business & mgmt.	$34,617	$31,415	$3,202	110%	25%
Architecture & related programs	$33,901	$33,127	$774	102%	41%
History	$32,890	$32,001	$889	103%	32%
Health & related sciences	$32,212	$31,597	$615	102%	68%
Other humanities	$29,808	$22,873	$6,935	130%	87%

	TABLE 5 (*Continued*)				
Major	Women's Average Starting Salary	Men's Average Starting Salary	Women's Pay Advantage	Women's Pay as % of Men's	% Degrees Granted to Women
Biological/life sciences	$29,539	$29,310	$229	101%	69%
Physical education	$29,269	$24,264	$5,005	121%	50%
Journalism	$28,600	$27,624	$976	104%	72%
Psychology	$27,504	$27,389	$115	100%	83%

pays women more than men—an additional $8,000 per year, or 116% of what men make. Women I know personally who have entered that field work long hours, but soon make well into the six figures.

A "find" of a different nature is public relations. It's a find because of its extraordinary flexibility—from working with a company to doing as my wife does, working out of the home as she raises the children. No matter what field you love, from books to medicine; no matter what pay you seek, from $40,000 to more than a half-million per year; and no matter what flexibility you need time-wise, public relations offers opportunities to piece it all together with acceptable trade-offs.

Now you've played the field and may feel it's time to settle down. If you're still saying to yourself, "I've already chosen a field," remember, you aren't dead yet.

When you choose a field, you don't take vows. Sometimes, being faithful to your family means keeping your partner but changing your field. Other times it means changing your subfield, or studying how your field and subfield are changing, or how your personal needs are changing. No harm in looking. Worse comes to worst, someone might admire you for just pointing them in the direction of their field of dreams.

TABLE 6   26 Occupations in Which Women with Bachelor's Degrees (Without Regard for College Major) Received Starting Offers Greater Than Men's[15]

Occupation	Women's Starting Offer	Men's Starting Offer	Women's Pay as % of Men's	% Women in Field
	(Ranked by Women's Average Starting Offer)			
Investment banking (mergers & acquisitions)	$56,667	$48,667	116%	14%
Process engineering (chemical)	$53,385	$52,704	102%	31%
Bioengineering	$52,750	$52,500	100%	80%
Production engineering	$51,841	$50,130	103%	27%
Other engineering	$49,239	$46,939	105%	26%
Research & development engineering	$49,088	$48,309	101%	34%
Manufacturing/industrial engineering	$48,182	$47,734	101%	39%
Project engineering	$47,887	$45,863	104%	14%
Field engineering	$47,247	$44,916	105%	21%
Systems analysis & design	$45,969	$42,855	107%	33%
Portfolio management/brokerage	$44,969	$40,876	110%	32%
Design/construction engineering	$44,737	$43,808	102%	21%
Urban/regional planning	$43,850	$38,372	114%	29%
Financial/treasury analysis	$42,925	$42,543	111%	49%
Auditing (private)	$39,329	$38,913	101%	58%
Purchasing	$39,271	$37,080	106%	57%
Distribution	$39,012	$34,844	111%	28%
Network administration	$39,000	$38,585	101%	5%
Finance, taxation, monetary policy	$37,051	$36,381	118%	52%
Fundraising/development	$37,000	$32,000	116%	50%
Medical technology	$36,866	$35,750	103%	67%
Military	$36,033	$34,690	104%	20%
Public relations	$31,441	$30,682	102%	73%
Religious occupation	$30,000	$20,400	147%	44%
Production (communications)	$26,407	$23,767	111%	75%
Dietician	$23,160	$17,680	130%	67%

The Field-with-Higher-Yield Formula: One to Five

promised in the Introduction that I would show how our focus on discrimination *against* women has blinded us to opportunities *for* women. We've already discovered more than 50 fields of high-pay opportunities for women; let's match these fields to our personalities and take a look at the trade-offs.

Of the 25 ways to increase pay—or the high-pay formula—10 involve choosing the right field: the field-with-higher-yield formula. All 10 are a bit much for one chapter, so take a break after the first five, and I'll complete your field of dreams after a good night's sleep.

1. Choose a Field in *Technology* or the *Hard Sciences,* Not the Arts or Social Sciences
(Pharmacology vs. Literature)

Perhaps the best reason to consider the hard sciences is that, well, one study suggests science, engineering, medicine, and dentistry graduates live longer than arts graduates (or law grads).[1] So whatever money you make you can keep a little longer.

The Field-with-Higher-Yield Formula: One to Five

1. Choose a field in *technology* or the *hard sciences,* not the arts or social sciences (PHARMACOLOGY VS. LITERATURE)

2. Get hazard pay without the hazards (FEMALE ADMINISTRATOR IN AIR FORCE VS. MALE COMBAT SOLDIER IN ARMY)

3. Among jobs requiring little education, those that expose you to the sleet and heat pay more than those that are indoors and neat (FEDEX DELIVERER VS. RECEPTIONIST)

4. In most fields with higher pay, you *can't* psychologically *check out* at the end of the day (CORPORATE ATTORNEY VS. LIBRARIAN)

5. Fields with higher pay often have *lower fulfillment* (TAX ACCOUNTANT VS. CHILD CARE PROFESSIONAL)

Doubtless one contributor to living longer is not just what your job pays, but knowing you can get a job that pays to begin with: career security. In the first few years of the twenty-first century, when the economic headlines reflected as deep a recession as Silicon Valley, and when technology was at the head of the recession's class, the Information Technology Association of America nevertheless estimated that U.S. firms needed more than 900,000 additional tech workers per year and, despite the recession, were able to hire only 475,000.[2] In brief, technology is not job security, but career security. Career security matters more than job security, and both can matter more than the exact amount you are paid.

What the tables in Chapter 1 on high and low pay make clear is that engineers and computer scientists dominate the high-pay professions, while liberal arts, languages, journalism, and social work dominate the low-pay professions. When we note (in Table 1) that women engineering managers average $83,000, but only 10% of the people in the field are women, we can project those lost pay opportunities.

If you love languages, the challenge is not just high pay, it's any pay;

the challenge isn't a benefits package, it's avoiding settling for a job as a cashier and practicing your French on a customer who leaves you her bewildered smile ("What's an educated girl like you doing working here?") for a tip. But if you're willing to make a trade-off from your love of languages to an employer's need for linguists, you'll consider substituting Arabic, Farsi, Urdu, or Pashto, be a godsend (and therefore receive a paycheck) to the FBI, which is desperately seeking Arabic, Farsi, Urdu, and Pashto linguists for careers in the national security industry.[3] Then, with that paycheck, you can learn your French in France.

As for high-tech jobs, ironically, wages for women have been increasing faster than for men. Specifically, the wages of young white women who took high-tech jobs went up 23%, as opposed to 9% for their male counterparts. Among young African American women, wages increased 42%.[4]

A recent study of U.K. graduates found that the choice of major explained as much as 88% of their subsequent wage gap.[5] The subjects most popular with women, such as literature and art, are also more likely to leave women unemployed and overeducated.[6]

Is this beginning to change—are women entering high-tech jobs in increasing numbers? Mostly no. As white men's share of high-tech jobs increased 60% throughout the 1990s, women's decreased 22%, and Latinas' share dropped even more.[7] Is this due to racism or sexism? Neither: Young African American women increased their share of high-tech jobs.

What this *does* have to do with is attitudes and goals. In a 2003 Gallup poll of teenagers, careers in computers were the number one choice of boys, but not even among the top 10 choices of girls. Similarly, being an engineer was the number four choice of boys, but also not among the top 10 for girls. What were girls' top choices? Acting, music, and teaching.[8] Los Angeles, of course, has thousands of jobs for actors—in restaurants.

What holds women back from pursuing degrees in tech fields, but not in medicine and law? It depends on which woman you ask. When Judith Kleinfeld examined an American Association of University Women study, she concluded, "More women want to be an attorney-in-an-office than a Dilbert-in-a-cubicle."[9]

Zoe Woodworth, who switched fields from computer science to art at Carnegie Mellon University (CMU), weaves a more complex tapestry. Since I promised not just to sell these 25 ways to higher pay, but give you a sense of the trade-offs as experienced by women, here is Zoe:

> Of the six girls in CS [computer science], three of us dropped out. (I felt pretty bad, because there are guys who are 10 times smarter than I am, who wanted to get into CS at CMU their whole life, who didn't get in, and for me it was a last-minute decision.) Anyway, the guys and girls in the program were like of different races (and I say this as someone who entered CMU feeling there are no mental differences between the sexes). And yet, it wasn't like I clicked with the girls, either. I thought the other five girls and me would be best friends, but I didn't like them as people. They were just so one-dimensional.

When asked about what made the sexes appear so different, Zoe pondered, "What the guys found fascinating I found frustrating. For me, correcting a programming error and doing the iteration, and still not solving the problem, made me want to jump off a cliff! The guys liked the challenge. Ironically, though I left computer programming for art, working with computers is a form of art, and a scientific background helps my work in art."[10]

Science and high tech appear to be challenging to many women. But let me share some often overlooked reasons as to why science and high tech are more female-friendly than they appear.

Zoe's perception of the overlap between art and technology becomes even more relevant to women when we see how male-friendly technology can facilitate a female-friendly working style. Sally Helgesen, the author of *The Web of Inclusion* and numerous books on men's preference for communicating hierarchically and women's for communicating more as in a web, points to the ways technology supports the web style of communication.[11] Prior to computer technology, for example, a nurse was dependent on getting information from a head nurse who got much of it from a doctor. Technology allows the nurse to get information for herself and communicate it to peers, patients, head nurses, or doctors and, in turn, receive it from each. No matter what business a woman is in, if she runs into a stumbling block, or needs more depth in an area, the Internet helps her receive from one web to give to another.

A woman who is proficient in technology, and therefore has access to the world's expertise, is also more able to be something else that is female friendly: her own decision-maker. This image of woman-as-decision-maker runs counter to the stereotypical image of woman-as-secretary-at-the-bottom-of-the-hierarchy. That latter image comes from looking at traditional women's roles in the workplace. If we move our scope to women's decision-making in the home, we discover a different picture.

A traditional woman's role in the home was to run in effect a small business—and practically speaking, with her husband away at work, she ran it her way. She did not need to present monthly spreadsheets to someone who had been chosen by someone else to supervise her (who in turn would be fired if he didn't fire her should she fail to produce the numbers). In contrast, her husband was chosen more by her; since divorce was stigmatized until recently, he did not have the leverage a boss did. Thus when we look in the home, women were CEOs without stockholders or boards of directors able to fire them. As we look at the degree to which women are now running their own businesses, we will see that making their own decisions is one of the strong motivators.

Men's roles taught men almost the opposite lesson: The farther up the ladder he climbed as a leader, the more experience he must have as a follower. Early on, a man learned only to take orders; promotions then required him to take-and-give. A small percentage of these men became mostly order-givers, but virtually every man still had to take orders, and be accountable to a boss—the president had the voter; the general had the president; the CEO had the stockholder and board of directors; the superintendent of schools had the board of education and the parents; the Pope had God. . . .

A woman, in her traditional role, was freer to run things her way than her husband was in his traditional role. And technology frees women to do this in the workplace.

If you're uncertain whether your personality and science and technology are a match, make no assumptions until you check out how different subfields appeal to different personalities. In the section of this chapter on subfields, we'll get some depth as to how to do that, but here's a hint from Cathey Cotton, founder of MetaSearch:

I love technology because you can pick the industry then pick the kind of technology segment that you love, and you just live it. I mean like biotech and environmental people are older and less cutting edge, but in my segment—database analysis and decision support technology— I deal with great technologists who are 29 and running companies. Instead of going to the expensive French restaurant, I take clients out dancing! Honestly! I go out dancing with my clients. There's a lot of relationship building that goes along with that. And I love it cause everything changes so fast that if you immerse yourself for 10 years you can be the industry expert.[12]

Perhaps the one technical area that has been traditionally female friendly is nursing. And with the nursing shortage, the opportunities are booming.

Nurses: Supply Down; Opportunities Up
The U.S. Department of Labor predicts that nursing will represent the "fastest-growing occupation" between 2004 and 2012, and the need for new nurses likely will remain strong for the foreseeable future, with thousands of nurses expected to retire.[13]

If you are just starting as a nurse and are willing to go where the supply is down and the opportunities up, the Visiting Nurse Service in New York City offers starting nurses more than $60,000, plus a signing bonus of $3,000.[14] Nurse anesthetists make around $100,000 in places like California and New York City.[15] But that's only the beginning of what's changing.

The specialties projected to be in greatest demand include critical care, preoperative care, and emergency services.[16] And, as we will see in Chapter 5, "On the Move," traveling (a.k.a. "gypsy") nurses are also in high demand.

Nursing, like most professions, has a diversity that allows choices for people with a variety of personalities and life stages: If you like research, you can do a public health study; if you like organizing, you can run a clinic. If you're single and want to discover where you'd like to live and be paid a lot to do it, be a traveling nurse. If you like traveling overseas, work on a battleship. If you like more of an office environment, work for a pharmaceutical company or a dermatologist or administer an insurance plan. If you need flexible time but decent money, work as a consultant; if you are a great salesperson, be a drug or medical supply rep. You can serve the poor or the rich, travel or stay put, or you can teach nursing. If all else fails, work in a hospital!

Whenever there is a shortage of this magnitude, it is not just pay that goes up. Employers start becoming more flexible, universities accelerate degree programs and offer financial incentives, and the government creates financial advantages. All of that is already happening.

The New York University Medical Center now offers nurses free tuition at NYU, health benefits, 30 days of paid holidays and vacation, and a generous retirement package.[17] And that's just for starting nurses—perhaps enough incentive to get you through the prerequisites of math and chemistry.

Speaking of which, suppose you love money but hate math, and have no chemistry for chemistry? Well, they need nurses so badly that you can be tutored for free in California. It's part of California's Nurse Workforce Initiative, and it proposes to allocate an additional $60 million to meet the need for an additional 3,600 nurses per year.[18] Neither you nor your tutor get the entire $60 million, but at a time when college financing is being severely cut back by California, the government will hold your hand on your journey to becoming a nurse.

If women are sometimes blind to high-tech opportunities, men are just as blind to opportunities in nontraditional fields such as nursing. Yet the nursing shortage has led the nursing profession to look for men. Of course it helps that, as Americans are more obese, and heavy medical equipment is getting more ubiquitous, men tend to have the upper body strength needed for lifting the obese patients and ubiquitous equipment.

When we take a look at the pay opportunities in nursing, pharmacy, chemical engineering, and computers, we can see that these professionals will earn in 15 years what a high school teacher with a master's degree earns in 30. Knowing the size of the pay gap helps you to generate options. For example, you might choose to be an engineer for 10 years followed by 8–10 years doing anything you wish.

There's *L.A. Law,* but No *L.A. Engineering*

Do women avoid fields like engineering because of the tendency of male-dominated fields to discriminate against women? Probably not. Prior to the women's movement, engineering was no more male-dominated than medicine and law. And women have entered medicine and law by the droves. When women do enter male-dominated fields, they tend to enter the more glamorous occupations. And the media reinforces this. There was *L.A. Law,* but no *L.A. Engineering; ER* doesn't mean *Engineering Room.* Women receive six layers of encouragement to enter fields involving engineering, computers, and math and science: first, better starting salaries than men's; second, special programs for girls in high school; third, female-only government scholarships; fourth, female-only corporate grants and scholarships; fifth, the advertising that reaches out to women to create a more female-supportive atmosphere; and sixth, special grants for science programs at leading women's colleges.

An example of layers three to six is this ad by IBM. (Since the print in the ad is tiny, and I don't want you to have to interrupt this very important reading moment to find a magnifying glass, I'll paraphrase its essence.) IBM uses pink booties on the right and blue on the left to symbolize gender's inhibition of girls' choice of careers in engineering, computers, and so on. The text describes IBM's 90 programs and grants to encourage women's entry into engineering, computer science, math, physics, and chemistry. And, lest women be uncomfortable being the only female in a class of male engineers, IBM also

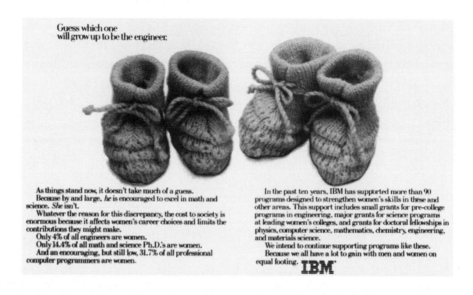

Guess which one
will grow up to be the engineer.

As things stand now, it doesn't take much of a guess.
Because by and large, *he* is encouraged to excel in math and science. *She* isn't.
Whatever the reason for this discrepancy, the cost to society is enormous because it affects women's career choices and limits the contributions they might make.
Only 4% of all engineers are women.
Only 14.4% of all math and science Ph.D.'s are women.
And an encouraging, but still low, 31.7% of all professional computer programmers are women.

In the past ten years, IBM has supported more than 90 programs designed to strengthen women's skills in these and other areas. This support includes small grants for pre-college programs in engineering, major grants for science programs at leading women's colleges, and grants for doctoral fellowships in physics, computer science, mathematics, chemistry, engineering, and materials science.
We intend to continue supporting programs like these.
Because we all have a lot to gain with men and women on equal footing. **IBM**

gives "major grants for science programs at leading women's colleges." In brief, 100% women-only support.

These programs took place between 1975 and 1985 in the hope that by 2000 women would be more than the 4% of the engineers the ad states they were at the time. However, despite all six layers of encouragement, by the century's turn only 2% of women with a bachelor's degree or more chose any of over three dozen fields of engineering, or engineering-related technologies, as a field in which to receive their degrees.[19]

Nothing exemplifies the Cathy cartoon's point more than women's avoidance of hazardous fields. Thus it will be tempting for a woman to skip this section. Don't. It contains some of the most important

cathy®   **by Cathy Guisewite**

insights in the book because what leads women to safety is central to the male-female dance, and so the hazard section is also about that dance. It's long, but it will take you a long way. And many of the other ways to higher pay will make more sense with its insights. For example, why do women in hazardous professions get equal pay with many fewer hazards?

2. Get Hazard Pay Without the Hazards
(Female Administrator in Air Force vs. Male Combat Soldier in Army)

Our focus on discrimination has distracted us from spotting numerous opportunities for women in the hazardous professions—opportunities that give women equal pay to men for fewer hazards. As a result, we continue to have a gender divide and a Catch-22.

The Catch-22 of Hazardous Occupations Creates a Female "Glass Cellar"
There is what might be called a Catch-22 of hazardous occupations: The more hazardous the job, the more men; the more men, the less we care about making the job safer (Table 7).

The Catch-22 of hazardous occupations creates a "glass cellar" which few women wish to enter. Women are alienated not just out of the fear of being hurt on the job, but by an atmosphere that can make a hazardous job more hazardous than it needs to be.

Of the deaths that occur in the workplace, 92% occur to men.[20] The gender divide between hazardous and safe jobs gives us an important hint. Understanding the gap is a key to understanding men and women, and therefore the underlying psychology behind why men earn more. We'll see what it will ultimately take to get around this Catch-22 and, since that can only be realized decades in the future, some more immediate secrets for women getting the benefits of hazard pay with virtually none of the hazards.

First, though, let's take a hazardous occupations IQ test. Name 3 of the 10 most hazardous jobs. Okay. Now find them in Table 8 (on page 29), the "Top Ten Most Hazardous Jobs."[21]

You probably guessed police, soldier, and firefighter. Although the

TABLE 7 Hazardous Occupations[22]	
Fire fighting	97% male
Truck drivers	96% male
Construction	98% male
Extractive occupations	98% male

Safe Occupations	
Secretary	99% female
Receptionist	98% female

most visible hazardous occupations, they are *not* among America's 10 most dangerous jobs. It's more dangerous to be a "driver-sales worker." Willy Loman finally gets his due.

While lists like this give overviews, they can be misleading and therefore camouflage opportunities. For example, the Pilots and Navigators category might scare you away from being a major airline pilot until we understand that, for starters, Alaskan pilots, who have a one in eight chance of dying during a 30-year career, skew the statistics.[23] Also, piloting for a major airline is lumped together with bush pilots, air-taxi pilots, and crop-duster pilots, among whom deaths occur at a far higher rate than among pilots for major airlines.[24] Moreover, these pilots get paid just over half of what a jetliner pilot gets paid—$52,000 versus $92,000.[25] What appears to be a hazardous occupation is in fact safe and lucrative.

I promised two secrets. Secret #1 is how women can get equal pay for fewer-than-equal hazards. Secret #2 is how to make a good living via hazardous occupations without *any* of the hazards. Since Secret #1 gives us the psychology of hazardous occupations that allows Secret #2 to work, let's start with Secret #1.

Secret #1: How Hazardous Occupations Give Women Equal Pay with Unequal Hazards

Your daughter says, "Dad. Mom. I want to join the armed services." You look at her beautiful face, her life flashes before your eyes, and you see a body bag.

TABLE 8

THE TOP TEN

MOST HAZARDOUS JOBS

RANK	OCCUPATION	DEATH RATE*
1	TIMBER CUTTERS	118
2	FISHERS	71
3	PILOTS & NAVIGATORS	70
4	STRUCTURAL METAL WORKERS	58
5	DRIVER-SALES WORKERS	38
6	ROOFERS	37
7	ELECTRICAL POWER INSTALLERS	33
8	FARM OCCUPATIONS	28
9	CONSTRUCTION LABORERS	28
10	TRUCK DRIVERS	25

*Deaths per 100,000 people per year.
Source: Bureau of Labor Statistics, 2003.[26] Image by Daryoush Parsia

Now's the time to let her know the biggest military secret: She can join the military and be as safe-from-death as she would be at home. How?

In the war in Iraq, not a single woman has been killed in the Air Force. Nor has a single woman been killed in the Marines. And only one has died in the Navy. Your only job is to keep her out of the Army (Table 9).

While women comprise approximately 15% of active-duty military personnel, and 10% of those deployed in Iraq, only a bit more than 2.3% of the soldiers killed in hostile action in Iraq were female.[27] Since suicide bombings and ambushes that allowed for less protection of women-as-women were more common during the war in Iraq, the percentage of women noncombat deaths was higher, at 3.4%.[28] Overall, women constitute 2.6% of the deaths, men 97.4%.[29]

Put another way, women who serve in Iraq will get equal pay with only about one-fourth the chance of being killed compared with men. Among women who serve in the military as a whole, their chance of being killed is only about one-sixth.

Exactly how safe does this make a woman in wartime Iraq? On an absolute basis, of at least 13,800 women who have served at the time of this writing, 24 have been killed.[30]

So if your daughter insists on giving all the armed services equal consideration, she'll still have at least 575 out of 576 chances of returning alive from Iraq. But again, in the Marines and Air Force it's a 100% chance of returning.

There's more good news. Your daughter is much more likely to choose, or be chosen for, the military's safer fields, such as health care, administration, or scientific-professional fields; women are disproportionately represented in these safer fields by a ratio of about two-and-a-half to one.[31] Of course, if you have a son joining the mili-

TABLE 9   War in Iraq: Women's vs. Men's Deaths (March 2003 to July 2004)

Military Service	Female Deaths[32]	Male Deaths[33]	Number of Soldiers Deployed[34]
Marines	0	195	26,000
Air Force	0	11	23,000
Navy	1	20	16,000
Army	23	656	73,000
Total	24	882	138,000

tary, selecting those fields is also a good way of making sure you see him raise your grandchildren.

If you can't get your daughter or son to think safety, put it to them this way. Starting salaries for enlisted soldiers is peanuts: about $16,000.[35] Hazard pay adds a mere $1,800 per year.[36] A sales clerk at a clothing store makes almost $27,000.[37] The only way to do the military is to live—after 20 years if you make it to general you'll also make over $150,000.[38] And oh, what a difference in benefits. It pays to live, not to die. Even rebels like the idea of beating the system, of having their cake and eating it, too.

It's difficult to read a section like this without wondering how there could be, in an era of equal opportunity for careers, such unequal opportunity for life. What's the dynamic that creates women's eight-to-one safety ratio?

Why Hazardous Jobs Can Be So Much Less Hazardous for Women

>   ITEM. Mohammed and Jessica. In the war in Iraq, an Iraqi attorney, Mohammed, witnessed P.O.W. Jessica Lynch being slapped and abused. He was upset enough that he walked 6 miles, found a U.S. Marine patrol, and, at the risk of his own life, alerted them to her whereabouts.[39]

Mohammed represents Everyman. He represents the biological instinct in men to save a woman-in-jeopardy, even at the risk of his own life.

However, the publicity for the woman-in-jeopardy reinforces our belief that women are more likely than men to be in jeopardy. For example, we all remember P.O.W. Jessica Lynch, and many recall the name Shoshana Johnson as the second female P.O.W., but few of us recall the name of even one male P.O.W.[40]

This greater publicity for a woman-in-jeopardy hides this secret: Hazardous occupations are far less hazardous to women than men. The discovery of this secret creates this opportunity for women: **Women can get equal hazard pay for fewer-than-equal hazards;** she can receive what I call a "death professions bonus" with not much more physical risk than in everyday life.

The dynamics that lead to this outcome are woven into every aspect of our biology, socialization, and institutions. They are the unconscious motivations behind the 25 ways to higher pay and to why men earn more. "The rest," as they say, "is details."

The way this works can be quite touching. For example, in South Africa, the laws eliminating apartheid also gave women the option of working in hazardous jobs such as mining. Many women—almost all single moms—have done so; some have tripled their pay.[41] But in the same time period during which 300 male miners lost their lives underground, not a single woman lost hers. Why? That's the part I find touching . . .

A male miner teaching a woman safety must teach her to sensitively "listen to the rocks," to listen to their creaking and groaning as they adjust to the shifting weight of the mountain above, a symphony of stress and strain. (Or as the miners might prefer, like a rock band.)

In male-dominated professions, traditional men tend to compete to be sure that women are cared for, mentored, and protected. In return they ask for appreciation. And respect.

Similarly, pay is higher and hazards lower for women than men in some of the most treacherous occupations like working on a floating commercial cannery in Alaska. Lance Hough, an Alaskan canner I interviewed, put it this way:

> The time pressure is enormous. You're on an assembly line, having to process 10–20 tons of fish before the next boat comes in with tons more. Power tools like band saws that cut through 500 fish in an hour, or fish injectors with maybe 50 needles (that inject salt into fish fillets), get jammed, and the time pressure tempts the men to try to undo the jam without shutting down the machines. Instead of the fish getting sliced or stuck with needles, your arm gets sliced or your hand is crushed and stuck by the 50-needle fish injector. . . .
>
> During salmon runs the pressure is even worse, 'cause you're only allowed 24 hours in certain areas to fish (for environmental reasons). Hands and arms get stuck and cut, and men get thrown into the icy waters and freeze to death. I've seen men who freak out and want "out," get dropped off on the closest piece of land, which could be a tiny island. Whether they find a way off or not I don't know.[42]

"Are there any women doing this?" I asked.

"A few. Maybe one or two out of a hundred."

"What's it like for them."

"I hate to say this, but if they're at all attractive, they get to wash clothes or clean, and avoid that assembly line."

"Do they get paid less?"

"No, they get paid more—it's considered a higher ranking."

Whether in a South African coal mine, on an Alaskan fishing boat, or in the American military, men's protective instinct toward women, and women's protective instinct toward themselves (and children) keeps men more disposable than women. Here's an example of the dynamic at work in the military.

At the military's SERE (survival, evasion, resistance, and escape) schools, concern about the well-being of women was so prevalent among male students that trainers now work to desensitize men to sexual assault and other abuse of women lest their sensitivity be used against them in war.[43] We think of women in the military as being safer in part because they are still prohibited from the most dangerous assignments.[44] But this prohibition is just a reflection of the traditional male's instinct to protect women.

The "Protection Dilemma": The Warrior vs. The Worrier

ITEM. The Navy provides pregnant women with housing, health care, and a benefit package that leads to twice the percentage of single mothers as in the civilian population.[45]

The military currently faces a "protection dilemma": protect-the-country versus protect-the-soldier. Traditionally, protecting the country meant preparing the soldier to die for his country. Boot camp's job was to train each soldier to be disposable, to be an unquestioning cog in the military machine. Why? Questioning and focusing on rights slow the machine down, compromising the country's safety. Traditionally, preparing to give one's life for one's country is preparing for disposability. Now that traditional mission has been altered.

The involvement of women, traditionally a group that men died to protect, has left the military with the dilemma of preparing warriors who may also be worriers—worrying about their own rights. The military has responded by worrying about the warrior. Currently, then, if a woman in the Navy becomes pregnant, as the previous Item notes, the Navy provides her such an array of benefits, from housing to health care, that the Navy now attracts twice the percentage of single mothers as are in the civilian population.[46]

These benefits are now available for women without the same price men have traditionally been expected to pay. When a 1985 Navy study found that most women were not able to perform any of the eight most critical jobs required for people on ship, they redefined the jobs to be inclusive of women. For example, the job of carrying a stretcher, previously a two-man job, changed: It is now a four-person job.[47] And the definition of "passing" changed: Women at West Point are given 5:30 minutes to complete an obstacle course that the men must complete in 3:20 minutes.[48]

If joining the military is not your thing, no problem. The same principal of the government incorporating women into the protector role and protecting the women who protect applies to police officers, firefighters, and rangers for the U.S. Park Services—all creating the same outcomes of equal pay for women, and often with fewer hazards.

The opportunities for women do not stop with working-class hazardous professions. Among white-collar professions under government jurisdiction, such as the Drug Enforcement Administration (DEA), CIA, and FBI, the "protection dilemma" leads to the government providing women with equal pay for fewer hazards. For example, in the DEA, all but 2 of the 47 agents killed have been men.[49]

In brief, all the portions of government that train and hire protectors face the "protection dilemma": The process of creating a protector is a process of sacrifice, of willingness to be disposable, to be a servant. (The very word "hero" comes from the word "serow" from which we get our word "servant."[50]) But personal empowerment also involves having the self-respect and self-esteem to care about one's own life. As the government incorporates the worrier's demand for personal protection with the country's need for the warrior's protection, it becomes the perfect time for women to become involved.

Why do so few women know about these "fewer hazards for equal pay" opportunities? Because we fear that if these special ways of giving women advantages are publicized they will undermine the country's commitment to affirmative action. And this is probably true—it's hard to have it both ways for a long time. But **the political necessity of a low profile, which makes it a "big secret," is also what makes it a big opportunity for the woman who knows the secret.**

The Costs and Benefits of Choosing Safety

The death rate for journalists in the war in Iraq was about 10 times as high as for soldiers in 2003: approximately one-tenth of 1% for soldiers versus 1% for reporters.[51] Yet, though 38% of the journalists in the world are female, only 7% (1 of the 14) journalists killed were female.[52]

Choosing safety is a choice of life over career. As BBC correspondent Katie Adie puts it, "Prizes handed out go to those people who go to wars and not to the people who go to the flower shows."[53] The price, though, includes more than exposure to physical harm: Journalists who cover wars have significantly more psychiatric difficulties than journalists who do not report on war.[54] Specifically, they drink more heavily and show higher rates of post-traumatic stress disorder and major depression.[55] In particular, women war reporters were seven times more likely to be heavy drinkers than other women reporters, a much higher ratio than men war reporters.[56]

Women bring a unique perspective to war coverage. They appear to focus more on the toll war takes on civilian women and children.[57] Ironically, although women's propensity to avoid danger makes them less prone to reporting from war zones, once in the war zone they focus more on the danger to other women and children and less on the danger to the men (who are more likely to be dying!).

Industrialization's Unconscious Transition in a Mom's Way of Risking Her Life

Are women too risk averse to realistically be expected to enter hazardous occupations—even for equal pay with fewer risks? Yes and no. Focusing on the workplace misses the fact that women have historically risked their lives in childbirth, and in nonindustrialized countries, they still do.

Industrialization is creating an unconscious transition in the way a mother is expected to risk her life for her children. While industrialization has indirectly contributed to significantly fewer risks in child-birth, it has also increased the affordability of divorce. As we see with the example of the women coal miners in South Africa, it was the single moms who responded to the pressure to take a hazardous job. What was previously a dad's way of loving his family (to risk his life so his children wouldn't have to risk theirs) could be evolving, at least partially, into a single mom's way.

A single mom knows her children need her love in the form of time as much as in the form of money, so the single mom today has a new question to ask: "Should I take a dangerous job to make more money in less time, so I can have both money and time for my children?"

The surface answer may be a reflexive "no": "If I lose my life, my children will have no mother, no money, no time—so 'no way.' " But let's go beneath the surface. Many moms dial a cell phone while driving over the speed limit on a highway, or pulling out of a parking lot onto a main drag; others delay fastening a seat belt, or go biking. . . . Chances are you've far exceeded the risk a police officer takes, and you weren't feeding your children.

How Men in the Hazardous Professions Are Their Own Worst Enemy

Jimmy Harris, a cabdriver in Jacksonville, Florida is completing his last fare after midnight Sunday. The passenger takes out a gun and refuses to pay the $5 he owes. Jimmy argues with him—into the barrel of a gun. Jimmy is shot 8 times, sustains 12 bullet wounds (some shots causing more than 1 wound, à la JFK). Some are in his chest. He is hospitalized for 12 hours. The next evening, on Monday, Jimmy returns to work![58] Jimmy said on TV that he could tell he would have been shot in any case, which is why he fought. Maybe. The reactions of his buddies when he returned to work the next day? Seeing his multiple bullet holes, they nicknamed him "Mr. Sprinkler."

While Jimmy is over-the-top, he's only an extension of the genetic heritage that selected for men who would risk their lives to put salmon on our table, fight our wars, cut timber so our homes can be built, and mine coal so our homes can be heated. This heritage makes it more difficult to imagine a woman stupid enough to argue into the barrel of a gun over a $5 fare.

When we apply to cab driving this male willingness to make the dangerous even more dangerous, we find opportunities for women that can lead to higher pay per hour for fewer hazards.

My assistant and I conducted interviews with fleet owners and cab-drivers in New York, Los Angeles, Chicago, and Philadelphia.[59] All the owners agreed that while cab driving can be dangerous (cab-drivers are 33% more likely than police officers and detectives to get killed on the job), it is much *less* dangerous for women because women work the less-dangerous shifts (daytime rush hours) and the safer areas (airports, business districts, wealthier neighborhoods).[60] Both sexes prefer these shifts and areas, but women are more likely to be granted them. Men are more likely to work 60–70 hours per week, especially if they have children, and so cannot limit their choice to more selective hours or areas.

Women cabbies experience fewer risks in many ways. By averaging 20-plus hours more per week than the women, men are more vulnerable to accident-by-fatigue. They are more likely to lift baggage, both increasing back injuries and, by being out of the car, increasing danger due to being unprotected by the Plexiglas barrier separating them from passengers. Although a woman would technically be an easier target for robbery, men, the sex more likely to rob, also have a biological instinct to protect a woman, but not a man. Beyond that, murders of cabdrivers often emanate from a robbery's conflict escalating out of control, perhaps à la Jimmy Harris.

If women cabbies experience fewer risks, is it possible that they could nevertheless earn more? Yes. Of course, the women's total pay is less, but women earn more per hour (by working the better routes during the better hours). And all the owners agreed that, despite not helping as much with the baggage, the women received larger tips. (One owner felt the women earned these tips by being more courteous, but all felt that both sexes tended to tip women more, especially the men.) Finally, some male cabdrivers hurt their own income by giving free rides—to guess which sex?!

Given these advantages to the female cabdriver, are there many applications from women? No. The consensus is that about 98% of the applications are from men.

What are the underlying reasons behind these differences—

behind women's strength as their facade of weakness, and men's weakness as their façade of strength?

Men's Weakness as Their Façade of Strength; Women's Strength as Their Façade of Weakness

Women's fewer risks even in hazardous occupations also derive from women asking that their safety concerns be heeded even as boys are learning to associate being abused with being loved. More on abuse-as-love in a minute, but let's look first at what women do to keep themselves safe.

While I was writing the first draft of this section, a Goodwill rep called to cancel a pickup at my home. Why? The driver said it was too dangerous for her to travel with her truck down the narrow, curving streets to my home. Since they had picked up for 17 years, I couldn't help but ask if Goodwill had gotten larger trucks. The answer? No. The good news? A woman was the new truck driver, and she had asked that her safety concerns be heeded. The bad news? I never met her. A year or so later I called again and Goodwill came. No problem. But also no woman driver.

When women enter a hazardous field such as construction, they take the time to wear the helmets, double-check the rafters, etc., and are more likely, via such manifestations of concern, to signal to a man their openness to his taking the risk for them. Thus, a male-female dance emerges: The women want to be thought of as equal, nevertheless they are receptive to special protection. Men resent women receiving special protection, nevertheless they offer it. And sometimes they compete to offer it—with the conscious or unconscious hope it will be rewarded by her smile, her warmth, her flirtation, or, sometimes, something more.

This male-female dance is magnified by our role models. While women's heroes in the war in Iraq were women who were saved, the closest to a male hero was a man who died. Inspired by 9/11, Pat Tillman sacrificed a more than $3 million NFL contract playing safety to keep his country safe.[61]

Pat Tillman had fulfilled the very purpose of football. Thus boys' heroes become football players such as Donovan McNabb, who quarterbacked virtually an entire game with a broken right ankle (yes, his team won).[62] Or the Tampa Bay Buccaneers' Kerry Jenkins, who became a hero because he played with a broken leg from September through November.[63] When did Jenkins sit out? When it was determined his fractured fibula had deteriorated to such a point that he was no longer as valuable as his potential replacement. That is, the only purpose of reducing his personal pain was his team's gain.[64]

"A team's gain over personal pain" becomes to dads what an "infant's gain over personal pain" becomes to a mom in labor. Both sexes endure their respective "labor" pains.

The lesson for women in all this is an understanding that guys who enter hazardous occupations are prone to take even more risks than are needed. For example, on oilrigs men who only work an 8-hour day are contemptuously called "nine-to-fivers." In stark contrast, women are more likely not to take risks, even when the risks are minimal.

What's the message to our sons? **Our praise of our sons when they risk physical danger teaches them that a willingness to be physically abused creates love.**

Abuse-as-love? Yes. Think of both the risk of injury and the potential for a boy to attract "love" associated with not just football, but ice hockey, rugby, NASCAR racing, boxing, and the high-risk versions of skateboarding, surfing, skiing, and snowboarding. What does risking concussions, bulging disks, broken collarbones, lacerated kidneys, shattered kneecaps, torn ligaments, torn Achilles tendons, and cracked vertebrae lead to?[65] A cheerleader becoming that boy's first love; to parental praise being interpreted as parental love. . . .

For males, risking physical abuse increases the probability of feeling the love and praise of parents and finding a first love. It becomes a primal, if sick, connection.

The injuries at the time of playing are small compared to the injuries with which time has a chance to play. By their forties and fifties, the former heroes and the never-known linemen have an increased risk of heart attacks, severe back and spinal pain, arthritic spurs, and worn-out knees, ankles, and elbows.[66] Degenerative arthritis in the knees and back make getting out of bed, or getting into a car, an excruciating experience. For someone whose identity was physical prowess, the pain is more than physical. As a former NFL team physician puts it, "We are creating a generation of super football players who will be crippled for the remainder of their lives with arthritis."[67]

While we call role models "leaders," most "leaders" are really followers. Most "leaders" follow their bribes. And we are the people who offer the bribes. We in essence give men two bribes to risk their lives: pay and praise. We praise them as heroes, a word that has etymological roots in the words servant, slave, and protector (hence "public servant"). Our appreciation keeps the slave a slave. The outcome? **A man who self-selects for a death profession expects his body to be used in exchange for pay.** The unspoken motto of the death professions is "My body, not my choice."

All of this had a purpose historically and biologically. Societies that survived had an unconscious investment in the disposability of their individual women and men. But women's risk of disposability came mostly biologically, via childbirth. Men's came more via socialization. Technology has minimized women's risk, but we still profit from the risks men were socialized to take.

If men were not socialized to call it "glory" to die in war, another society that wanted its land or its resources would eventually conquer it. If men were not trained to be disposable as coal miners, hunters, and lumberjacks, they couldn't transform the resources into food, homes, or electricity. If they were not socialized to risk their lives as firefighters, they couldn't protect the homes into which those resources had been transformed.

While this is useful for a society, it is not necessarily healthy for an individual man. It affects a man's psyche beyond the job. Thus, police officers are two to three times more likely to take their own lives than to be killed on duty.[68]

Our unconscious investment in men's disposability is reflected in our institutions' absence of educating men about their personal safety needs. Thus men die sooner of all 10 leading causes of death, but there is no Office on Men's Health while there is an Office on Women's Health. One of the most hazardous jobs is coal mining. Yet instead of expanding the government agency responsible for preventing mine accidents and respiratory diseases (the Bureau of Mines), the government has, for all practical purposes, shut it down.[69]

Secret #2: How to Make a Fortune in the Death Professions Without the Death or the Dirt

If you are a woman, oh my . . . you can take advantage of a window of opportunity during which government agencies, universities, and other businesses are required to have a certain percentage of their construction contracts with women-owned businesses. And since so few women have started their own construction companies, you've got government agencies, universities, and large companies with federal contracts that are competing for you and your business.

"Wait," you're saying, "I don't want to be a construction worker." "Wait," I'm saying, "You don't have to be a construction worker." We're talking about women-*owned* businesses, and about working in hazardous occupations *without* the hazards: Put the two together and consider running your own business, hiring the best construction workers and subcontractors, and putting together the team. After all, how many men have owned businesses in which they had no experience? I never saw George W. Bush play professional baseball, or Marge Schott for that matter, yet Schott owned the Cincinnati Reds and Bush put together the partners who bought the Texas Rangers.

Does the idea of taking on responsibility for ownership, of which you've had no experience, freak you out or just not compute? Really? Have you ever thought of being a mother?

Still skeptical? Barbara Kavovit's story will make you a believer.[70]

Barbara was fired from her first job. But it didn't take the fire out of her belly. I won't tell you anything up-front about what she was doing when I caught up with her some years ago, at the age of 31. I'll let you take the journey with me.

The Barbara Kavovit Story

My mom always said, "You should do things on your own." My undergrad degree in finance prepared me, at least in theory, to do mergers and acquisitions, but in my first job my boss treated me like a glorified coffee gopher. We frustrated each other so much he once flipped my desk over in anger. I coulda sued him. But I thought: "Maybe I should do something on my own!"

I recalled a friend complaining about how construction workers never seemed to pay attention to the details—and that once paid, they weren't around for problems that were discovered later. I thought, "I'm good at detail and follow-up." One problem: I knew nothing about construction. But I didn't think that should make a difference!

One other problem: I didn't have any money or family to finance me. So I made some business cards and fliers on the computer for about $200. I had no money for advertising either, so I sat outside this very wealthy shopping center in Westchester County and I targeted my market to just women. I dressed up in a navy blue suit and as the women came out, I went up to them and told them I started a home improvement company in the local area and I'd like to give them a price on any home improvement ideas they might have. I must have given out 700–1,000 cards. Soon people starting calling, "The tile in my bathroom, it's cracked" . . . "Can you change the door hardware?" . . . "Paint the room" . . . very small projects.

Meantime, I was digging through the *Pennysaver,* calling a bunch of unknown carpenters, getting references, inviting a carpenter to come to each project, and have him give me an estimate. I'd make an offer that allowed me about 40%, and then, I kept my fingers crossed that the carpenter was good. But I kept involved with him and the client every day making sure the client was happy.

The jobs started getting bigger and bigger. Since I always thought large, after a year of building a track record I said to myself, "IBM is near where I live; they should know what I'm doing." So I wrote a letter to IBM. Nothing. I tried again and again. Nothing and nothing. Finally, 6 months later the senior buyer up at their Stamford office awarded me an interview. I went in there very corporate-like, and said, "I have a small crew of guys, and we can accommodate you with 24 hours' notice."

He looked at me like I had two heads. I was 24 at the time. He said, "How could you possibly do anything for us?" I showed him the resumes of the men I was working with and said, "Give me a chance, and I can show you." He tried us out.

Six months later he called and said, "We have 2,000 sq. ft. over

here; the whole department is moving to the other side of the building. We need to take down the walls and put in a different configu-
ration of walls. New electric. If you had to start at 7 o'clock at night
and work through the night, could you do it?" Whatever it was, I
didn't care, I was doing it. That led to being awarded a 2-year contract to do all the work at corporate headquarters. From there, they
extended my contract to cover a facility they were purchasing. Now, I
was on the map.

I figured if I could get into IBM, I could get in anywhere. So I
started writing letters to all the Fortune 100 companies. Now, 8 years
later, I'm 31, and my company, Anchor Construction, just finished the
renovation of Carnegie Hall.

What we learn from Barbara Kavovit serves us beyond the hazardous professions:

- Barbara felt that men in construction tended to miss the careful
  attention to the customer both during and after the project.
  Fields that are either male- or female-dominated tend to ignore
  contributions the other sex would likely make were it present.
  Thus if you're interested in a field dominated by the other sex,
  you may be able to start a business that specializes in filling that
  gap.
     Similarly, a man might look at the school system now domi-
  nated more by female values of book-learning, orderliness, child
  safety, and protectiveness, and be inspired to start a private high
  school that specializes in risk-taking, entrepreneurial skills, dis-
  ciplining by consequences rather than repetition, and the interactive, participatory, total immersion, take-responsibility-type
  learning of the Outward Bound or Tony Robbins genre.
- Every complaint points to a path for potential profit. Barbara
  Kavovit heard a complaint and followed it to her path for profit.
- You don't need to be an expert to organize experts. You mostly
  need to be a good communicator and organizer.
- A good substitute for raising money is starting small.

3. Among Jobs Requiring Little Education, Those That Expose You to the Sleet and Heat Pay More Than Those That Are Indoors and Neat
(FedEx Deliverer vs. Receptionist)

> *A woman told me she'd do anything I want for $50.*
> *I said, 'Paint my house.'*
>
> —HENNY YOUNGMAN[71]

The Exposure Professions

Check this out the next time you're in your car in the rain and the only thing between you and the downpour is the windshield and a little wiper running for its life. Your gas gauge is low, but you don't want to join the wiper, so you treat yourself to a gas station with a full-serve pump. Now, what are the chances a woman will pump your gas?

If there is a woman working at the gas station, she is indoors; if there is a man working there, he could be indoors or outdoors, or rotating between the two.

Now imagine being the owner of the full-serve station. Other things being equal, to whom would you give a raise—the one who will just work indoors, or the one who will work indoors and outdoors as needed, no matter what the weather? If you had to let someone go, who would it be? If you had to hire just one employee, who would have the edge?

It is one thing for a woman's lesser upper body strength to limit her ability to pitch in loading boxes during a slow period. It is another for a woman to limit her value by not wanting to get herself wet or cold.

Once a woman has made herself credible as a stereotype-breaker in one field, she makes herself credible to try something new in another field. And beyond her self-interest, she creates a reason for women not to be the last hired and the first fired during tough times.

I call professions that require being frequently outdoors the exposure professions. Landscapers, housepainters, and park rangers; UPS and FedEx deliverers; garbage collectors, ditchdiggers, and firefighters; highway workers and construction workers; roofers, welders, and linemen all expose themselves to the sleet and the heat, to summer's humidity and winter's windchill, to rain, snow, lightning, and in some cases, fire.

Some exposure professions pay terribly. Ditch digging, once the work of all-male chain gangs, was protested as exploitive of prisoners.[72] Their appeal? They just pay better than the alternative: children starving. For jobs requiring little education, most exposure professions pay more than one requiring little education and no exposure (Table 10).

If you have little education, want to work indoors, and still want high pay, are there alternatives? Yes. The government can use taxpayer money to pay more for indoor work than the market might bear. Thus a U.S. Postal Service (USPS) clerk only gets paid about $1,250 less per year than a mail carrier ($40,400 vs. $39,150).[73] Plus there are all the government holidays and benefits.

When Affirmative Action Marries Technology and Invites Women into the Family

Fortunately, technology now allows many ditches to be dug by someone in the cab of a backhoe protected from the rain, rather than at the bottom of a ditch where the rain can be a pain.

TABLE 10   "Exposure Professions" Requiring Little Education

Occupation	Earnings
U.S. Postal Service Mail Carrier	$40,000
Line Installers and Repairers	$37,000
FedEx Couriers	$34,500
Meter Readers	$22,000
Exposure Profession Examples	Average: $33,250

Occupations That Are Indoors and Safe, Requiring Little Education

Occupation	Earnings
Counter and rental clerks	$23,000
Telemarketers	$20,000
Hosts and hostesses, restaurant, lounge, and coffee shop	$17,000
Cashiers	$17,000
Indoor Occupation Examples	Average: $19,250

Source: Bureau of Labor Statistics, 2004 and Salary.com[74]

Technology is suddenly making professions that have been expo-sure professions for thousands of years into minimum-exposure pro-fessions, and that, combined with affirmative action, is making these professions more inviting to women. For example, among mail carri-ers, the slogan on the façade of the main post office in Manhattan is "Neither snow nor rain, nor gloom of night stays these couriers from the swift completion of their appointed rounds." (Borrowed from Herodotus' similar description of Persian messengers around 400 B.C.!)

For more than those 2,400 years the exposure professions kept men exposed. I experienced a smidgeon of what Herodotus wit-nessed when, as I mentioned earlier, I delivered mail in Waldwick, New Jersey, during Christmas (in those days we didn't say "holiday") vacations to earn money for college. On my skinny-as-a-rail frame (I wish I could still claim the same), my back and shoulder endured a mailbag stuffed with Christmas mail and a gift of slush, courtesy of passing cars.

As I ended that job, an era also ended. Soon after, the USPS pur-chased mail trucks. Suddenly, the speed of mail carriers is dependent more on city speed limits than heroism, the rain splattering on the roof of the truck rather than on the head of the mail carrier.

And not too long after that, affirmative action gave women special advantages as mail carriers. Thus technology and affirmative action led to women as mail carriers. And that change created more changes. For example, I am now slushless in San Diego. Shortly after a female mail carrier had the window of her truck broken, the fear of a woman-in-jeopardy led the USPS to order 300 larger and stronger vans with windows reinforced with wire mesh and equipped with telephones.

Just as the fear of putting women in jeopardy now makes the death professions less deadly, so technology plus the fear of putting women in jeopardy have now made the exposure professions less exposed. And less exposure, to the sun at least, means less deadly effects, since sun exposure has doubtless been a factor in men being about seven times as likely to die of *work-related* skin cancer.[75]

Affirmative action and technology are together making exposure professions such as construction workers, mail carrier, park ranger, UPS and FedEx deliverers, and telephone line workers more available to women with more pay and less exposure than were typical of those professions in the past. And sunscreen, cancer prevention awareness, and medical advances are doing respectable battle with the increased risks.

If you are the type of woman who watches HGTV (the Home & Garden channel), loves gardening, is creative, is a people person, and likes high pay, landscape architecture is an up-and-coming field. (If you are a guy, don't disqualify yourself if you don't watch HGTV!) Even with all the security and benefits of working for a firm, a good landscape architect can make $80,000–$100,000 per year.[76] As with most jobs, there's an inverse relationship between fulfillment and pay: Commercial landscape architects generally consider themselves to have less-fulfilling jobs but more-fulfilled wallets. For a residential landscape architect, the reverse is true.

When we hear, "Full-time working men earn more than full-time working women," we seldom hear someone say, "Wait, have you adjusted for men's greater willingness to earn more by being in the death and exposure professions?"

Many of these men have little education. So when we hear, "Men still earn more when both sexes have equal education," **we ignore a working-class man's equivalent of education: a willingness to risk his life in the death professions and exposure professions.** That is a working-class man's way of increasing pay.

Any study that claims to have found a gender pay gap that has not adjusted for involvement in the death and exposure professions is a study that has not adjusted for its sexism. It reinforces women's propensity to focus on education to increase pay, and to ignore opportunities in two types of professions—hazardous and exposure professions—that are becoming female-friendly. It keeps women in an outdated mind-set.

4. In Most Fields with Higher Pay, You *Can't* Psychologically *Check Out* at the End of the Day
(Corporate Attorney vs. Librarian)

The Bell cell ad makes it clear as a bell that even if we take the man out of the office, we must not take the office out of the man . . . that even a man out of his office is a man in his cell.

More accurately, the male profile is closer to the profile of successful people of either sex. Unfortunately, most successful people are like 7-Elevens—they never close. Cathey Cotten, founder and managing principal of MetaSearch (tech recruiting), would keep an alarm clock in her office reminding her to go home—at 2 a.m. Christmas was not sacred, except insofar as work was sacred.[77]

The most successful women I interviewed had to be the ones standing on the mountaintop, calling not their home office, but often their home and office. Some married their careers. Some forfeited children. Some stood alone. But a psychological check-out job was not an option.

Successful women were ambivalent about checking out. When I

interviewed Lillian Vernon (of Lillian Vernon Corporation), she commented, "Many people who dream about their own businesses and don't have one, are not prepared to work that hard—to think about their job while they're getting dressed, showering, waiting for somebody—to think of every minute as an opportunity."[78]

While most successful women echoed that feeling, they added caveats. Theresa Metty, senior VP of Motorola, generally agreed, saying, "Successful people don't see after-hour 'demands' as demands, but as opportunities. The opportunity to surprise, invent, create . . ."[79] But then she added, "I'm trying to teach myself to check out even occasionally—maybe work out, or check in to church, rediscover my Catholic roots and get a spiritual life."

Women who do not know how to cut back often end up cutting out, especially if their children are paying the price. When Nadya Shmavonian quit her post as executive VP of the Pew Charitable Trusts, she explained, "I was beginning to dream about work, not the children."[80]

When a department store clerk physically checks out, she or he can psychologically check out. Trial attorneys rarely check out psychologically: They make opening arguments in their dreams, think about billing in the bathroom, and make closing arguments while making love. (Don't ask me what the surgeon is doing!)

When we can psychologically check out from our work, we tend to call it a job; when we can't, we call it a career. We get prestige and pay to become psychologically enmeshed, or, if you will, career codependent.

The big question in choosing between a job in which we can psychologically check out and a career in which we cannot, is whether the career choice is creating eustress or distress. Eustress is positive stress that strengthens the immune system, like the stress of doing a dozen things to get ready for a dream date, or the stress of meeting people at a dinner in which you are being honored. If your career makes you proud of yourself and excites you after hours, chances are it is creating eustress—and eustress strengthens the immune system.

Eustress is a virtue on a slippery slope, however. We've all heard the expression, "The good die young." Despite the doubtless great genes of the great performers, and some perpetually visible exceptions (Bob Hope, George Burns), it appears that the extreme pressure on great performers (both external and internal), their propensity for risk-taking, the uncertainty as to who really loves you for you, and the tendency to burn the candle at both ends lead to drugs, accidents, and many hints that perhaps, in fact, the good may die young (Jim Morrison, Jim Croce, Jimi Hendrix, John Belushi, John Lennon, John Keats, Janis Joplin, Jesus, all three Bronte sisters, Alexander the Great, Buddy Holly, Charlie Parker, Patsy Cline, Elvis, Martin Luther King, Mozart, Gershwin, the Kennedys . . .). Eustress can be like a snowfall that becomes a blizzard overwhelming the snowfall's beauty. Too much eustress breeds stress just as too much success breeds failure.

If a career in which we cannot psychologically check out is creating distress, the question is whether the level of pay is an adequate compensation. As we will see in Chapter 4, "Doing Time," men are more likely to put in more hours at work. As we saw among physicians, they are more likely to be self-employed, which allows for less ability to psychologically check out, and they are more likely to work much more when they start their own businesses.

5. Fields with Higher Pay Often Have *Lower Fulfillment*
(Tax Accountant vs. Child care Professional)

> *"In computer sciences I always felt I stuck out like a sore thumb; in art, you can't stick out—you're expected to be who you are. In art, I'm free to pursue projects of my own creation, not just do assignments."*
> —ZOE WOODWORTH, A FEMALE STUDENT WHO SWITCHED FROM COMPUTER SCIENCES TO ART AT CARNEGIE MELLON UNIVERSITY (CMU)[81]

Zoe said, "Obviously, I'm going to be a starving artist, or, ideally an art professor. But my roommate at CMU, who stayed with getting a computer science degree, is now driving a BMW, living in Santa Barbara, and working at Intel. But I couldn't live doing something that upset me so much."

Work to live, or live to work? That is the question. And that is also the false dichotomy. Fulfilling work can make "living" and "working" almost synonyms. But as I cautioned earlier, when we follow our bliss, it's often money we'll miss. If a workplace primarily offers fulfillment, *we* would be *paying the workplace*—the workplace wouldn't have to pay us. If the workplace is extremely fulfilling, it is more like a workshop, and we pay to attend workshops.

What is the most fulfilling work? A large Australian study found that volunteers are the most satisfied Australians, and a close second are stay-at-home moms.[82] Stay-at-home moms scored the highest in happiness with their personal relationships. Volunteers, most of whom were women over 55 who worked less than 20 hours a week, had the highest personal well-being score of all employment groups. The volunteers were happier than any other group with their health, spirituality, amount of leisure time, their job, working hours, and community connections.

The Australian study also found that people working more than 60 hours a week in caretaking roles (usually stay-at-home moms) were more satisfied with both their health and their work than people who worked for money between 40–60 hours per week. More precisely, the caretakers who worked more than 60 hours per week were the second happiest of all employment groups; the people who worked for money between 40–60 hours per week were the least happy of all employment groups.[83]

The implications of the Australian study are that:

- Caring for children is fulfilling and healthy.
- Doing things we perceive as for the public good and social good (what volunteers usually do) contributes significantly to one's personal well-being—that is, it is highly fulfilling.
- We can't expect to get paid much for doing things that are highly fulfilling. (Volunteers aren't paid much.)
- If we're doing what is fulfilling we can do it more than 60 hours a week and be happy.
- Doing the average paid job is usually stressful and unfulfilling when done for more than 40 hours a week.

I now know why I am happy writing this book more than 60 hours per week, and paid very little to do it!

The Gender Fulfillment Gap

A London School of Economics (LSE) study tracking 10,000 graduates from 30 universities between their 1993 graduations and their
careers as of the early 2000s, found a 12% gender pay gap in men's
favor.[84] Why the 12% gap?

The women graduates were more likely to major in education and
the arts, and the men in engineering, math, and computing. More
precisely, "Just over half the women (vs. 32% of the men) stressed the
importance of a socially useful job, whereas men were almost twice as
likely to stress salary."[85] Once differences in fulfillment and flexibility
were accounted for, there was only a 2% remaining pay gap. In brief,
the gender pay gap is better explained as a gender fulfillment gap.

The LSE study did not inquire about the number of hours worked.
But as we will see in "Doing Time" (Chapter 4), the gender "hours-
worked gap" by itself can account for as much as 70% of the pay gap.

Women Penetrate Glass Ceiling, Find Wisdom, Leave

*"I'm an incredibly happy person now. I definitely never
want to be an executive again."*
—JAMIE TARSES, FORMER PRESIDENT OF ABC ENTERTAINMENT,
AFTER HER RESIGNATION

Once a woman or man has made it to the top rungs of her or his
profession's ladder—a rung high enough to look down through the
glass ceiling—most observe their family waving from a distance;
standing near their family is a pale ghost of themselves that they
yearn to make real. Whether Jamie Tarses of ABC or Brenda Barnes
of Pepsi, women are more likely than men to shoot a hole in the
alleged glass ceiling and escape through the exit. And women considering the top consider more than the top . . .

When Sonia Gandhi successfully led her Indian National Congress
Party to an unexpected victory over the opposition in 2004, she was
poised to be India's next prime minister. But she declined the post.[86]
Reaction? Shock. Party members threatened suicide if she did not
agree to be India's prime minister.[87] She was called selfish. And selfless.

The confusion as to whether Sonia Gandhi was selfish or selfless exposes our lack of understanding of men's and women's roles. As a woman, Sonia was not limited by the male role. **The male role was designed to align selfishness with selflessness.** We gave men medals, promotions, titles, glory, power, and immortality to bribe them to make their own lives secondary to saving the lives of others (e.g., Kennedys and Gandhis, generals and privates, firefighters and coal miners, Achilles and Christs)—to make every man feel, whether he was poor or rich, that there was something bigger than self to die for. Thus almost all the suicide bombers, whether from Israel or Palestine, Iraq, Iran, or Saudi Arabia, are men.

Indians who threatened suicide if Sonia Gandhi did not serve were using the male style of making a contribution to persuade a woman to use the male style. They did not understand that a woman unconsciously learned she was to be protected by male sacrifice, not to use herself as a sacrifice. As a woman, she could permit herself to be sacrificed for only one purpose—her own children. Rather than conflict being something she must overcome, it was for her something to be weighed; and when her Italian birth and halting command of Hindi became a political issue, she opted to exercise power behind the scenes.

Neither sex is a prisoner of these instincts, but understanding the differences helps us uncover the motives of both sexes. For example, it helps us understand that capitalism and patriotism have special appeal to men because they have to date been modeled on the traditional male role—the alignment of selfishness with selflessness.

We see this not only in business and politics, but in women's sports, public service, and the arts. Notice this wisdom in Steffi, Nadya, and Sinead's understanding that the glass ceiling may be a steel trap, that power can become powerlessness . . .

Steffi Graf's $22 million prize money exceeded that of any woman athlete. She retired at age 30, still ranked number two in the world, but saying, "For the first time in my career, I didn't feel like going to a tournament."[88] In 2004, 5 years later, *Inside Tennis* magazine noted, "Faster than you could ask, 'Are Steffi and Andre [Agassi] really an item?' she vanished from the public eye to embrace romance and marriage, motherhood and a Garboesque solitude."[89] There she remains, a German living in Las Vegas; a younger former tennis star cheering her older still-a-star husband from the tennis stand; as committed to giving her children love at home as she was to giving her opponents love on the court.

Nadya Shmavonian (the executive vice president at the Pew Memorial Trusts), assessing her life, concluded, "I was absolutely flat-out. All I managed to do were the kids and my job. I could have continued to do this indefinitely, but I would have been a shell of myself."[90]

Nadya gave a resignation speech to her co-workers, explaining how dreams about her children had morphed into dreams of work. After her presentation, she walked through the Trusts' offices. One by one, she counted 10 different people who pulled her aside, asking if they could have a moment with her. Then, in the privacy of an office, all close to tears, each poured out how much her speech resonated with their own aching to have time with their family, to balance work and home. She said she was "struck by the deep well of pain and yearning in these colleagues."[91] And she was struck that all of these colleagues had one thing in common: They were men.

What even the most publicity-seeking women seem to have, to a greater degree than their male counterparts, is permission to act on their desire to retire at an early age, though not without ambivalence. Sinead O'Connor, the singer-activist who first announced her retirement at age 25, expressed her ambivalence when she resurfaced, and then retired again by age 32, and then resurfaced and retired for the third time (in 2003) at age 36.[92] She articulated the powerlessness of her power when she expressed how each time she responded to a fan in the street, she gave away a piece of herself, until she felt she had nothing left to give.[93]

Hospital Nursing's Fulfillment Failure

All the opportunities I discussed for nurses who are not in hospitals are occurring at the same moment that insurance-companies-playing-doctor and government-playing-regulator have made in-hospital nursing less fulfilling. Dedicated nurses are spread so thin that failure is built-in. Physical exhaustion, second-rate resources, safety hazards, and the inability to complete care are pushing nurses out of hospitals even as higher pay and better conditions are pulling nurses into them.

While these are the baseline conditions for nurses of both sexes, male nurses are finding the profession to be even more alienating. Male nurses are almost twice as likely as women to leave the profession within 4 years of graduation.[94] When an in-depth Gallup survey investigated, it found male nurses felt less fulfilled and engaged in the workplace in all 12 areas of measurement.[95]

The survey found the biggest gap between the male and female nurses is in the development of friendships at work. Male nurses are much less likely to feel "I have a best friend at work," which leads to feelings of isolation and the fear that co-workers won't be there when needed.[96]

Just as a woman can feel especially isolated in male-dominated fields, so a man can feel parallel isolation in a female-dominated field. The big difference is that for the past 35 years, diversity training has been helping women achieve fulfillment in male-dominated fields by sensitizing men to women, but not sensitizing women to men. For example, men have been taught how sexual harassment can make a woman feel distracted at best, or, at worst, isolated, objectified, unvalued for her work, and violated; how constant discussion of sports, or dirty jokes, or teasing, can feel isolating to women. Men have also been taught how, on the other hand, solicitation of a woman's opinions and interrupting less can make her feel more valued; how child care and flexible hours not only make her job more possible, but make her feel the company wants her enough to adapt to her needs.

A parallel diversity program to make men feel more included would begin by addressing the dozen areas in which male nurses feel more alienated, educating female nurses about the positive functions of male teasing and humor, confronting the discrimination against male nurses seeing naked female patients even as female nurses can see naked male patients, and so on.

Small Business: Fulfillment's Price Tag

As we explore in Chapter 8, women's and men's different reasons for starting small businesses magnify the usual differences between men's pay and women's fulfillment. Women who start small businesses are more likely to be seeking fulfillment, flexibility, family time, and autonomy. And these last three—flexibility, family time, and autonomy—are just ingredients in fulfillment's feast.

Fulfillment's price tag? Despite the numerous forms in which the government subsidizes women-owned businesses, they earn 49% of what their male counterparts earn.[97]

Less-Is-More Fulfillment

Martha Tacy typifies women leaving larger and less personal workplaces for the greater fulfillment she felt a small company affords. Martha left IBM's Lotus Development Corporation, where she was a marketing director, and became a vice president at Collaborative Communications, a public relations company in Cambridge, Massachusetts. In a company with fewer than 40 employees, she receives greater fulfillment. "Now, when I have an idea, I get to act on it immediately instead of sitting around arguing about it in a meeting all day."[98] She had to both figure out sales strategies and execute them. "Until I started this job, I didn't think I'd ever have the confidence to make a sales call. Now I'm doing it all the time, and it's really built up my self-esteem—and my resume."[99]

The Golf of Teaching

Teaching is one of the best blends of fulfillment and income. As for fulfillment, teaching is a bit like golf: often frustrating, but when you hit it just right, you become an addict. Unlike golf, you don't have to be in the top 200 to make a living doing it, you don't have to travel, you can be home for the kids, it has excellent benefits and a great retirement package, you know you can make a difference in dozens of young lives (even if you fail with your own children!), and you have up to 180 days a year "off" (albeit many are spent preparing for the days you are "on").

While the average U.S. teacher earns $44,000 a year, in many states the pay exceeds $50,000[100]; and with a master's and enough experience, it's into the $80,000-plus range. Moreover, what is sometimes missed about teaching is the fringe benefits beyond summers off. The monetary value of the benefits equals 26% of a teacher's salary, versus about 17% in the private sector.[101] In states such as California, teachers can get discounted mortgages and car loans, and tuition reimbursement. And in many states, retirement benefits are substantial. In Missouri, teachers can retire at age 55 with a pension paying 84% of the last year's income, plus benefits and cost-of-living adjustments.[102]

We often hear that paying teachers so poorly is a sad commentary on our values. On one level it is: Paying more would attract the cream of the crop to teaching and child care. On the other hand, it also reflects positively on our values. Here's why. People love children so much that millions of parents in essence pay to raise them (via lost work hours and actual expenses). If caring for children is so fulfilling that people pay a lot to do it, and tens of thousands of mothers home-school for "free" (usually paid indirectly by their husbands' salaries), it is little wonder we pay people little for doing it. It is in part because we value raising children so much that the supply of child-raisers is so great and the pay so moderate. **If everyone hated children, and hated raising them, we would have to pay more to get someone to do it. That would be a sad commentary on our values.**

How can someone teach and be the primary breadwinner of a family with children? Two ways. First, become an expert on distinguishing wants from needs. Second, become an expert on investing, especially in real estate. No profession offers longer breaks to research investments. (Without developing this expertise, I could not have sustained the last two decades of my writing—the politically incorrect decades.)

The Next Decade in Teaching

As women earn more, they'll increasingly want husbands who are not only good dads, but who can get home when the children get home, yet still make a stable income with benefits that include the option of also covering their wives. Fortunately, this coincides both with the needs of children and with the future of men in teaching. Here's why.

I predict that the biggest opportunities in teaching within the next decade will be for men in elementary and junior high school. Why? Schools will discover the need for men *enough* to make the school system safer for male teachers. Here's what is in process . . .

As of the early twenty-first century, men throughout the world are dropping out of teaching as quickly as boys are dropping out of school.[103] And boys are dropping out of school as quickly as men are dropping out of teaching. Divorces have led to the absence of dads in the home, and the fear of being sued or fired for being hands-on has made the potentially best teachers of both sexes avoid teaching. When a boy goes from a single-mother home to a female-dominated school, he may not experience a positive male role model until he's in junior high. It is little wonder he may seek a gang for identity, or a bottle to numb his emptiness.

What, precisely, is a male role model likely to add to the mix? Usually, it's the encouragement of risk-taking, tough love, boundary enforcement, roughhousing, and pushing both girls and boys to discover within themselves a potential they did not know existed. To a male teacher or coach, team sports are less a game than a preparation for life. Michael Lewis poignantly describes this attitude in his tough-love high school coach whose challenges transformed Lewis from a self-described lazy, wise-cracking failure into a student ready for admission to Princeton, with enough self-starting skills to become a best-selling author.[104]

Here's the rub. This coach—who also trained Peyton Manning, perhaps the world's best pro football player—is now being forced to give up the style that triggered the spark in so many of his students. Parents are objecting to their sons being pushed too hard. Schools are fearful of lawsuits, and therefore of litigious parents, and are pressuring coaches to take it easy. Good-bye, tough love.

How does men's teaching and parenting style differ from women's? Women tend to encourage children by creating very achievable opportunities for success, by being hands-on in their guidance, and praising each attempt. That's precisely what some children need, and what all children need some of the time.

Conversely, men tend to encourage by making life into a game, setting high expectations, and pushing—with less focus on protection and more on "I'm here to guide you toward that spark inside of yourself that you'll discover when you ignore the excuses, kick aside the barriers, and achieve exactly what you told me you couldn't do. You don't need to be protected from psychological or physical hurts; you need to learn how to deal with them and get beyond them. I'm not here to push you beyond your limits, but to show you how many of those limits are only in your mind." That's also precisely what some children need, and what all children need some of the time.

What's the outcome for the child deprived of good male role modeling? We now know that the absence of men creates the presence of problems. For example, the five D's—depression, disobedience, delinquency, drinking, and drugs—are much more common in the child brought up in a single-mother home than in a single-father home.[105] When the single-mother home and the female-dominated school system impact the same child, the outcome is more likely to be problems with assertiveness, empathy, physical health, and academic achievement, especially in math and science. Add to that a greater likelihood of nightmares, bullying or being bullied, feeling like a victim, attention deficit disorder, suicide, homicide, and teenage, out-of-wedlock pregnancy.[106]

Obviously, not every man would teach in the same way. But as the outcomes that are now documented become better known, school systems will face increasing pressure not just to find men teachers, but to make the system safe for the type of man who brings these qualities to his teaching. They will discover, I believe, that every community does best when its children have about equal exposure to mothers and fathers, and men and women teachers. And since it will be a while before communities with a lot of single moms have equal numbers of single dads, there will be an even greater need for those communities to have 50%–70% men teachers in elementary school, and especially the primary grades to balance out the mother-only influence in their students' homes. And therein lies a "best bet" opportunity for men, and the women who may wish to have children with good dads, worldwide.

When a woman has chosen such a man, she frees herself to take financial and emotional risks in business without guilt about neglecting the children at home. And those risks are the sixth way to choose a field with higher yield.

CHAPTER 3

The Field-with-Higher-Yield Formula: Six to Ten

In ways six to ten to a field-with-higher-yield, we learn as much about men and women as we do about pay per se. We peer into how we can more effectively prepare our daughters for risk-taking, which male-dominated professions our daughters will find more user-friendly due to technological transformations that are replacing muscle with mind. We discover some special career "finds" in places we wouldn't be prone to look, we explore the flexibility we can give ourselves by studying subfields, and we continue to uncover which male-female work differences create enough of a pay difference to make the gap in pay disappear completely.

6. People Who Get Higher Financial Rewards Choose Fields with Higher *Financial* and *Emotional* Risks
(Venture Capitalist vs. Supermarket Cashier)

A venture capitalist can expect to earn between $100,000 and $300,000 per year.[1] That's even more than a supermarket cashier! But the venture capitalist, a bit like the NFL coach, had better be a win-

The Field-with-Higher-Yield Formula: Six to Ten

6. People who get higher financial rewards choose fields with higher *financial* and *emotional* risks (VENTURE CAPITALIST VS. SUPERMARKET CASHIER)

7. Many fields with higher pay require working the worst shifts during the worst hours (PRIVATE PRACTICE MEDICAL DOCTOR VS. HMO MEDICAL DOCTOR)

8. Some jobs pay more to attract people to unpleasant environments without many people (PRISON GUARD VS. RESTAURANT HOSTESS)

9. Updating pays: Currency begets currency (SALES ENGINEER VS. FRENCH LANGUAGE SCHOLAR)

10. People who get higher pay also choose *subfields* with the "high-pay formula" (SURGEON VS. PSYCHIATRIST)

ner. You'll invest millions of dollars of your company's money, from which you will be expected to acquire new companies—or make new investments—that will make your company a lot more money. Or you'll use your own money, and take a big cut and risk being undercut. As you might have predicted, 91% of venture capitalists are men.[2]

I first experienced this male-female gap in financial and emotional risk-taking some years ago when I lived in New Jersey. I had just been admitted to graduate school at UCLA, but no summer job I could find could give me enough money to handle the costs of travel, tuition, room, and board. Except, perhaps, just maybe . . . selling encyclopedias. I decided to go for it. At the time, my mom was also working.

One week I would bring home a paycheck about four times the size of hers; but the next three weeks, no paycheck at all. And so it would go. At the end of the summer, though, I had earned more than she. I asked my mom, "Would you prefer to get steady paychecks even if you were quite sure you would earn less, or get variable paychecks even if it meant you would probably earn more?" She responded immediately, "I'd definitely prefer the security. Bringing home no paycheck for three weeks in a row would drive me crazy." My mother felt this way even though her paycheck did not handle any of the family's necessities—it did not create security in the absolute sense, only the latitude to spend with less questioning by Dad.

Since selling encyclopedias is 100% commission, the company (Collier's) lost little by giving virtually anyone who applied a chance. Hundreds applied. But now that I look back, I recall that the hundreds were all men. During the two summers I sold encyclopedias, a woman never applied.

Selling encyclopedias involved a lot more than financial risks. It also involved the emotional risks of handling the rejection at each door, seven hours a day, then returning the following day to the hot asphalt of a sweltering midday in mid-August in New Jersey, only to be rejected again, hour after hour for two–three weeks in a row. It was not a combination of experiences we ask young women to endure as preparation for the world of business.

The marketing manager at Collier's told us at the time that once we could handle that job, we'd be able to do almost anything in the world of business. He was right. Women who didn't apply lost many opportunities.

As I've gotten older, I notice women often work with money (cashiers, accountants, bookkeepers, even more than half of the nation's financial managers), but rarely choose full-time careers in which they put high percentages of their personal finances at risk (venture capitalist, inventor, private investor).[3] There's no perfect formula for financial success: People who make a fortune are more likely to have lost a fortune, à la Donald Trump. But overall, informed risk-taking pays off.

Men are more likely to think of financial failures as financial investments—an education at the school of hard knocks. Women still prefer the security of a degree. So before we say that women with equal education suffer from discrimination because they earn less, we have to ask whether they and the men are taking equal financial risks. And before we criticize women for not doing it, we need to do a better job socializing them for the option.

Preparing Our Daughters to Take Risks

Risk-taking is a mind-set. Our sons do too much of it; our daughters too little. Fortunately, the genetic heritage of men-as-risk-takers and women as protection-seekers can be either magnified or tempered by parenting. Not parents' lectures, but by hands-on parents who don't become so invested they can't bear to be hands-off; who expose their children to the right blend of pushing and protecting, freedom and monitoring, rewards and consequences.

We often discourage our daughters from risk-taking without knowing we are doing it. Many parents never encourage their daughters to go to the playground with a basketball and "pick up a game," even though they would make the suggestion to their sons. Few parents educate their daughters to call a boy for a first date—not as an exception to the rule, but as the rule. (Not just if she's less attractive, but especially if she's very attractive.) Few suggest she earn enough money to be able to buy a car so she can also pick up the boy she asked out and take him for dinner. And it is the rare parent who would give a daughter the message that it is okay to be the first to take a boy's hand and kiss him the first time, even though they would expect their son to pick up the messages to do that.

Of course, there are practical reasons we don't do this with our daughters: "It's more dangerous out there for a girl," or "Such behavior is looked upon differently if a girl does it—she'd be setting herself up for rejection, or for guys to take advantage of her." These responses, whether accurate or not, are the reasons we discourage our daughters from taking risks; they do not dispute the fact that we are less likely to do it.

Take the example of earning enough money to buy a car to pick up the boy she asked out. A son learns, "More money means more car, more flowers, more dinners, more drinks, more love." In brief, he learns money equals love, and therefore 25 ways to increase his pay are 25 ways to decrease his rejection. Since he is more likely to take about 150 risks of rejection between eye contact and the end of rejection (also called sexual intercourse), even a hazardous job feels like it will hurt less than all that rejection.[4]

Some of my other books discuss how to encourage our daughters to develop a risk-taking mind-set without compromising their safety or reputation (*Why Men Are The Way They Are, Father and Child Reunion,* and *The Myth of Male Power*), but here are some of the ways our daughters may be encouraged to apply this mind-set to the world of financial risk-taking.

Taking the Financial and Emotional Risks

My interviews with highly paid women revealed the inseparability of financial and emotional risk-taking. Money gathering was often mentor gathering and venture capitalist (VC) gathering, which meant a woman discovering the right match between herself and her mentor or VC. The process proved to be a growth experience for each woman. Selling an idea was more about selling herself as a person than the idea per se; selling herself meant deepening her self-confidence. It also meant developing the openness to take advice and the wisdom to reject advice, especially when the advice was tied to the money she might receive.

Most every high-paid woman stressed perseverance, but Kay Hammer, the CEO of Evolutionary Technologies International, uses her spiritual development to inform the direction of her perseverance:

> I'm not the workshop-attending, spiritual type, but some of my co-workers were, so maybe out of self-defense, I attended one. Sure enough, it came complete with a shaman. The shaman painted two paths—that of the warrior and of the adventurer—that changed my approach to the world.
>
> The goal of the warrior's perseverance is to defeat evil; the adventurer is focused on the journey. So when a warrior sees someone who is wrong, it is his duty to try to defeat him. Consequently, a warrior spends most of his life at war. When an adventurer sees evil on the road, he'd just as soon go around it, behind it, under it, or through it and fight only as a last resort. That image changed my approach to the world. I started saying, 'I don't care that this guy is wrongheaded, I just don't want him to get in my way.' It allowed me to enjoy the journey.

In her study of highly paid women, Barbara Stanny, the author of *Secrets of Six-Figure Women,* emphasizes that top-earning women ask for jobs for which they are *not* completely qualified—they "feel the fear and do it anyway" (as Susan Jeffers puts it in a book of that title).[5] In my interviews, this quality was a crucial outcome of early socialization to be comfortable with taking risks.

One of the most useful applications of risk-taking is asking, "What do I know that might produce more income?" For example, Cathey Cotton, the founder of a tech-recruiting firm, noted that many women are good at, and enjoy, matchmaking.[6] Cathey saw the connection between matchmaking and recruiting. So she kept an eye out for people with this interest. The difference? The pay. Usually making a good match means a wedding invitation. But Cathey reports that in tech recruiting, "There's no reason you can't make a quarter million dollars a year." Then her employees have a choice: They can take the quarter million to the bank, or bankroll the wedding.

The jump start to financial risk-taking has different motivations. For Sue Buchanan, the cofounder of Aurum Software, it was her financial security that made her willing to take financial risks: "I have money saved, and I know if things don't work out my track record and support system are strong enough to get me a good job anywhere, anytime."[7]

Raising Money vs. Saving Money

Some risk-takers are penny savers; other risk-takers are penny wasters. The type of financial risk-taker who raises venture capital—more than 90% likely to be a man—tends to be a penny waster.[8] The type who raises money on credit cards—usually a woman—tends to be a penny saver, even though there's hardly a better way of wasting money than to incur credit card debt.

Fortunately, the pride of the entrepreneur to make a profit turns almost all entrepreneurs into penny savers. For example, Ru Scott started a clothing store named Punch. To save money, she used shower curtains instead of real doors for the dressing rooms.[9]

Although Small Business Association loans often give women business owners a preference, women are still more likely than men to use personal credit cards to finance their firm—32% of women versus 21% of men.[10] The risk women tend not to take is the search for venture capital—involving much more rejection, but a much better way to spread both the risk and the reward. Its big downside is the loss of autonomy, and many women seek to run their own business exactly for independence. These reasons doubtless contribute to chief executives receiving only 5% of the venture capital.[11]

7. Many Fields with Higher Pay Require Working the Worst Shifts During the Worst Hours
(Private Practice Medical Doctor vs. HMO Medical Doctor)

If we think of "shift work" occurring late at night to early morning and on weekends, then there are three kinds of shift work: blue-collar, white-collar, and self-owned business. They have three things in common: First, they increase pay or employment opportunities (or both). Second, they increase either stress or damage to physical health (or both). Third, men are more likely to take shift work to get the pay.

Blue-Collar Blues
If you possess more flexibility than education, or desire more flexibility to get more education, then blue-collar shift work offers options. A night shift usually means extra hourly pay, to the tune of about 10%.[12] Because a night shift is usually less intense and less supervised, working the night shift as a security guard monitoring a highrise's TV surveillance or as the attendant at a 24-hour parking garage, for example, can offer an opportunity to study for one of the above-mentioned high-pay professions.

If you have preschool children and your spouse works during the day, a night shift can allow you to care for the children during the day while your spouse cares for the children at night. The upside? The children get love and food. The downside? Mom and Dad don't get each other.

If you are unemployed, night shifts are often easier to get, since fewer people compete for them. And it is higher pay than unemployment.

Before you pick up the phone to pick up a night shift, let me shift direction. The night shift has a shadow side. People who work nights average only 5.5 hours of sleep per day, versus 7.5 by ordinary day workers.[13]

The blue-collar shift worker is disproportionately young, Black, and male.[14] Men constitute 64% of total shift workers working at least 35 hours per week.[15] A Korn/Ferry study documents that men are more willing to take these shifts not just for the money, but as an alternative to unemployment.[16] They are more likely to gain weight, neglect exercise, and get divorced. When the company offers special training, it's when they are sleeping.

If night shift workers are single, they often feel out of circulation. If they are married, they frequently feel out of sync with their family. They feel, in brief, lonely. Like "a car going the wrong way down a one-way street."[17] Night shift workers are on one of the lowest rungs of the workplace ladder.

In Japan, women fight for the right to work late-night shifts, but once achieving that right, rarely take the shifts.[18] (In Tokyo, unlike in many American cities, working late at night is not a hazardous occupation.) The typical job rotation in Japan is a week on a day shift followed by a week on a night shift (10 p.m. to 5 a.m.). As one Japanese woman put it, "When you see the men after their week on the night shift, their cheeks are sunken in and they look thinner. They just look dead."[19]

Precisely because of these downsides, a woman who endures the rigors of shift work earns the respect of workers. Few workers want to be supervised by someone unwilling to "pay their dues." Theresa Metty found her night shift supervision to be one of her most rewarding experiences in her climb to the top of Motorola: "The men were so real, it kept me connected. It inspired them when they felt listened to and worked with, and it inspired me."[20]

White-Collar Warrior

ITEM: Until work rules were changed, first-year residents in obstetrics-gynecology averaged 91 hours per week with surgical residents averaging 102 hours per week.[21]

ITEM: Medical residents who are on call average 2.7 hours of sleep per night.[22]

We just saw (in "Blue-Collar Blues") that the average amount of sleep for night shift workers is 5.5 hours per night. But the on-call medical resident averages less than half of that—2.7 hours. With the night shift worker, we quickly see the powerlessness of sleep deprivation; however, the pay and prestige of the doctor blinds us to the powerlessness of the medical resident's sleep deprivation. Obviously, for some of those surgical residents, their workweek is almost three shifts.

When the medical profession was virtually all male, its culture—of white-collar warriors—did not allow these demands to be questioned. It was the white-collar man's way of training to be a hero, of risking his own survival to ensure the survival of others. I discussed how every society that survived developed an unconscious investment in training its men to be willing to die so others might live. Biological instinct and social applause kept the slave a slave.

Fortunately, women changed this in two ways. When, in New York state, the exhausted doctors' excruciating hours led to mistakes that resulted in the death of a female patient, her influential father worked for legislation to restrict doctors' hours. The female patient died in New York state; New York then became the nation's first state to require that doctors' shifts max out at 24 consecutive hours, and that they not work more than 80-hour weeks.[23] Women could then enter a profession that was becoming conscious of how the quality of life of the savior might affect the person the savior sought to save.

This is the pattern of safety regulations in many of the hazardous professions: When male disposability backfires into female disposability, the political will surfaces to pass legislation that forces the modification of rules.[24] For instance, when a rafter fell to the street and killed a woman pedestrian, only then were regulations passed requiring rafters to be safer in the construction industry.

Self-Owned Slaves

We don't think of people who own their own businesses as shift workers. But if we define a shift worker as someone who works outside the normal 8 a.m. to 6 p.m. framework, then many business owners feel that, unlike a normal shift worker, they work all the shifts. This is especially true at start-ups.

Most start-ups rarely shut down (unless they go out of business). People who run their own businesses often feel like self-owned slaves.

When Barbara Kavovit started her own construction company, she committed to organizing her cadre of independent contractor construction workers to take on a project with 24-hour notice, and to be able to start at seven o'clock in the evening if necessary.[25] Since in the early years she organized and oversaw all her projects, this committed her to shift work oversight to be certain the men were committing themselves to shift work construction work. The person holding the whip is the prisoner of the whip.

Lost in the Dark

The money men make from their willingness to work the least desirable hours is not a sign of discrimination against women, but a sign of the willingness of mostly married men to lose sleep to feed the family as their wife loses sleep to feed the child. A willingness to do the uncomfortable shifts is one reason married men earn more than twice what never-married men earn.[26]

Men's contribution, made at night, need not be lost in the dark.

8. Some Jobs Pay More to Attract People to Unpleasant Environments Without Many People
(Prison Guard vs. Restaurant Hostess)

You don't have a college education, but you'd like a government job that will allow you to creatively use your people skills? You'd be okay with earning $70,000 per year? You could retire at age 50, with more than $63,000 per year for the rest of your life if you've put in 30 years. In California, there's a 10% vacancy rate, and the state is anxious to hire to avoid overtime.[27] The position? Prison guard.

Jobs in dirty, unpleasant environments with little people contact—like auto mechanic, steelworker, sewer maintenance, plumbing, fumigating, and short-order cook—are often avoided by women. But a closer look within these fields uncovers three "finds."

First, some of these jobs pay women more than men (as is often the case in male-dominated fields). Second, technology is transforming many jobs requiring heavy lifting from muscle to microchip and machine. Third, while many women prefer people contact, other women—and men—think "alone time" is a gold mine.

The first "find": The weekly salaries of women who are engine mechanics for heavy vehicles, as well as for women who are automobile body repairers, or helpers in construction trades, are all *greater* than the salaries of their male counterparts. Note I did not limit this to starting salaries, but *average* salaries.[28] For female engine mechanics, that's over $40,000 per year (vs. $31,000 for men).[29]

The second and third "finds"—in technological transformation and "alone time"—are well illustrated by what is happening to manufacturing and the steelworker.

Most steelworkers at the new Steel Dynamics plant in Indiana make between $60,000 and $90,000 per year, including overtime.[30] The person who makes that is almost always a man, but technology is transforming this job into a female-friendly occupation. Here's why . . .

Our current image of manufacturing is reflected in the Latin origin of the word *manu factus,* or handmade.[31] And we still think of the factory worker as a blue-collar worker, wearing a blue shirt to hide the dirt. In the past, his work was so grimy, greasy, and dirty that homes in blue-collar towns such as Erie, Pennsylvania, had separate basement entrances so the husband could rinse and change rather than get the home dirty. (A man's home was his castle as long as he obeyed that little unwritten sign: "Husband must enter through the basement . . . with a paycheck"!)

The current manufacturing plant is different from the old image. Steel mills now look more like air-traffic control centers with men supervising computerized machines. A steelworker, rather than being in the mix, may literally be above it all: in the cabin of a crane, 70 feet above the factory floor, guiding a cauldron of molten steel— as much as 120 tons of intensely hot liquid—over the heads of his co-workers.[32] He, or she, had better not fall asleep or lose concentration.

As for alone time, well, there are 164 stairs from the cabin of the crane to the floor, so if you don't want to delay production, you heat your meals in a microwave in the cabin, and wash up in its makeshift bathroom. If you want to reach that $90,000 per year level, you'll need to clock in some overtime—and some more "alone time."

While some may reject this as impossible for a woman to do, the opposite is true. Men do so much worse in school in part because they have a much harder time being physically still for long periods. Keep us guys still for too long, and we fall asleep—not a great idea if we're supposed to be guiding those 120 tons of molten steel over the heads of our co-workers! And since the average woman is smaller than the average man, she'll have some extra breathing space for her alone time.

As the assembly line is replaced by proprietary technologies in the United States and many industrialized countries, brains will be replacing brawn, thus making manufacturing more female-friendly. For example, a company manufacturing an innovation-intensive computer component, or a new medical device with technology it wishes to protect, keeps that item in the United States even as it may outsource an assembly-line job to an overseas location.

A degree from a technical school can be the foundation for working with many of these new technologies. For example, the robots that manufacture what the manufacturer manufactures are themselves manufactured by robotics technologists, who can expect to make about $40,000 per year.[33]

Another occupation that deserves close attention is cook. More women than men are trained to cook. Yet about 90% of all short-order cooks are men. A good short-order cook is indispensable, and will always have a job. In the right setting, she can apprentice to be a chef. With skills that are good enough, she can create flexibility. For example, kids go to school? Apply in the business district to work a lunch shift only, from 10:30 a.m. to 2:30 p.m. Can't get a job? Keep calling. Keep leaving your number. The turnover is frequent; the absentee rate, high. Soon you'll be calling when you're needed.

Why do few women apply to be a short-order cook even in the same restaurants where there are plenty of women hired in positions like host and waiter? The host has contact with people in an air-conditioned environment in the part of the restaurant designed to please the eye. The short-order cook has contact with garbage and grease over a hot grill, often on a hot day, in the part of the restaurant unconcerned with pleasing the eye. The restaurant host often hears the customer's thank-you and sees the customer's smile. The short-order cook rarely hears a thank-you and seldom sees a smile. He or she hears "Where is it? Finally!"; "You overcooked it . . . gimme another"; "You undercooked it."

How important is the work environment? Personnel managers tell us that most people seeking a job want contact with people in a pleasant environment, not contact with a hot grill on a humid day. It is obviously more fulfilling to work with humans than in sewers, with children than with pesticides, over people than under cars. The man endures the hot grill for the higher pay. Or for low pay rather than no pay.

We cannot assume sex discrimination until we measure women and men serving equal time under the cars, over the grills, and in the sewers.

9. Updating Pays: Currency Begets Currency
(Sales Engineer vs. French Language Scholar)

> ITEM. Women are 53 times more likely to go for master's degrees in education than in the physical sciences.[34] (In the mid-1990s, women were only 46 times more likely to do so.)

With the exception of nursing, almost half of the master's degrees awarded to women are in fields characterized by their lack of a pressing need for updating.[35]

Updating requires more than just keeping up-to-date. "In tech recruiting I research the next tier of products, those in the developmental phase," explained Cathey Cotton, founder and principal of MetaSearch. "Then I ask myself how they will impact hiring from a manager's standpoint. Then I look at how I can find candidates to fill that need, and begin developing a method of finding those candidates. Sometimes, by the time I have finished that, another technological development makes it wiser to throw everything out than to sail against the wind."[36]

It's not just that fields requiring a lot of currency pay a lot of currency. It's that they turn someone from a job seeker into someone sought after. An engineering major is over five times as likely to receive a job offer prior to graduation than is the average college grad.[37] And as we've seen (in Table 6), her starting salary is likely to be higher than a man's.

Being sought after creates leverage—the leverage to work for the government, a university, or a Yahoo!; the security to join an exciting start-up (if it fails you'll be wanted on another dance card); and the knowledge you can move to San Francisco or Sydney, go urban or rural.

When James Gander studied faculty salaries at more than 500 universities, he discovered that while the men earned more than the women, once he had accounted for men's greater tendency to join research-oriented universities that required staying on top of their fields, and then looked at the productivity of those faculty members, "most female faculty receive on average salaries comparable to male faculty or as much as 7% higher . . ."[38]

It is not just the high-paid fields that require updating; the need for updating is also perhaps the primary quality of the fields the *Jobs Rated Almanac* ranks as the best fields—the fields in which people are a blend of the happiest, most secure, most highly paid, and so on. As we saw in Chapter 1, science, math, and computer skills dominate the top six fields:[39]

1. Biologist
2. Actuary
3. Financial planner
4. Computer systems analyst
5. Accountant
6. Software engineer

Of course, computers and accounting are not for everyone. Myself included. As a student, I always scored considerably higher in math than in verbal exams; with my dad being an accountant and my math teacher, Mr. Perticone, asking me to substitute-teach our eighth grade class most Fridays, math felt natural. But it did not inspire me. When I chose instead to write about topics that needed less updating, I knew I would sacrifice income.

We've looked at how we can choose a high-paying field. But almost every field has subfields in which most of these choices reappear, which we now turn to.

10. People Who Get Higher Pay Also Choose *Subfields* with the "High-Pay Formula"
(Surgeon vs. Psychiatrist)

A nurse anesthetist can make twice the pay of a general nurse. An auto mechanic specializing in Mercedes makes more than one specializing in Fords. We don't have to change fields, or wish we had taken a different major in college, to earn more.

The pay gap between people in the same field, but different subfields, is often much larger than the 20% gap between men's and women's pay. So when we see headlines proclaiming "Male Engineers Earn More Than Female Engineers" and don't ask whether they are working in the same subfields, we are ignoring, for example, that an aerospace engineer earns about $73,000 while a transmitter engineer earns about $32,000.[40]

When I taught at the School of Medicine at the University of California in San Diego, I noticed that my female students were choosing subfields that had in common three characteristics: (1) contact with human life (for example, child psychiatry) rather than with human suffering and death (surgery); (2) the fewest round-the-clock emergency demands at unscheduled hours; (3) less specialization beyond the basic residency and internship. All three are low-pay formula choices, emphasizing fulfillment and flexibility.

It was apparent to me that by the end of the first year of medical school, both sexes knew that, for example, surgery would require about twice as many hours of work per week and more training, but paid more than child psychiatry. *Yet every field of surgery was systematically avoided by women, as was anything to do with death or dying.* For example, nationwide, men are 11 times more likely to become thoracic (chest) surgeons, 8 times more likely to be urological surgeons, and 9 times more likely to be orthopedic surgeons.[41]

The distinction is not just between surgery and nonsurgical choices, but between medicine that puts doctors in contact with life versus medicine that forces the doctor to deal with death. Thus men are four times more likely to choose cardiac care, but only about one-third as likely to choose child psychiatry or pediatrics, and only about three-fourths as likely to choose family practice.[42]

For precisely these reasons, headlines saying "Male Doctors Earn More Than Female Doctors" encourage women to focus their binoculars on victimization rather than on the subfields that lead to women earning as much or more than their male counterparts. In medicine, women would miss fields like pediatrics, or general and family practice. And, as we can see in Table 11 on medical specialties, female physicians also earn more than men when the subfields of psychiatry, dermatology, neurology, aerospace medicine, general preventive medicine, physical medicine and rehabilitation, public health, occupational medicine, and radiation oncology are aggregated (averaged).[43]

We can see from Table 12 how, on the surface, it seems male doctors are paid much more than women, but as soon as the doctors work equal hours in the same subfield and practice setting (e.g., wealthy urban), then the pay gap shrinks to only 2%. With a few more factors accounted for we can see there is no pay gap.

So, is there a gap in pay between men and women medical doctors? Most likely. Here's why. The figures in Tables 11 and 12 are for 1990, the last time the male-female pay differences were calculated by the Survey of Young Physicians. Yet the trend has been for women's earnings to increase. For example, in 1986 men physicians

TABLE 11	Physicians: Specialties in Which Women Under 45 Earn the Same or More Than Their Male Counterparts[44]	
Medical Specialty	**Men's Pay as % of Women's (when all variables are controlled for[45])**
General and family practice	87%
Pediatrics	93%
Obstetrics and gynecology	100%
Radiology, anesthesiology, or pathology	100%
The aggregate of psychiatry, dermatology, neurology, aerospace medicine, general preventive medicine, physical medicine and rehabilitation, public health, occupational medicine, and radiation oncology[46]	98%

TABLE 12 How the Appearance of Unequal Pay Disappears the More Men's and Women's Work Is the Same: Physicians[47]

Variables Considered	Men's Pay as % of Women's
Yearly income only	141%
Hourly income (i.e., equal hours)	114%
Same hours, specialty, and practice setting	102%
With study's other variables also equalized[49]	100%

who were just starting their practices earned 7% more than women for equal work; by 1990, the women physicians just starting were earning 3% more.[48]

Why hasn't the Survey of Young Physicians' gender data been updated? Well, no one will say for sure, but a pattern emerging from my research is that each time a study discovers there is no pay gap, that portion of the study is not repeated. That is, the portion measuring the pay differences based on gender is dropped from the next study. Or the study itself is dropped or fundamentally changed. That's what happened with the Survey of Young Physicians' gender data; we'll see this next in the section on size of responsibility (the PATC survey), then with comparisons of net worth, and so on.

If the survey were repeated, and more of these 25 ways to higher pay included, it would most probably report that the *women* now earn *more* than men for truly equal work.

The irony is that the women-as-victim headlines should really be women-as-balanced headlines: The female doctor has more free time (relative to her male counterpart), has more control over *when* her life is free, is entering more life-enhancing fields—she has, therefore, more real power in her life and career. The male doctor who feels that being a child psychiatrist, for example, isn't enough, but feels pressured to accept the bribe of money, loses control of his own life—his time, his flexibility, his 20s, his 30s, his 40s . . .

However, Table 12 suggests that extra working hours may pay off. Do they?

Since life is time, let's look in the next chapter at how we spend it and when the time is worth the money and the extra time it may buy.

CHAPTER 4

Doing Time: People Who Get Higher Pay . . .

Our choice of field and subfield has the biggest impact on the *quality* of our work time; "Doing Time" is about the *quantity*. Taken together, they affect the quality of our lifetime.

Europeans look at Americans and say, "You live to work; we work to live." "Doing Time" introduces six decisions we make about time that will help you know where on that continuum is best for you, or whether some out-of-the-box thinking is possible. Decisions such as how many hours per week it's worth working, when years of experience in a field pays, what happens when you take long leaves, using technology to reduce absenteeism, and some fascinating re-thinking of commuting time.

Of course, we'll also see the effects of "doing time" on the gap between men's and women's pay. For example, men teachers average $46,000 per year versus women teachers' $42,000.[1] But isolating for the issues of time alone, we see that men who teach are 25% more likely to have had at least 20 years' teaching experience, and they have 10% more time with their current employer.[2] The men also spend approximately two hours more per week on all teaching duties than women.[3] And until 1996 the men had an average of six more years of experience teaching, though now it is down to one year.[4]

The big takeaway from knowing how to invest your time to produce the most income is the flexibility it provides a family to create a
better quality life, which starts with knowing how many hours per
week it's worth working.

11. People Who Get Higher Pay Work More Hours—And It Makes a Big Difference

Everyone knows that if you want to get paid more, it helps to work
more. But few people know how much more money the extra hours
are worth. Take a guess . . .

**If Mary works 40 hours per week and Jane works 45 hours
(13% more), on average Jane would make about how much
more than Mary?**

❑ a. 5%
❑ b. 15%
❑ c. 25%
❑ d. 35%
❑ e. 45%

The U.S. Bureau of Labor Statistics reports that the average person
working 45 hours per week earns 44% more pay—that is, 44% more
pay for 13% more work.[5] Put another way, she or he gets more than
triple pay during those extra hours. Not at the same job, usually—the
willingness to work more hours helps land jobs that pay more per hour.

Is the Gender Pay Gap Mostly an Hours-Worked Gap?
When we hear John Kerry say in the third debate with George Bush
that full-time working men make a dollar for each 76 cents earned by
women *for the same work*, Bush did not dispute the claim.[6] Aside
from being outdated (it's now 80 cents)—few people know that we
are comparing apples and oranges: The average full-time working
man works 45 hours per week, while his female counterpart works 42
hours per week.[7]

What does that three-hour difference amount to in pay? Well, the
average *person* who works 45 hours per week earns 14% more than

the 42 hours per week worker.[8] The 14% covers 70% of the 20% pay gap between men and women. So it is possible that up to 70% of the pay gap between men and women is accounted for by the differences in hours worked.[9]

However, looked at from another perspective, we can see that the number of hours we work is even more crucial.

Do Women and Men Who Work *Equal* Hours Receive Equal Pay?

We wouldn't expect men and women who work equal hours to receive equal pay given the 24 other ways to higher pay men engage in to earn more money *during* those hours (technical careers, night shifts, fewer career interruptions . . .). So when we look at the pay of men and women who do work equal hours (see Table 13), two discoveries are quite astonishing:

- When women and men work *less* than 40 hours a week, the *women* earn *more* than the men;
- When men and women work *more* than 40, the *men* earn more than the women.

Why this difference? Could it be that the men who work more hours are more likely to be supporting a family, and therefore respond to the pressure to make more money by making the 24 other money-creating trade-offs?

If this is true, then we would expect unmarried men who work a lot

---

TABLE 13   The Power of Hours

Hours	Weekly Earnings		Women's Earnings as % of Men's
	Men	Women	
25–29	$115	$154	134%
30–34	$173	$231	134%
35–39	$346	$371	107%
40–44	$577	$481	87%

Source: U.S. Census Bureau, 2003.[10]

of hours to have a smaller pay gap versus unmarried women—the unmarried men would have less pressure to make workplace sacrifices. And sure enough Figure 2 shows the median earnings of both unmarried men and women who work 50+ hours per week at a dead heat—$31,000 a year.

This astonishes almost all of us, because so often we hear the opposite. The Women's Tennis Association, for example, complains that men will earn more at Wimbledon than women ($756,000 versus $700,000).[11] The WTA doesn't clarify that men's matches are the best-of-five sets and women's are the best-of-three. We hear only the complaint that women are paid less, when in fact the women are paid more—93% of men's pay for 60% of the work. And we hear nothing about what real equality in tennis would look like, as I discuss in the 25th measure of equal pay (productivity). Surrounded only by the image of women as victims of unequal pay, a more balanced picture astonishes. On the other hand, men haven't spoken up, and women can't hear what men don't say.

FIGURE 2

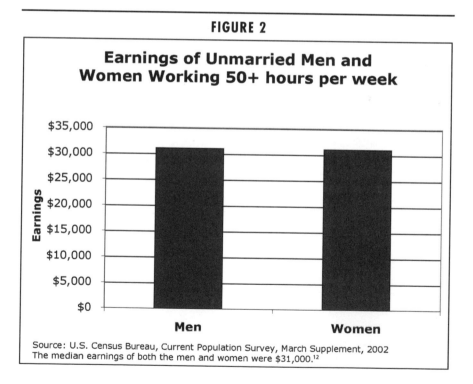

Source: U.S. Census Bureau, Current Population Survey, March Supplement, 2002
The median earnings of both the men and women were $31,000.[12]

7-Eleven Pay

Why the disproportionate pay to people who work longer hours? It's "7-Eleven pay." If our infant needs diapers at three o'clock in the morning, no one objects to paying twice the Costco price for them at a 7-Eleven. When we want what we want when we want it, we pay 7-Eleven pay.

Employers do the same thing. When the Ford truck plant in Michigan discovered a much greater demand for Expeditions and Navigators than anticipated, some factory workers who put in consistent 60- and 70-hour weeks made $200,000 a year.[13]

How does an employer spot an employee for whom 7-Eleven pay is worth the cost? 7-Eleven hours. Michael Bloomberg (the mayor of New York City who also founded Bloomberg Information Television) explains it well in his description of his rise to the top at Salomon Brothers. He started with a salary of $9,000. His severance check 15 years later was $10 million: "I came in every morning at seven, getting there before everyone except Billy Salomon. When he needed to borrow a match or talk sports, I was the only other person in the trading room, so he talked to me."[14]

In the evening, Bloomberg stayed later than everyone except the managing partner, so when the managing partner "needed someone to make an after-hours call to the biggest clients, or someone to listen to his complaints about those who had already gone home, I was the someone."[15]

Of course, just being there is not enough. Bloomberg became a top-selling equity salesman and a computer whiz. His willingness to put in 15-hour days is part of an attitude. It is the attitude that makes 13% more time worth 44% more money. Part of that attitude is being there when needed.

However, that attitude has a competitor that is upping the pay ante.

Many mothers are teaching fathers how important it is to be there when needed for their children. And many dads now treasure time with their children both for the child's sake and their own. So dads—who used to show their love for their family by being *away from* the love of their family (at work)—can no longer be expected to raise children just by raising money. So the employers have to increase the pay "bribe" for extra hours.

I believe that conflict is part of what is magnifying the disproportionate pay we give those who put in the extra time. Here's how the "Family Time Era" is creating more than 7-Eleven pay, but also CEO pay.

How the "Family *Time* Era" Begets CEO Pay

If you're a woman who wants to break through the glass ceiling, for how many years must you put in the hours? If we look at the CEOs of Fortune 1000 companies, they typically paid their dues with 15-hour days for a period of about 20 years, usually six days per week.[16] That's 90-hour weeks for two decades. Chances are you're not interested unless you have no children (or your husband gives you headaches!).

For almost all the CEOs I interviewed (or know) who have good marriages and at-home children, there's a shift from love-equals-money to love-equals-time. This reduces the supply of balanced and qualified people willing to continue putting in 90-hour weeks.

What we think of as outrageous CEO pay, then, may be due at least in part to the short supply of qualified people who, after two decades of forfeiting family time for dollars, want still more dollars to wallpaper over the cracks in their family home. Which is why the sharing of top positions that I discuss in the Conclusion will become increasingly viable.

Breaking the Glass Ceiling Time Barrier

Women today are less than half as likely as men to work in excess of 50 hours per week.[17] (Again, working women put in more hours at home.) It is rarer still for women to sustain that commitment for 20 years and then, without having burned out, increase her hours still more as a CEO. But exactly because it is rarer, women who are willing stand out as more exceptional.

Women, it turns out, are far more "European"—working to live rather than living to work. But the glass ceiling is rarely cracked by healthy, balanced people who work to live.

How 7-Eleven Pay Creates the Option for Women of Succeeding at Work Without Failing at Home

Most people who succeed at work risk failing at home. Especially if their children are young and they don't have a stay-at-home "wife." Thus most successful women complain, "I need a wife."

But if 10 more hours each week at work can mean almost twice the pay at home, then a career woman has the option of marrying a stay-at-home dad.[18]

Am I suggesting a career woman "marry down"? No, I'm suggesting she "marry up"—that she respect herself enough to "marry up" to a man who will care for both the children and the home while she brings home the bacon. She gets her career and a "wife." And the children get a full-time parent. She avoids both career neglect and kid neglect. And, of course, neglected kids have a way of subjecting dual-career parents to the neglected kids' tax—bills from psychologists, medical doctors, private schools, and private colleges, all predictably leading you to your own psychologist and hospital bills, and sometimes to divorce court.

If you're a woman who is already married to a successful career man, don't assume he would never give up or cut back his career to care for the children. Ask him. A recent Harris poll asking men and women in their twenties if they were willing to give up pay to spend more time with the family found that 70% of men (versus 63% of women) would forfeit money if they could have more family time.[19] Men, they are a changin'.

What do men of any age need to change? When I did the research for *Why Men Are the Way They Are*, I discovered that the key question for most men is "Will you respect me on payday?" If he feels you value his time with the children more than his paycheck, he makes a shift; his assumption that he must earn more often evaporates almost as quickly as your assumption that he must earn more.

Many men's motivation to be a full-time dad involves becoming a different dad than their dad had the opportunity to be. Younger men have often grown up without Dad (raised by single moms), and older men with minimal Dad. Mid-career men, often burned out with work, sometimes need to see just one successful person take parental leave to be inspired to do the same.

Single women often fear that the men they are going out with wouldn't be comfortable with less career and more child. Perhaps. If a woman selects for a man with a lot of career ambition, she'll get what she selected. The solution? Choose among men who would love to be married to a career woman who valued his being home full-time with the children for a few years. Can't find these men? State your interest on your Match.com profile—the Internet's the best net to catch the right fish. You'll be surprised. I've started hundreds of men's groups, and such men are all over the place, waiting to be wanted. (And no, I'm not starting a matchmaking service!)

How Many Hours Are Optimal?

An overview first. Most people would prefer to work part-time. That's especially true for women. In reality, working part-time is a minefield of trade-offs with a rainbow (but not a pot of gold!) for those who don't get blown away en route. For example, precautions are necessary to prevent a part-time job from becoming a full-time job with part-time pay. When precautions are taken, part-time work is usually more satisfying.

What's more satisfying than working part-time? Working the number of hours you prefer. For example, women doctors who work their preferred number of hours not only found their job more rewarding, but also their marriages.[20] However, working reduced hours did not by itself produce these outcomes—working the preferred hours did.

As we saw from the survey of Australians, more satisfying than working part-time is volunteering, followed by being a full-time homemaker.[21] Then, when fulfillment is high, time is not an issue. Volunteering and homemaking are two roles that seem to satisfy the deep need to feel that we are making a difference in the lives of a human, a community, or a cause. It's certainly what keeps me motivated.

If one of the minefields of working part-time is your job becoming a full-time job with part-time pay, how do you prevent that? For starters, if you can, charge by the hour, not by the project. Projects—like writing this book—always take longer than expected. Most authors, artists, and freelance writers are paid for the completed project. Although they have flexibility of hours, they make much less than they anticipate, and for the 99% who are not famous, they make less-than-minimum wage. Second, let your employer or clients know which days, or what hours, you'll be available, so they don't see you as "not returning calls," and you prevent a part-time job from becoming an all-the-time job.

The likely pursuers of part-time flexibility are moms with children who average about half the number of hours per year as their husbands.[22] But it usually works both for the women and, if there is a commensurate reduction in pay, also for the companies. A McGill University study tracked professionals and managers who had cut back to 30–34 hours per week, with commensurate reductions in pay. Of those who pursued this route, 90% were women.[23] There was virtually no overall negative impact on the company, and 91% of these employees reported greater work–home balance. In fact, 62% considered the overall experience a success.[24]

12. People Who Get Higher Pay Have More Years of Experience— Especially in Their Current Occupation

ITEM. A woman today is 50 times as likely to be a stay-at-home mom (home full-time while her husband works full-time) than is her husband to be a stay-at-home dad.[25]

ITEM. About 94% of women attorneys working at the top law firms in 1987 left their jobs between one and eight years later.[26]

ITEM. Working women are eight times as likely to spend 4 or more years out of the labor force than are men.[27]

Men average about an additional year and a half in their current occupations, and between five and nine years longer in their overall work lives.[28] Each additional year in their current occupations gives men roughly another 3%–4% annual pay increase.[29]

Perhaps the real significance of these extra years is how they contribute to benefits packages. The retirement package is often calculated based on the final years of income, and for many entering the work market today, retirement life may last as long as work life.

When we don't take years of experience into account, it is easy for a woman to become discouraged when she reads headlines such as "Study of TV News Directors Finds Discrimination Against Women." When a woman in the mid-1980s read that TV news directors who were women got paid about 27% less than men directors, it might have made her avoid the field, fearing it had a "buddy-boy" atmosphere that was anti-women.

If, on the other hand, a headline more accurately reflecting the study's core findings, summarized in Table 14, read "Female Man-

TABLE 14   TV News Directors' Experience[30]

	Male	Female
Median years working in news	14.8	5.6
Median years in managerial role in news	6.6	2.1
Median years in news prior to getting into management	8.2	3.5[31]

agers Become TV News Directors Three Times as Quickly as Men," well, that would have made a woman feel wanted. (It may not have made her brother feel wanted, but that's another story.)

In fact, women today can climb the corporate ladder more quickly than men, leaving them the option of retiring earlier. Here's why.

The Women-First Club

ITEM. Prior to age 40, women are 15 times more likely than their male counterparts to become top executives at major corporations.[32] (Of top female executives at major companies, 21.4% are under 40, while only 1.4% of the male executives are under 40.[33])

ITEM. In a study of the top five executives at almost 3,000 of the country's largest firms, the women's average age was 48; the men's, 53.[34]

While the glass ceiling made the news and made women feel unwanted, the women-first club got huge and so secret it never got a name.

Executive men are about four times as likely as women to have 25 or more years' experience with their company.[35]

Do women reach executive levels sooner because these women work twice as hard? The study checked. And fortunately for women, the answer is no. The male executives work more hours, travel more, move more, earn more MBAs, have more job continuity, and make more of almost all of the sacrifices discussed in this book.[36]

In brief, the road to higher pay is a toll road. But at this point in history, there are female tollbooths and male tollbooths, and the toll charged to women is lower. This should encourage every woman who wishes to embark on the road to higher pay to take it while the tolls are still low, and every man who wishes to be with his children—or just wishes to support the career-focused woman he loves—to be aware that there was never a better time to be a great dad and go with your wife's flow.

One caveat. Because women who show promise and commitment are promoted more quickly, and at a younger age, they often have less experience. Therefore, they may be paid less for the same position. A woman who sees this as discrimination against her—and not the result of discrimination in favor of her—may be perceived as a woman who wants to have her cake and eat it, too, making the company fear her rather than desire her. For example, because 73% of women surgeons are under 45, compared to 40% for men surgeons, a hospital is likely to have many more men surgeons over 45, thus paying more for the average male surgeon.[37]

The pendulum seems to be swinging back to center over the issue of hiring with or without experience. For example, one of the women CEOs I interviewed, V.J. Horgan, president of TXU Energy Trading, was already noting "the failures of companies in the energy industry who hired whiz kids with too little experience."[38] Note, though, that "whiz kids" in technical fields usually implies men. Most women feel they must already know a job prior to taking it. Since women tend to err in the direction of taking too few risks, my advice to most women fearful of taking on something they feel unprepared for is *carpe diem*, learn-as-you go, dance. Just be gracious enough to temporarily accept less pay, until you have equal experience.

As we saw in Table 14 on news directors, experience comes in many forms, and not all experiences are paid equally. Experience in TV news is overall experience in an occupation, which is distinct from seniority with a specific employer—especially recent, uninterrupted experience with that employer. How much does that matter?

13. People Who Get Higher Pay Have More Years of Recent, Uninterrupted Experience with Their Current Employer

ITEM. A study of more than 14,000 executives found women executives earn 45% less than men.[39] But when we looked at why the men earn more, seniority alone accounted for two-thirds of the gap.[40]

ITEM. A working woman is nearly nine times more likely than a man to leave the workplace for six months or longer for family reasons.[41]

What price does a woman typically pay for a workplace leave? The first year back she experiences about a 33% wage loss in comparison to the person who did not take the leave.[42] Even after three to five years back, she takes a 20% loss.[43] Obviously, for jobs that require sophisticated technological skills, the loss is greater.

There's some good news here. In 1984, women were 135 times more likely than men to leave the workplace for six months or longer for family reasons.[44] How did it get reduced to only nine times as likely today?[45] Men have increased their leaves 12-fold, and women have cut back 25%. Yet even today a third of full-time working women take these extended family leaves.

Why is the income loss for workplace leaves so huge? Consider Toni, a computer sales rep to hospitals. When Toni left for a six-month maternity leave, her employer hired Barbara to temporarily replace her; but not uncoincidentally—women are much more likely to take temporary contracts.[46] Barbara didn't work out. Her employer had to reinterview and rehire. Finally Nancy was hired. Nancy knew at the outset the job was temporary. Yet she worked out well, began building her expectations, and then, when Toni extended her maternity leave, Nancy's expectations grew.

When Toni wanted to return, Nancy argued that she had done a lot of recent training that Toni was missing, and she now had continuity and new clients.

Both Toni and Nancy were threatening lawsuits if things didn't go their way. The employer wondered whether he should have taken a harder line with Toni, not allowing her to extend her maternity leave, but he had wanted to be family-friendly. He was responsible for cutting costs, but the only way he wouldn't alienate half his employees was to hire both of them. And even if he let Nancy loose, he'd still have to put together a severance package, retrain Toni, and hire a consultant to help repair the damage. Now his own morale was declining.

The employer eventually resolved the issue by keeping Nancy and offering Toni another position requiring less retraining and less technical updating. The new position, though, paid considerably less. In brief, that's just one example of why the income loss can be so great for people who leave the workplace for extended periods, especially in the sciences.

Is reversing traditional roles viable, so that men take more family leave? With 70% of American men in their twenties preferring family time to more money, men's 12-fold increase in working and parenting from home in less than two decades can be expected to continue.[47]

14. People Who Get Higher Pay Work More Weeks During the Year

ITEM. Women are almost 40 times more likely than men to drop out of the workforce between March and July.[48]

The almost 40 times greater likelihood of women to drop out of the workforce between March and July holds special significance because the surveys by the Bureau of Labor Statistics are based on work behavior during March. By July almost 3 million more women have dropped out of the workforce.[49] But here's the rub. If they have dropped out for less than half a year, the women are still counted by the bureau as "working full-time, year round."[50]

Thus if we read a newspaper account saying that women are only 5% less likely to work full-time, year round, that's based on the March data.[51] It misleads us. And it misleads us because it does not incorporate any of the weeks missed by women on maternity leave.[52] Nor does it include any of the weeks missed by temporary workers, 72% of whom are women.[53]

In brief, we are left thinking women are subject to discrimination rather than knowing how to help women earn as much as men. Exactly how much pay does working fewer weeks per year, or women's extra absenteeism (factor #15 below) cost women? Until now, it's been rare to even acknowledge that there is this difference between men and women. Common sense dictates there's a cost, but women don't know how much it costs. We can't measure what we won't admit exists. And if knowledge is power, this leaves women less powerful.

15. People Who Get Higher Pay Are Absent Less Often from Work

Women lose about twice as much time from the workplace as men.[54]

Why this difference? In part, doctor visits are 70% more likely to take women away from work than men.[55] But more important, the much greater tendency of women to have responsibilities divided between home and work doubtless leads women to take off days when their children are sick, or when they catch their kids' flu and have to take time off again. Similarly, women's greater likelihood of working as teachers predicts their being subject not only to children's colds but to children's tendency to use their teacher as a substitute Kleenex.

Solutions? When I interviewed Dr. Carol Scott, president of The Medical Education Group, she reported that absenteeism among women who worked for her was greater when the women had mobile commuting capability, especially laptop computers, but the impact of the absenteeism was less.[56] Hiring a nanny, on the other hand, allowed women to stay at work, be in a reasonable amount of contact, and yet be secure that her children were cared for.

A better solution than a nanny? Daddy. Of course, then dads will be earning less and going to the doctors more.

16. People Who Get Higher Pay Commute to Jobs That Are Farther Away

Even workers without a family at home want to be close to home. In a study of male and female entrepreneurs, all of whom had MBAs from the same top business school, 90% of women entrepreneurs *without* children said working close to home (or at home) was nevertheless important; 50% of the men without children also said this was important.[57] No one wants to commute.

When wish translates into responsibility, full-time working men commute 36% more than their female counterparts—about 8 additional miles per day.[58] Commuters putting in these extra miles make about $1,500 more per year.[59] The man commuting into the city, while his wife limits her job selection to the suburbs to assume family responsibilities, doubtless expands his pay options.

Why do businesses in the city pay more? Because it's still easier to raise money in the city, and easier to raise children in the suburbs. Money is the bribe to get a working parent to bridge the geographical gap. As I grew up in the New York City area, my dad's bridge was the George Washington, and between bridging the Hudson and the job itself he was usually away from home from about 7 a.m. to 7 p.m.

Commuting adds to pay not just because of the job's higher wage, but because it opens more options that allow you to find a job in which your qualifications fit like a hand fits a well-matched glove.

All this is true for commuting in the traditional sense. But technology is making commuting hard to define.

To Commute or Not to Commute, That Is the Question

The answer? Yes. Liz Dowling (my wife—you met her in the Introduction) helps raise our children and our money from the same place, our San Diego home. Her business partner, Greg Dennis, works from his home in Vermont. A writer works with them, from Oregon; another independent contractor is in Arizona. Each has a home-based business. Do none of them commute, or do they all commute? Yes.

By the traditional definition, we all want to commute as little as possible. But today more people are like Karen Hughes, who was President George W. Bush's communications director prior to her decision to telecommute. See if you can decide whether Karen Hughes is commuting more or less. And whether she should be paid more or less.

Karen used to go to the White House every day from her home nearby. But she and her family missed their real home, in Austin, Texas. So she arranged a change of function and a change of venue—back to Austin. She still spends about 20% of her time on the road.[60] So, now that Karen goes farther to the White House less often, is she commuting more or less? Yes.

A more important question with only a slightly clearer answer is: What adds to or subtracts from Karen's job? And therefore how much should an employer reduce or increase pay when someone wants to "do a Karen Hughes"?

On the one hand, cell phones with headsets allow a mom to work while breast-feeding in the doctor's office. As long as the deal doesn't turn sour, the milk won't, either. A dad can change diapers at 1 a.m. and then, if he can't fall back to sleep, catch up on office e-mails.

But when we say Karen Hughes is "as close as the phone," we over-simplify Karen's challenge as a telecommuter. When President Bush needs Karen, he can call. When Karen needs Karl Rove, she can call. But Karen is no longer "running into" Karl Rove or Colin Powell in the hallway, or attending parties or dinners as often, or while visiting a Republican senator bumping into a Democrat who's wavering on a bill.

Cell phones and e-mails are least effective with the people with whom we most need to communicate—those with whom we dis-agree. It is hard to call our enemies out of the blue. But when Karen lived in DC, her son attended St. Alban's along with the children of many other politicians. An "enemy" by cell phone becomes another St. Alban's parent by the soccer field. Suddenly your child and your "enemy's" child are on the same side. The next week they're cele-brating your child's birthday in your home. You're meeting another "enemy" at church after the intimacy of prayer. And yet another has problems with a child similar to those that you've experienced, and wants to know your solutions.

It's easier to call someone to discuss a political solution after you've just partnered to parent both of your children. And those partner-ships are more common when everyday contact facilitates their dis-covery—whether in DC, a company town, or at a corporation, where the Democrats of company politics may be the human resources staff, and the Republicans the engineers.

In both cases, phones and e-mails are instruments of purpose ("I need to call Karl about the meeting"). Watercoolers and elevators are instruments of serendipity. Cell phones and e-mails cannot replace watercoolers and elevators as facilitators of contact. But St. Alban's in DC couldn't replace Karen's son's friends or the school he loved in Austin.

CHAPTER 5

On the Move: People Who Get Higher Pay Are More Willing to . . .

Aside from commuting, there are three basic ways to increase pay by being "on the move": relocating, especially abroad; *carpe diem* moving (for example, seizing an opportunity for construction work after an earthquake, but returning to home base); or on-the-job travel. Let's start with relocating and *carpe diem* moving.

17. People Who Get Higher Pay Are More Willing to *Relocate—Especially to Undesirable Locations* at the Company's Behest

> *I've regretfully passed over many great people—especially great women—because they couldn't (or wouldn't) move.*
> —THERESA METTY, SENIOR VP AND CHIEF
> PROCUREMENT OFFICER OF MOTOROLA[1]

A corporate secretary may change companies in the same town; a corporate executive is more likely to change towns with the same company.

A talented corporate secretary sees an invitation to relocate as an invitation; a future corporate executive sees an invitation to relocate as an opportunity—and an obligation.

Even for a single person, moving implies trade-offs. Frequent movers tend to be hard workers, and, as Robin Curle, the director of strategic marketing for Evolutionary Technologies, put it, "Moving means more time to adjust to work, which conflicts with the time it takes to develop friendships from scratch. With old friends, you can pick up where you left off. Nevertheless, I prefer that to spending all my life in Cleveland. No offense, Cleveland."[2]

When I began the research on this book in the early 1990s, only 17% of the people who moved for their work were women.[3] Today it's 46%.[4] Even more impressive is that married women are now 48% of the women who move for their work.[5]

Next Moves
A willingness to move, though, doesn't tell us that much. Dozens of employees may wish to move to San Diego or San Francisco, but not Fargo or Chicago. A willingness to move is the first move for a woman-on-the-move, but since the moves that count are ones that also serve the company, here are five next moves that are especially relevant to a woman who wants high pay and wants to climb high:

Next Moves

- Move overseas
- Move upon demand
- Move for two decades
- Strategize with your spouse if married
- Move to less desirable locations

Moving Overseas: The Farther Away, the Farther Up
The farther a woman moves, the more she distinguishes herself. While half of today's professionals are women, only 18% of all employees transferred abroad are women (including both married and single women).[6] With companies as American as McDonald's serving burgers in locations as foreign as China, new career opportunities are born as fast as a Big Mac replaces a Chairman Mao.

Opportunities abroad are in many ways greater than opportunities at home. Being a business pioneer in a foreign land creates both heroes and failures. Therefore the turnover is great, and a woman with experience who is ready-to-go becomes the right person in the right place at the right time when her boss is let go. Distance from the central office supervision allows a woman to run an operation in her own style, thus showcasing her potential.

Because so few women are willing to be transferred abroad, a woman who is should make that clear. The clarification increases her value even prior to making the move—she has given her company an insurance policy of flexibility, announced her commitment, and distinguished herself among women. That creates the leverage to legitimately ask for higher pay—companies pay for insurance policies.

Most women say they love to travel and love learning about different cultures, and foreign language skills and writing are women's strengths. But when it comes to moving abroad, these strengths take a backseat to stability, even for single women.

When I asked Theresa Metty, chief procurement officer of Motorola, what advice she'd give to those who want to do well in their careers, her first response was, "Take an international assignment as soon in your career as you can—before you have family. It teaches you to listen openly and respond flexibly." For example, early in her career, in Guadalajara, Mexico, for IBM, Metty listened to a woman express how she couldn't work late because she would be a disgrace to her family and community if she didn't cook dinner and have a family meal. "When I acquired a laptop computer for her, I secured for IBM the talents of a brilliant, conscientious woman, and she received her family's respect and more much-needed income."[7]

Moving upon Demand, and Moving for Two Decades

IBM used to be referred to as *"I've Been Moved."* To become an executive of a Fortune 1000 company, one can expect not only to be moved, but to be moved at the company's behest.

To become a CEO of a Fortune 1000 company typically requires a willingness to relocate as often as every 2 years for at least 20 years.[8] Not just when the children have all graduated from high school; not just during the kids' summer breaks; not necessarily, even, when your family can follow and be with you.

However, 25 years ago, about the time it takes to become a CEO, only 4% of all relocated employees were women. And this 4% figure *included* single women.[9] The good news for women-on-the-move is that women are now much more willing to move (46% of the professionals who move are women); we don't yet know whether women will keep that up for two decades, responding to the needs of the company at the expense of their families. The other option, of course, is that companies will change because they see that the type of people they want at the top are, perhaps, the type who are open to being pioneers in the executive sharing option (as outlined in the solutions section of the Conclusion).

Reconfiguring the Have-It-All Dance

With the much larger number of married women moving in recent years for their work, and the much greater willingness of younger men to care for the children, the next big shift is the marriage-career dance at the top of the ladder. **About 95% of the men CEOs of the largest Fortune 100 industrial companies economically support a wife who has never worked outside the home.**[10]

In contrast, a woman executive is much more likely to have two sources of income. Worldwide, women executives are almost *seven* times as likely as men executives to have a spouse who works full-time.[11] The implication? A woman executive who considers moving is also considering a cut in her husband's pay, which can mean a loss of family income. A man executive's move is more likely to mean a gain in family income.

As women executives become more comfortable supporting men economically, they will buy themselves "the wife" they often complain they are missing. Currently, men's incomes are still much more likely to pay women to manage the home, family, and social life; few women pay men to do the same.

In brief, an executive wife rarely has the luxury of a husband at home full-time supporting her and rarely has the economic burden of a husband at home full-time being supported by her.

Perhaps the toughest rite of passage is, though, location.

Location, Location, but Not *That* Location!

There are some locations most people love that also pay well. For example, a 2004 survey of nurse leaders (first-line supervisors to CEOs) found they averaged over $91,000 per year on the West Coast, whereas no other region of the country exceeded $72,000.[12] Sounds good, but . . . when high pay and great location are in the same package, everyone wants to be there, which opens up management opportunities in places where fewer people want to be that pay less.

To become a top executive of a Fortune 1000 company, then, one can expect not only to be moved, but to move to undesirable locations. Why undesirable locations? These are often the smaller, more remote places where the less-experienced employees are, and where, therefore, there may be more problems. New people can be tested with less risk at a small, remote, location.

This opportunity advantage offered by some (but not all) moves to undesirable locations also applies to noncorporate careers. Teachers in Alaska get higher starting salaries than teachers in any other state, yet Alaska is looking for teachers.[13] Why? Duh.

But exactly because of men's greater willingness to move to less-desirable locations, the less-desirable areas can be more desirable for a single woman. For example, in Alaska, there are almost one-and-a-half times as many never-married men as never-married women.[14] Most of the men are looking for a little warmth.

These five "New Moves" are mostly relocations involving one to five years. But *carpe diem* moving usually involves a more temporary move to a job or an assignment.

Carpe Diem Moving

Carpe diem moving, or "seize-the-day" moving, is based on the principle that every change creates an opportunity. No. Every change creates a myriad of opportunities. Technology creates silicon valleys, which create a real estate boom; a need for new teachers and hospitals; new construction but fewer trailer parks; more food but less agriculture, therefore more truckers and roads; less crime per capita, more crime per square mile. . . . Then the stock market bubble bursts, and we shift into reverse.

No matter what career we choose, the daily news gives us hints of new ways to seize the day to higher pay—not just nationally, but internationally. Consultants who respond to oil spills or earthquakes receive opportunities missed by those confined to their office.

Carpe diem moving sometimes means moving your family and home, sometimes means a temporary setup for six months alone and returning home as a once-a-month visitor, and sometimes means being single and moving for a year or two at a time for great money and location.

Natural disasters almost always create opportunities for reconstruction in construction; 9/11's insecurity created a myriad of opportunities to secure our security in the security industry. Security and construction allow for every level of skill and education to get good money in a good location. One person's crisis is another's career move.

Unlike many crises, the health care crisis will predictably be with us for much longer. The emphasis on cost cutting and universality of care predicts a long-term demand for nurses, but the varying locations of that demand have created a demand for medics-on-the-move, especially nurses commonly referred to as "gypsy" nurses.

Nurses-on-Notice
Want a luxury home with a gorgeous waterfront view in the San Francisco Bay Area—for "free"? Now it's possible because California is the first state to require a minimum nurse-to-patient ratio at the same time that it ranks 49th out of 50 states in its share of registered nurses.[15] That leads to pay for the "gypsy" nurse—or traveler—being higher in the Bay Area than anywhere in the country.

Translation? A nurse can sign up with a national staffing agency that will provide a steady flow of opportunities, including contracts for free, waterfront luxury homes, guaranteed overtime, signing bonuses of $2,500, and car allowances. The staffing agency also provides more permanent benefits such as health insurance, vacation time, and workers' comp. The contracts are technically for periods of one to three months, but in reality are often renewable.[16]

The benefits are more than temporary. Each place you go to gives you another layer of education that can prepare you for nursing administration or nursing consultation.

The jury is out on whether nurses-on-notice are good for hospitals, but it certainly offers an opportunity to the right person who can be in the right place at the right time.

Safe Zones That Appear Dangerous

As we saw from our examination of the real hazards in the war in Iraq—in which no woman in either the Air Force or Marines has been killed as of mid-2004, but journalists were 10 times as likely to be killed as the average soldier—we can experience either less danger in a "danger zone" than while driving under the influence of a cell phone, or more danger than a soldier in a war zone.[17] The lesson? Danger zones can be great employment opportunities if one does the research to distinguish disproportionately sensationalized danger from reality.

I saw this in a boy's way when I was fifteen and worked as a cabin boy on the boats of the Seine River in Paris. I looked at the newsstands and saw headlines and pictures of what appeared to be a war zone. A closer look revealed the "war zone" was but a couple of storefronts—stores I passed every day, across the river from the boat on which I worked and slept. Neither I nor anyone around me felt the slightest danger. The "bombing" was political, and apparently I wasn't a political threat. I made sure, though, to resist calling the headlines to the attention of my parents back in Holland.

A Danger Zone That Appears Safe

Paradoxically, perhaps the most dangerous move we can make appears to be the safest. . . .

After divorce, everyone needs money. Two homes, travel, and legal fees mean less disposable income. Moving away for higher pay and less conflict with the ex feels like moving out of a danger zone and "starting a new life." In fact, it's moving into a danger zone.

"Moving away" may work for the parent, but rarely works for the child. When I conducted years of research for *Father and Child Reunion*, one finding surfaced with clarity: Children of divorce do best when both parents live close to each other, and when they see both parents about equally.[18] "Close to each other" means that the children can see either parent without having to forfeit friends or activities.

The way to *high pay* after a divorce is to move to where the pay is. Except by coincidence, this will mean different cities for each divorced parent. One problem: For a child, growing up is getting to know both parts of oneself, or both biological parents. Being close to both parents is being close to her- or himself. Living close to both biological parents, and seeing about equal amounts of each, appears to be an even more important stabilizer for a child of divorce than for a child in an intact family.[19] Moving away from the other parent after divorce may be a safe zone for the parent, but it is a danger zone for the child.

Moving away may double your pay. Giving your child both parents: priceless.

18. People Who Get Higher Pay Are More Willing to *Travel Extensively* on the Job

Sales reps covering national and international territories obviously earn more than sales reps in department stores. While half of today's professionals are women, only 16% of the most-frequent flyers are women.[20] A woman who travels on the job distinguishes herself.

If we choose a field like diplomacy, then traveling goes with the turf. But if we choose to be a computer scientist, extensive travel is not part of what we have prepared for. Yet a computer scientist willing to travel the world to troubleshoot system breakdowns can expect to get paid more than someone unwilling to leave her or his office. Almost every field has national or international consulting opportunities for the person who listens to the complaints and develops a unique solution—as long as the will to travel accompanies the creative problem solving.

The first time a company asks for volunteers to travel, there is often competition for the assignment. But companies find that frequent business flyers quickly replace the fantasy of travel-as-romance with the reality of jet lag, sleeping alone, eating alone, "dining" on airline food, getting out of shape, and watching one's back become luggage's victim. While airline food used to be a cut above prison food, it is now mostly peanuts and rolls. A cut above bird food. For longer flights, the hot plate has been replaced by a cold white bag. Blue-collar-worker-with-brown-bag-on-the-street, meet white-collar-worker-with-white-bag-in-the-air.

One would think that with the greater number of male travelers, especially among those paying for *full*-price coach fares, the airlines would cater to men's larger sizes. Not so. Out-of-shape, overweight men are stuffed into seats designed for quasi-anorexic women.

Returning from a business trip is more likely to mean accumulated responsibilities than time off. Colleagues have little empathy: Even if you never saw the beach on your business trip to Hawaii you're still treated as if you were on vacation. For all these reasons, burnout is a business, and a woman in business will find opportunities if she's willing to step in where others have burned out.

Companies wanting to attract both the best women and the best men will also increase the use of videoconferencing to minimize travel, or airport conferences to reduce the time of the trip, or offer long weekend breaks after a trip so the traveling parent can reconnect with family. Fortunately, technology is once again making the work world more female-friendly, and allowing men in the future to also share the role of responsibilities divided between the world of work and the world of home.

Four Steps to Transforming a Traveling High to High Pay

One. Think of your interest in traveling or relocating as the equivalent of a skill, and therefore a bargaining chip.

Two. Ask about the different problems facing your company in different locations: Is there a mesh between your skills and your company's challenges in a location that interests you?

Three. If your company cannot use your willingness, consider whether another company's need for you to relocate or travel at its behest might lead to enough additional pay to make you consider transferring companies.

Four. If so, apply to other places and keep following up. Most people who relocate or travel at a moment's notice also burn out fairly quickly, or a change in their personal status diminishes their professional flexibility (for example, they become engaged or pregnant, or decide to heed the warning of their high blood pressure). It just takes that one follow-up call to coincide with the moment a company is being given notice from a key employee for you to become the right person in the right place at the right time: and a woman-on-the-move.

Responsibility, Training, Ambition, and Productivity: People Who Get Higher Pay . . .

In this buffet-of-a-chapter we discover what's theoretically been known, but practically speaking been unknown, for almost a quarter century: Companies pay men and women equal money when their titles are the same, their responsibilities the same, *and* their responsibilities are of equal *size*. We discover, therefore, the value of women knowing which type of responsibilities to pursue, and what size company to try on for size if she wants a man-size paycheck.

We learn at how early an age women's choices of career and family goals are formed, and why these choices alone have been found to account for the gap in male-female pay. Given women's family considerations, what alternatives can women pursue to have a high-paying career, children, and a marriage that doesn't topple over the closer she gets to the top?

As we round out the 25 ways to higher pay, we hold up the first 24 against 1: productivity. Is productivity the only one that really counts? And what is productivity, anyway? Is it different for a business, the government, for men, for women? . . .

19. People Who Get Higher Pay Take On *Different* Responsibilities Even When Their Titles Are the Same

You can't tell a salary by its title. Eminem, Madonna, and Marilyn Manson have in common two identical titles—singer and actor—but they all make more than people with three titles: singer, actor, and waiter. Often, you can't tell a salary by its title.

HR, PR, or the Bottom Line?

If women in 2004 are only 17% of the top earners in America's biggest companies, what can be done to change that?[1] Bottom line: The top earners take responsibility for the bottom line, for generating revenue, or for profit and losses. They include, for example, marketing managers or other managers responsible for the bottom line.[2] Yet less than 10% of these revenue-generating positions that lead to top earnings are held by women.[3]

Example? A *man* with the title of corporate vice president usually handles finance or sales; a *woman* with the title of corporate vice president more often handles human resources, communications, or public affairs. Of Fortune 1000 CEOs, 82% said these differences were a major deterrent to women's advancement.[4]

How can more women be encouraged to take on bottom-line responsibilities?

Fortunately, the National Association of Female Executives (NAFE) offers women its assessment of the 30 corporations most aggressively moving women into revenue-generating positions. Unfortunately, NAFE puts almost all the onus on the companies, not the individual women.

That's a problem for two reasons. It doesn't direct women toward solutions they can implement: how to assemble the right team of mentors, or how and when to take over a line responsibility in, for example, a foreign operation. But much more important, it doesn't help many women address an underlying issue . . .

Think about the difference between the human resources division, on the one hand, and the profit-and-loss (P & L) line manager, on the other. Aside from the first dealing with relationships (women's traditional bailiwick), and the second with money (men's traditional responsibility)—and, therefore, "the more we change, the more we remain the same"—perhaps something else is going on.

Qualitatively, in line management, cutting back monetarily almost always means making recommendations that lead to firing humans whose families you may have partied with. That's a trauma for both the fired and the person recommending the cutback.

And, as we have seen with Enron, Adelphia, and Tyco, people who handle finances can also be sued. Bottom line: The buck stops there. The IRS and the SEC can lead to the JAIL.

Helping women make the transition to line management requires training women to play, ironically, a much more vulnerable role—one more vulnerable financially, legally, humanly, and personally. Martha Stewart's "Recipes from Prison" will doubtless include comfort food.

Why, though, is the bottom-line manager paid more to begin with?

If the human resources' diversity program consistently wins awards, but the company consistently loses money, well, every employee soon loses a job. If the company consistently makes profits, but the human resources program is nothing exceptional, everyone keeps her or his job, stock options increase, pensions remain secure, and, therefore, there are fewer divorces and fewer children without a parent. Ultimately, if HR and PR don't take a backseat to the bottom line, it's Chapter 11 at the office and broken families at home. A company's survival is top priority, so a company pays top dollar to survive.

The same survival focus is reflected in the high pay of the super-salesperson—sometimes paid more than any corporate VP. Support functions, whether HR or back-office operations, will always be paid less than the profit-generators and the loss-preventers.

Headlines that tell the world "Women Corporate VPs Make Less Than Male Counterparts" create anger without directing women to either personal solutions or corporate solutions.

20. People Who Get Higher Pay Take On *Bigger* Responsibilities Even When Their Titles Are the Same

ITEM. The U.S. Bureau of Labor Statistics (BLS) found almost a quarter-century ago that companies paid men and women equal money when their titles were the same, their responsibilities the same, and their responsibilities were of equal size.[5]

As early as 1981, the BLS surveyed professional, administrative, technical, and clerical workers, all working in the same establishment, in the same field, with the same type of responsibility. But they added one crucial additional measure: size of responsibility. For example, rather than a buyer for a small boutique being compared to a national buyer from Nordstrom's, they compared buyers with equal-sized responsibilities.[6] Once the men and women had equal-sized responsibilities, they received equal pay.

Given what we have been finding, if this was true in 1981, is it possible the women are today earning more than men? As we saw in the Introduction, once a study reveals that men and women are paid equally for the same work, the study may be repeated, but the gender comparison is rarely funded.[7] Therefore, we don't know.

How important is the size of responsibility to a top executive's pay? Very. In Standard & Poor companies, women executives earn 45% less than men executives. But when we look at size of responsibility alone, 75% of this gap is accounted for: That is, the men managed companies with almost twice as much in sales; with twice as many employees; and among the top executives studied, the men were more likely to have worked their way to CEO, chairperson, or president, rather than, say, executive vice president.[8]

Is the next generation of women executives preparing itself differently when it comes to size of responsibility? A recent study of university graduates in the U.K. found the women seem to prefer the shorter commutes to the smaller firms that in the U.K. are more geographically dispersed.[9] This appealed even to young, unmarried women without children.

Are there ways women can take on larger responsibilities without becoming a member of the mostly male "good die young club"? Yes. (Would I have asked the question if I didn't have one of those solution-type answers!?) One way is by feeling freer to delegate. Many women have a tendency to feel they have to do everything themselves, as the accompanying Cathy cartoon indicates.

Mastering the skills of assuming larger responsibilities without larger heart attacks gives women the option to both earn more and live longer.

21. People Who Get Higher Pay Require Less Security

ITEM. It's 2004. I am presenting *Why Men Earn More* to the sales and marketing teams of my publisher (AMACOM). To illustrate financial risk as one of the ways to higher pay, I ask everyone in the room who is paid by commission to stand up. Eight men stand; no women. I then ask those paid by salary to stand: About equal numbers of men and women stand.

In Chapter 3 I discussed the risk-taking mind-set that leads to men being more likely to choose risk-taking fields such as venture capitalism. Even once a given field is chosen, though, women *within* the field choose the security, and men the pay. Usually. The marketing and sales people at my publisher are in the same field, marketing the same products for the same company, but only the men took less security for the potential of more pay—or, perhaps, seized a job opportunity that might not otherwise have been available were it not for their willingness to take only commission.

What are the financial risks worth? A British researcher reports the pay advantage of working in the private sector is 7%–12%.[10] In Britain, women are 61% more likely to work in the more secure public sector.

Are financial risks worth the loss of security? In the United States, probably no parents would consider the extra $1,800 per year in hazard pay worth it for their daughter or son to take the extra risk of being deployed to Iraq or Afghanistan.

The United States follows the pattern of men taking the financial risks even within a given field. Women physicians are three times as likely as men to work for the government or an HMO; men physicians are much more likely to be self-employed in a solo practice.[11]

The trade-offs are fairly obvious: The doctor in a solo private practice has no life; he or she can feel pulled between saving the life of a stranger and attending to her or his own child when sick. Ob-gyns are especially vulnerable to malpractice suits, making private practice a lawsuit-in-the-waiting. Family health benefits, vacation leave, personal days, and pensions must be provided on one's own.

Taking the secure route does not always mean less pay. Since the government has less obligation to make a profit, it can more frequently offer both security and pay, plus a sense of serving (as in public service). My younger sister, Gail, made more money as a teacher than I do as an author. A few months ago she retired at age 59 with a pension that will care for her for the rest of her life. I sense that her pension will create more than financial security for her—it will doubtless lead to a longer life. Teaching offered her pay, security, and a sense of contribution. One smart sister.

22. People Who Get Higher Pay Have More *Relevant Training* in Their Current Occupation

If we hear that a woman and man general surgeon with equal years of experience nevertheless have a gap between their salaries, it sounds like discrimination. Few of us know enough to point out that only 30% of women general surgeons are board certified (vs. 59% of the men).[12] In virtually every scientific area, men have a higher percentage of the Ph.D.'s. So comparing men and women professors, engineers, or scientists without accounting for relevant training is not exactly comparing apples to oranges, but Galas to Fujis.

Suppose, though, two people have a Ph.D. in literature from Harvard from the same year, and, in brief, they're both equally matched on all of the other 24 criteria. Could relevant training be a difference? Yes. At Harvard University, more than 86% of the recent doctoral dissertations in literature were "advocacy-based research."[13] That is, it was research whose purpose was the active promotion of either radical feminist perspectives or highly politicized perspectives on literature.[14]

At this point in history, saying a person is doing advocacy-based research is considered a positive at Harvard among those pursuing dissertations in literature or sociology or many of the social sciences. And right now, because of the bias of universities, advocacy research will doubtless help women obtain academic positions (via "the sisterhood-is-powerful network"). But when the pendulum comes back to the center, advocacy will be less valued than objective research. Most degrees, like Ph.D.'s, and board certifications, are awarded for the achievement of underlying skills like research and the mastery of the scientific techniques in one's field. Advocacy research will be considered poor preparation for making long-term contributions to the field.

On the surface, then, women Ph.D.'s in literature from Harvard will appear to have equal training to their male counterparts. But if these women's contributions to the mainstream journals do not eventually equal men's, we will assume discrimination when the reality could be that our daughters were seduced into academic "flashdancing"—more politics than professionalism. Hardly worthy of Harvard. Or our daughters.

23. People Who Get Higher Pay Have *Higher Career Goals* to Begin With

ITEM. Catalyst, a women's advocacy group, in 2003 found that 43% of women executives worldwide aspire to "join their senior management committee," but only 9% aspire to be a CEO or managing partner.[15]

ITEM. Small business owners whose goal is a more flexible life make less profit. Women own 95% of these businesses surveyed.[16]

ITEM. Though most work out of necessity, women are almost five times as likely as men to work "for extra money." Men are almost 50% more likely to work to support the family.[17]

Worldwide, women and men still say they work for significantly different reasons. In separate studies from Singapore, Australia, Poland, and the United States, women said they started their own businesses because of dissatisfaction with their current employers, a desire for autonomy, and a need for flexibility, usually for family reasons.[18]

Is this likely to change in the near future? A study of recent college graduates finds:

Women decide from as early as age 17, when they choose their degree course, on how to combine work and motherhood. They prefer careers such as teaching and nursing, where they can take an extended break to raise a family. And from the outset of their careers, choosing a socially useful job was more important to the women than the men, while financial rewards were less important (only 14% of women ranked financial rewards as "very important").[19]

How much impact do these different goals have on women's earnings? The same study of recent graduates determined that these early choices are the single most important determinants of the gender wage gap.[20]

The vision of a balanced life is common to women throughout the world—whether they are moms, executives, or small business owners. A recent survey of West European and Asia-Pacific women executives found this to be true for them; a survey of Australians reveals that most mothers prefer part-time work (26 hours per week).[21] In the United States, this vision of balance leads more than half of all women-owned businesses to be at-home businesses.[22]

The Corporate Catch-22

For business, the precarious outcome of this desire for balance is reflected by what a *Fortune* magazine poll uncovered: 87% of female executives were considering making a significant change in their lives, almost invariably by leaving their jobs.[23] When Denise Kuhlman discovered bankruptcy law was drudgery, she quit to study psychology.[24] Shoya Zichy quit international banking to take up painting.[25] Almost a third of the women executives had, in the past year or so, either left their jobs to not work at all outside the home or seriously considered doing so.[26] Others went back to school, took sabbaticals, changed their careers, or made a major personal change.

This reality can trigger the corporate Catch-22: "Don't be flexible, lose good women; be flexible, lose good women." Ironically, the women are often lost to the company exactly because of the flexibility. How?

Women often reassess their career goals when they take a leave of absence. When Colleen McMahon, the first woman litigation partner at one of New York City's top law firms, took a 10-month leave of absence after the birth of her third child, she reported, "I rediscovered things . . . music, playing the organ and singing, exercising . . . it broke the law's chain of custody over me."[27] When her 10-month leave was up, she announced she wanted to cut back her hours, whatever the financial consequences.

During the past quarter century, companies have found themselves the target of lawsuits as women who did not get promotions saw fewer women in top positions and automatically assumed that reflected "systemic" discrimination.

A Fortune 500 company was being sued by a woman who didn't get a promotion. The company hired a research company known for *defending* women to uncover the experiences and desires of its employees. A survey of 6,000 of its employees uncovered these revealing findings:[28]

- Nearly half the women said, if they had a choice, they would prefer to work part-time; only 18% of the men felt that way.
- Only 5% of women clerks listed "executive" as their ultimate

aspiration. The men clerks were more than four times as likely to aspire to executive positions.

- Overall, men were twice as likely as women to request promotion.
- Women were 25% more likely to get the promotions they requested.
- Among the employees who were married, men were about 13 times as likely to perceive themselves as the primary breadwinner.

In brief, all of the findings pointed to women and men having significantly different career goals. Perhaps more important, the men were willing to make more sacrifices to achieve their goals—to forfeit shift assignments they personally preferred, to take shift assignments more helpful to the company, to accept inconvenient transfers, and work more overtime. (Sacrifices that have their parallels for women at home.)

This creates the most important corporate Catch-22: a company listening to women's desires for fewer promotions, giving fewer promotions to women, and then being sued for giving fewer promotions to women. Yiddish has a word for this: chutzpah.

A better alternative? A woman communicating to a company that she understands this principle: A company creates opportunities for employees who create opportunities for the company.

A company that thinks this way is a company you want to be with—they'll be profitable enough to make good on your pension plan. Be suspicious of any company that *just* speaks of "opportunities for women." The company is patronizing women; underneath they will fear that creating these opportunities undermines profit—and therefore undermines even their women stockholders—so they'll become passive-aggressive (praise women more, promote women less).

What are clues that a company respects women? When it emphasizes opportunities created *by* women, when it modifies old policies to take advantage of those opportunities, and when it does the same for men.

The Shift in Men's Goals: His "Invisible Juggling Act"

Worldwide a shift is happening inside men's psyches that is expressed only when the men are directly asked. We saw evidence of that shift in the Harris poll asking men and women in their twenties if they were willing to give up pay to spend more time with their families, and finding that 70% of men (vs. 63% of women) would forfeit money if they could have more family time.[29] And new polls of Asia-Pacific men find that Asia-Pacific men and women executives now place identical priority on their balance between work and family life.[30]

At this moment in history, millions of "working dads" are desiring to do what they do not feel they have the right to do: be more devoted as a dad, less devoted as a worker. This feeling is far more ubiquitous among men executives than women executives in many areas of the world because, for example, Asia-Pacific women executives today are more than six times as likely to *not* have children than men executives are.[31] The Asia-Pacific executive man is about six times as likely to be a working dad as an executive woman is to be a working mom.

The executive man's juggling act is magnified by the fact that worldwide he is almost seven times as likely to be the sole full-time worker than is an executive woman.[32] So his desire to be with his children is frustrated by the reality of his father's Catch-22 of loving the family by being away from the love of his family. His frustration is a juggling act-without-a-name, and therefore without acknowledgment. Which can leave him feeling lonely and depressed.

24. People Who Get Higher Pay Do More In-Depth Job Searches

Jack and Diane both had managerial experience, and they both had preschool children. Jack did a nationwide search for his job; when he found it, the family moved. Diane waited until the children were in school and then did a local search for her job. Prior to the children, Jack and Diane both had careers. After the children, Jack was doing a career search; Diane was doing a job search.

Jack's search gave him a country's worth of options; Diane's search gave her a suburb's worth of options. To my knowledge, no one has measured the worth of a national versus local job search, but I'd venture a guess at about a 10%–25% increase in income, to say nothing about increasing one's options for field of work, working conditions, and benefits.

If you add to a nationwide search many of the other 24 ways to increase pay, you not only increase the likelihood you will be offered a job, but also increase your value for any job offered. For example, Jack was able to choose among jobs that required him to work late at night; Diane's search was limited to jobs that allowed her to pick their daughter up from school. Jack's and Diane's children had medical problems. This meant Jack, needing the money, had to be willing to move should his new job require it, and he knew he had to update himself in his field. Potential employers, sensing these flexibilities, were more likely to hire him and be willing to pay him more (as long as he articulated what he was offering to his potential employer).

None of this is women's or men's fault—it is a couple decision. But it results in the woman getting more income from her husband's paycheck, less income from her own. Just as she is taking care of their children, so he is taking care of their income, and the job search reflects both priorities, just as it reflects those priorities for her to be more likely to do a search for the children's clothing, their bedroom furniture, pediatrician, child care center, and which medicine to put on which rash. The couple's decision does not reflect discrimination against women at work, but the choices of a couple with children at home.

The Job Search Dilemma and Some Creative Solutions

When the unemployment rate is high, it's a boon for recruiters, right? Wrong. Between 2000 and mid-2003, the U.S. economy lost more than 3 million jobs in the private sector alone. Recruiters had a lot of job seekers with no place to go. In just one year, headhunters like Heidrick and Struggles International laid off 1,000 people, or 40% of its global staff.[33] That's the dilemma. What's the solution?

Exit the recruiter, enter the computer. Recruiters' online databases have gone from little-used to highly useful. They won't replace the recruiter in good times, and recruiting is still an excellent field for high pay if you're willing to adapt, wait, and dance with the times, but it's a better field for people like Cathey Cotten, the founder of MetaSearch, who is constantly retooling her recruiters with the likely trends of the future.[34]

The solution? In addition to the mainstream computer job

searches listed in this book's bibliography, consider fields that are out of the mainstream. For example, if you love children, try Toyjobs (Toyjobs.com); if you've been into sports, TeamWork Consulting can help place you with more than 120 sports organizations. If you're into food, catering, or hospitality, try Hospitality Executive Search at www.jspatt.com. (They have one of the highest placement rates.) If you're good with computers and want to go beyond the firms everyone thinks of, try Rusher, Loscavio and LoPresto (www.rll.com), who have a rep for starting people with start-ups.[35]

25. People Who Get Higher Pay Above All, *Produce More*

Imagine. . . . It's easy if you try . . .
Imagine a "senior citizen" in the National Football League protesting, "I've been playing football for 30 years . . . you're going to pay me *less* than a *rookie?*"

Imagine Caucasian men forming an all-Caucasian basketball league, and the CBA (that would be the Caucasian Basketball Association . . . you knew that!) complaining that CBA players were not being paid equally to the NBA.

These are scenarios so outrageous that if ESPN viewers heard them, they'd be checking to see if they were on Comedy Central. In the NFL, no one cares about years worked as much as yards gained. In fact, no one cares about any of the 25 ways to higher pay except productivity. From the perspective of a sports fan-man, the closest one can come to a demand for "equal pay for equal work" is "equal pay for equal productivity."

It's not that a guy into sports is unwilling to debate the meaning of productivity. In fact, sports gave him an incentive to learn how statistics could be used to assess productivity: first, how to define productivity (the value of a .333 batting average vs. a 3.33 ERA); second, that it took dozens of statistics to get a fair assessment of which teams and players were the most productive.

His third lesson was that the very definition of productivity is debatable. Productivity may not be limited to competence and goal scoring alone, but it also needs to include the ability to draw a paying crowd (Brandi Chastain drew crowds far exceeding her goal-scoring productivity after she celebrated her U.S. soccer team's Olympic victory by removing her shirt and revealing her sports bra on TV).

By the time this boy becomes a man, he's suspicious of any one statistic defining productivity. To him, hearing a simple "women earn 80% of what men earn" does not imply discrimination any more than "Caucasian basketball players earn 80% of what African Americans earn."

What would real equality in sports look like to most men? Women and men competing in one league—just like Caucasians compete with African Americans in basketball. This doesn't mean the male psyche objects to a Women's Tennis Association or a Women's National Basketball Association. Any secure man would applaud it, and every good father is glad his daughter has the role models. To these men, forming most any group is progressive; demanding equal pay at Wimbledon without equal productivity is regressive. **Separate leagues are about opportunity; demands that they be paid equally are about entitlement.**

Do Men Earn More Because They're More Productive?
A study of court reporters finds that men court reporters completed 29% more work (controlling for accuracy) than the women in the same time period.[36] Another, of ob-gyns, found that the men ob-gyns put more hours into direct patient care and did more deliveries, but they also worked four more hours per week—so they produced more in a week, but not necessarily per hour worked.[37]

University professors love studying themselves, so we have studies that indicate that men professors in more than 500 universities publish more in both peer-reviewed and non-peer-reviewed journals than the women professors—but then again, the men professors got paid more. The men professors were likely to be paid the same or just slightly less than the women professors in cases of equal productivity.[38]

We saw Army and Navy studies in Chapter 2 about how West Point created separate definitions of adequate preparation for women and men, requiring men to complete an obstacle course in just over three minutes, but giving the women more than five minutes.[39] But the

Navy example has more pay implications. Recall how the job of carrying a stretcher, previously a two-man job, was redefined as a four-person job when it was discovered that two women couldn't usually carry a stretcher with a dying man on it?[40]

Here's the productivity-pay dilemma: If a man assigned to carry a stretcher needs only one additional man, but a woman needs three additional people, should the man receive extra productivity pay if he partners with a man to carry the stretcher, freeing two other military people for other functions? If a man is less likely to drop out of the armed services, more willing to be deployed, and more willing to do what it takes even at a much greater risk of being killed, is that productivity in military terms? And if so, should the men be awarded extra pay?

In conclusion, defining productivity is different for business, the government, and the individual. For business it's profit. For the government it may be protecting the country as efficiently as possible. Or it may be trying social solutions that may not benefit monetarily but could benefit socially—in this case, troubleshooting the problems created by the integration of women into the manual labor part of the workforce.

Conclusion to Part One:
Twenty-Five Ways
to Increase Your Pay

It is my hope that Part One of *Why Men Earn More* has begun to create a different attitude toward the workplace, so that when we hear "men earn a dollar for each 80 cents women earn" it will trigger for women 25 paths to higher pay rather than one path to victimhood.

More fully, I hope it has uncovered not just 25 but hundreds of little payoffs—such as the dozens of ways to be a nurse, engineer, or computer specialist—with a choice tailored to your personality and needs at any point in your life. That it has opened doors never previously considered eligible for your consideration—from safe ways of being in the armed services to ways of making money in construction without ever having to pick up a hammer. That its specific information such as the value of extra hours worked creates additional choices for parenting and working. It is my hope it has done this for men as well as women.

It is also my hope that Part One has created a *method* of looking at the workplace—of looking not just at field of choice, but a subfield; not just a field as it was or is, but a field as technology will create it to be; a field transformed by the evolution of men caring more for children and women creating more money; of how fields will adjust to economic hard times and easy times; of the importance of assessing not just pay but the trade-offs . . .

A good method should give us clues about the future. If Part One has been read well, Table 15's projection regarding the greatest growth potential of careers will be of little surprise. You won't be surprised at the inclusion of the health industry or of hazardous waste removal. And you'll be aware that knowing which jobs will be in demand predicts not only high pay but the likelihood that you'll be able to find a job where you'd also like to live.

Part One is but the foundation of *Why Men Earn More*. For thousands of years women chose men based on their ability to provide.

TABLE 15   Fastest-Growing Career Areas, 2002–12

#	Occupation	Employment 2002	2012	Projected Change*	Earnings Quartile (First Is Lowest)	Usual Education or Training
1	Medical assistants	364,600	579,400	59%	2nd	Moderate-term on-the-job training
2	Network systems and data communications analysts	186,000	292,000	57%	4th	Bachelor's degree
3	Physician assistants	63,000	93,800	49%	4th	Bachelor's degree
4	Social and human service assistants	305,200	453,900	49%	2nd	Moderate-term on-the-job training
5	Home health aides	579,700	858,700	48%	1st	Short-term on-the-job training
6	Medical records and health information technicians	146,900	215,600	47%	2nd	Associate degree

TABLE 15 *(Continued)*

#	Occupation	Employment 2002	2012	Projected Change*	Earnings Quartile (First Is Lowest)	Usual Education or Training
7	Physical therapist aides	37,000	54,100	46%	2nd	Short-term on-the-job training
8	Computer software engineers, applications	394,100	573,400	46%	4th	Bachelor's degree
9	Computer software engineers, systems software	281,100	408,900	45%	4th	Bachelor's degree
10	Physical therapist assistants	50,200	72,600	45%	3rd	Associate degree
11	Fitness trainers and aerobics instructors	182,700	263,900	44%	2nd	Postsecondary vocational award
12	Database administrators	110,000	158,600	44%	4th	Bachelor's degree
13	Veterinary technologists and technicians	52,700	75,900	44%	2nd	Associate degree
14	Hazardous materials removal workers	37,600	53,800	43%	3rd	Moderate-term on-the-job training
15	Dental hygienists	148,000	211,700	43%	4th	Associate degree
16	Occupational therapist aides	8,300	11,800	43%	2nd	Short-term on-the-job training

TABLE 15   *(Continued)*

#	Occupation	Employment 2002	2012	Projected Change*	Earnings Quartile (First Is Lowest)	Usual Education or Training
17	Dental assistants	266,000	379,000	42%	2nd	Moderate-term on-the-job training
18	Personal and home care aides	607,600	853,500	40%	1st	Short-term on-the-job training
19	Self-enrichment education teachers	200,400	280,800	40%	3rd	Work experience in a related occupation
20	Computer systems analysts	468,300	652,700	39%	4th	Bachelor's degree
21	Occupational therapist assistants	18,500	25,700	39%	3rd	Associate degree
22	Environmental engineers	47,100	65,100	38%	4th	Bachelor's degree
23	Network and computer systems administrators	251,400	345,300	37%	4th	Bachelor's degree
24	Environmental science and protection technicians, including health	27,600	37,700	37%	3rd	Associate degree

TABLE 15   *(Continued)*

#	Occupation	Employment 2002	2012	Projected Change*	Earnings Quartile (First Is Lowest)	Usual Education or Training
25	Preschool teachers, except special education	423,600	576,900	36%	1st	Postsecondary vocational award

Note: The national average percent change is 14.8% for the 2002–2012 employment projection series.
Source: U.S. Bureau of Labor Statistics, Office of Employment Projections. Table adapted from America's Career Info Net.[1]

The more women increase their mastery of the workplace, the more they open themselves to partnership with a new type of man.

It is my hope that Part One has begun a paradigm shift in the way we view men. As we saw women doing financially better than men in male-dominated professions, it hopefully offers a more generous view of the male attitude toward women in the workplace. As we contemplate making sacrifices to earn more, it is my hope we appreciate the sacrifices men have made to nurture the family by being their family's "financial womb." Especially the sacrifices of "working dads" and of dads' "invisible juggling act."

Reprinted with special permission of King Features Syndicate.

Part Two will deepen that paradigm shift. When we look at how quickly we passed laws designed to integrate women into the workplace even as we resist divorced and unmarried dads' equal participation with children, we will see how difficult it is for both sexes to make transitions from the rigid roles of our past to the more fluid roles of the future.

Part Two will allow us to see that men may be way behind in creating choices for themselves, but have actually been quiet supporters of the choices women want for themselves (even as they try to keep up with the changes in those choices!).

The deeper purpose of a more positive attitude toward men is a better life for the children who are parented by the men who are their dads and stepdads; less shame for our sons who will become men; and, for our daughters, a deeper understanding of men's desire to please that leaves them feeling their willingness to please is not unrequited but returned—allowing our daughters to feel less lonely and more loved.

If we earn more and love less, we pay for a home in which we do not live.

PART TWO

Women in the Workplace

CHAPTER 7

What Women Contribute to the Workplace

Women make many concrete contributions to the workplace. For example, recent studies of women teachers find they are more likely than men to devote time to collaboration with other teachers, verifying the findings of Sally Helgesen in *The Web of Inclusion* and *The Female Advantage*.[1] Whether they work in the armed services, in coal mines, or as cabdrivers, they are less likely to be killed or injured, creating less need for insurance and contributing to higher morale among workers.[2]

What Men Love about Women (at Work, That Is)

When I conduct workshops for corporations, I warm up by asking women and men to turn away from each other, and share "anonymously" what they like the most and least about working with the other sex.

Here is what men say they value most about working with women—with the important caveat that some women do not possess these qualities and some men do:

"They don't mind asking for directions."

"When they *give* directions, they don't mind if I ask questions— they don't make me feel stupid."

"They listen well."

"They are nurturing."

"They are good at organization and detail."

"I feel treated more like family—with respect."

"I like their energy."

"They seem to anticipate needs."

"They care about you as a person—what's happening with your life outside the workplace."

"They're serious and attentive . . . almost like they're trying to prove themselves."

"It makes it more fun coming to work."

"They bring a different approach, a different point of view."

"They are good at multifocusing."

"They are good at writing reports and letters."

"They are very articulate."

"They don't seem to lose their temper and swear at you as much."

"They care about the process, not just the goal."

"They care about contributing to society, not just the bottom line."

"They care about the ethics, not just the profit."

Often the men in my workshops make a distinction between women who are managers and those in nonmanagerial positions.

Women who are managers, they say, are often more similar to men—"even worse than men." So that's the first challenge: making sure we don't force women to become imitation men; that we don't force women to adapt in the way Hollywood might force an independent filmmaker to adapt and lose what makes him or her special. Which doesn't mean women can't also learn a lot from men.

It does mean engendering an awareness of the different ways women and men are likely to be motivated. For example, when we study boys' and girls' reactions to computer games, we find boys are more likely to want congratulations only when they have accomplished a victory. Girls are more likely to want acknowledgment for their effort, and want the acknowledgment throughout.[3] Additionally, boys are more likely to be motivated by the need to finish—and win. Girls remain motivated and involved when they are interacted with, and are more likely to quit if bored.

One of the clearest insights into women's contributions comes from what they emphasize in their work as legislators.

Mrs. Clinton Goes to Washington

Male legislators focus on punishment and consequences; female legislators on rehabilitation, job training, and education.[4] Both sexes generally agree about the importance of each other's different priorities. Women legislators help guarantee that the prevention argument holds its own; men that enforcement is not neglected.

Beyond crime prevention, female legislators on both the national and state levels are much more focused on women's issues, children's issues, issues of family law, and health care.[5] Legislators who are men are more likely to concentrate on finance, budget, taxes, and defense.

Ironically, whether Republican or Democrat, our leaders reinforce the traditional stereotype of this division of labor. We saw this even with the nontraditional Hillary Clinton, with her focus on health care both as first lady and in her more independent Senate career. Nevertheless, both sexes are as important in the legislative world as they are in the raising of children.

When "Dr. Mom" Becomes Mom-the-Doctor

In the medical profession, science, drugs, and technology, along with the belief of doctor-as-infallible, had been turning many doctors into machines, making patients feel more like replaceable parts than valued humans. Women's demand for better bedside manners and their push to take responsibility for knowing their own bodies (starting with the feminist Boston Women's Health Book Collective's *Our Bodies, Our Selves,* first published in 1984 and still going strong) began the push for women to enter the medical profession at every level.

Women's contribution in health care has been phenomenal: They have helped expand the definition of acceptable medical treatment to include meditation, stress reduction, prayer, exercising, vitamins, diet, herbs, chiropractic work, acupuncture, psychotherapy, massage therapy, music therapy, and art therapy.

In the 1960s, almost 100% of MD's would have pooh-poohed almost all of these approaches as nothing more than a placebo effect.

Yet even as the medical establishment acknowledged the placebo effect, it was hesitant to give credence to the mind's ability to promote healing via meditation and prayer. When someone said "chiropractic," they heard "quack" practice. The influx of women into medicine created permission for women like Caroline Myss (a "medical intuit") and Joan Borysenko (a New Age medical doctor) to make these alternatives to traditional medicine available and allow people to judge for themselves. This same influx also allowed many men who are medical doctors, such as Deepak Chopra, Andrew Weil, Bernard Seigel, Robert Atkins, Arthur Agatston, and Nicholas Perricone, to earn millions by helping millions in a way for which they would have been professionally ostracized in the 1950s.

From Mom-and-Pop Back to Mom-and-Pop

When Catalyst, an advocacy organization for executive women, surveyed Fortune 1000 companies, they found that 52% of women who were board members felt it was their job to encourage corporations to have more benefits—what the women called family-friendly policies (health care, child care, maternity leave, paternity leave, flexible work hours, or job sharing).[6]

Many men executives had seen these family-friendly benefits largely as disadvantages, because they drove up the cost of business, which obviously could mean the company could be less profitable, thereby actually making employees less secure. Child care, for example, involves liability insurance, the use of potential office space, hiring new employees, and the possibility that moms will be dividing their attention between work and the children. Male executives tended to view family-friendly benefits as attracting women at a time in their lives when their attention would be unpredictably pulled away from work by the urgency of family needs. And some felt that security packages attracted security-focused employees rather than entrepreneurial, creative employees who would speak up, innovate, and take risks.

The perspective of the men executives was not invalid, it was merely incomplete. Women gave companies the opportunity to try family-friendly policies and see if they could make them work for both the company and the parents.

In a sense, in the area of child care, children's relationships with parents' working has come full circle. We have gone from the mom-and-pop store (or mom-and-pop farm), with its integration of child care and work, to children-at-home and dad-at-work; to the mom-plus-daddy working at home, with its integration of childcare and work again. From mom-and-pop back to mom-and-pop.

Bad Cop Gets a Good Cop

In the atmosphere of the police station, a police officer's potential for compassion is rarely nurtured: It is considered a weakness. The addition of women can prompt men to consider that their true weakness may be their facade of strength. This not only highlights the strength of the women officers per se, but creates men more tuned-in to those circumstances in which the addition of compassion can make them stronger.

Women accomplish this best when they are more than a tiny minority, because small minorities are expected to adapt.

Women officers play a powerful role in domestic violence disputes, which can result in more danger to the police than any other area. But when women join men as police officers called to the dispute, the danger decreases. Open ears calm more tempers than closed handcuffs.

In those same domestic violence disputes, a woman police officer is freer to play "good cop" exactly because a man might be more willing to play "bad cop." Open ears *and* the possibility of closed handcuffs—to be used when no alternative is left—work best in tandem.

The entrance of women into hazardous work also affects initiation rituals. Men's hazing rituals, especially in hazardous professions like police work, have evolved so gradually and unconsciously they have not been questioned. Women, generally uninspired by hazing, and prone to ask for protection from it, can motivate hazardous professionals to do more functional initiating. For example, firefighters might call a new recruit into a room that appears to be collapsing—but really isn't—to check whether the new recruit is willing to risk her or his life to save a partner. Some partners might wish to know this sooner rather than later.

The positive value of these hazing rituals is that they weed out people unwilling to risk their lives to save their partner. They offer information about trust. When hazing is ritualized to test for trust, a woman who skips hazing skips being trusted. Of course, any woman who valued herself would want to skip past the dehumanizing hazing. But in the process, she would miss part of the point of hazing in a hazardous profession: to see whether she can devalue herself enough to sacrifice herself in order to save someone else.

But hazing rituals that test only for toughness are incomplete. Hazing is meant to desensitize; domestic violence requires police sensitivity. Thus part of women's contribution will be the development of initiation rituals that also test for sensitivity, and that question hazing-without-purpose. In the process men can discern that rituals of put-downs rather than compliments, of repressing feelings, of every-adjective-as-a-swear-word, can quash what might otherwise be opportunities for bonding that would enhance teamwork. Women and men in dialogue can sort out functional from dysfunctional initiation and create new ways of building trust and teamwork.

The male police officer's sensitivity affects more than his police work; it affects the way he loves his wife and children. And a man who is happy at home is more effective at work.

If so much of what women contribute to the workplace emanates from their differences, why do men seem so threatened by women? What misunderstandings about our differences are making the integration of gender roles more difficult? Let's begin, in the next chapter, with understanding why men and women approach work so differently.

CHAPTER 8

Why Women and Men Approach Work So Differently, Yet So Similarly

This chapter reveals the underlying male-female dynamics reinforcing the pay gap. The most transparent view of men's and women's work-life choices are the choices they make when a boss isn't telling them what to do.

Male- and Female-Owned Businesses Reflecting Work-Life Decisions

Men- and women-owned businesses magnify the findings that men's choices lead to higher pay while women's lead to better lives (or, at least, more balanced lives).

When it comes to pay, women do a lot better *with* bosses. Working for someone else, women's different work decisions lead to 80 cents to men's dollar; as a business owner, women net only 49% of what men earn who own their own businesses, or about $6,600 per year.[1]

But for most women, money is not the primary goal of starting their own business: A study by the Rochester Institute of Technology found that just 29% of the women said building wealth was a major priority (vs. 76% of the men).[2]

The different goals are backed up by different ways of running their business. More than half of women business owners run their business out of their homes; in comparison to men-owned businesses, women-owned businesses are almost twice as likely to be home-based (54% for women vs. 29% for men).[3] This doubtless reflects women's greater likelihood to be juggling the raising of children with raising money for children, and therefore their need to choose busi-ness opportunities with convenience, flexibility, and direct access to the family.

Women business owners also differ from male owners in their will-ingness to pay others to help them. Just 16% of women-owned com-panies have employees (vs. 27% for those owned by men).[4] Of that 16% who hire, women are twice as likely as men to hire only part-time employees (25% vs. 12%).[5] Thus the women spend less per employee: $21,000 per worker (vs. $27,000 per worker for men-owned businesses).[6] However, among the small amount of women owners who do hire full-time employees, women express a desire to create family-friendly policies to a greater degree than men business owners do (65% vs. 29%).[7]

Table 16 gives us insight into four additional differences. Usually business owners put in less time and effort the longer they run their businesses; but as we can see, although men business owners have been running their businesses about 50% longer than women, they work close to 40-hour weeks versus 30-hour weeks by women. Men business owners also commute an extra 50-plus miles per week, and invest more in employees. In brief, the men both invest more of

TABLE 16   Differences between Men and Women Business Owners

	Men	Women	% More Done by Men
Hours worked per week	38.6	29.9	29%
Years running business	11.9	7.9	51%
% with 25 or more employees	4.8	3.5	37%
Miles commuted per week	169	115	47%

Source: Raw data from the U.S. Census Bureau's *Survey of Income and Program Participation* (*SIPP*), 2001 Panel, Wave 6. Latest survey as of 2004.

themselves in their business and invest in more employees. The very purpose of many women for owning a business is to facilitate investing more in their families, while still generating some income.

I questioned this data, wondering whether women-owned businesses hire fewer people and pay them less because banks were less willing to give them loans and financing. So I checked this out. A study of whether lenders discriminate found that women and men have the same access to capital and are charged the same interest, when the size of the firm and the age of the firm are accounted for.[8] Men have been running their businesses longer and hire more employees—and banks invest more in businesses that have spent a longer time investing more in themselves.

The bigger question of this chapter is not the differences between men- and women-owned businesses, or even the differences in behavior between men and women workers, but the underlying male-female dynamics reinforcing the pay gap. Some of these dynamics have been part of our survival instinct for perhaps millions of years; people for whom survival needs are no longer as dominant have the freedom to explore which of these male-female dynamics are still functional for them. So I'll start with a look at these underlying dynamics and how we apply them to everyday areas such as hiring help—an area that seems to differentiate men and women business owners.

Why Do Men and Women Seem to Approach Work So Differently, Yet So Similarly?

Money and Love: "A Diamond Is a Girl's Best Friend"
Throughout history, men learned that survival, respect, and women's love were all achieved by killing—whether killing animals, or enemies, or "making a killing" on Wall Street. Women received the money that men produced by loving. Men came to feel themselves as *unlovable* without the money, property, or the heroism it took to make them equal to a woman's love.[9] Women came to associate men spending money on them as a statement of how much they were valued—even loved—by the man. Her ability to love became her source of security: "A diamond is a girl's best friend." Essentially this

dynamic is true in almost all societies and all classes throughout history.[10] **The division of labor evolved into more than a division of labor. It became a division in the way the sexes received love.**

As men learned that being loved was conditional on producing money, they became insecure enough to be willing to risk their lives for money (or was it for love?). They worked in unsafe coal mines and construction sites so their wives could have better homes and gardens; and they fought in wars so *everyone* could have safer homes and gardens. This created a work ethic that required making any sacrifice necessary—including the sacrifice of his life—even for a stranger (e.g., firefighter, soldier). Men built this responsibility into the law (e.g., male-only draft registration). And into their socialization. Hence, lumberjacks, long-distance truckers, Alaskan crab fishermen, big-city taxi drivers, and construction workers all risk their lives every day. (Three construction workers die every day in the United States.[11])

It is not that men's underlying values were so different—they, like women, valued their family, home, security, and community. But men's focus on work demonstrated their devotion to the family, whereas women's focus on the family demonstrated their devotion to the family. The fact that men were paid to be away from love, while women were paid to love, made women far more lovable. That in turn reinforced men's willingness to fight to protect women when women asked for that protection, even after divorces.

These divisions were especially predominant in early human history when survival was the primary preoccupation, and the sexes played very different roles. Because the division of labor created a division of interests, opposites attracted each other because they needed each other, not because they understood each other. Expressions like "You can't live with 'em, and you can't live without 'em" reflect the frustrated outcomes for both sexes. **The sexes have been role mates, not soul mates.** Men got love by performing, not communicating; and to this day men have been unwilling to communicate their feelings about being accused of earning more because they have more power and privilege—about how they were trying to attract someone to love them, or to protect the family they loved that grew from that attraction.

This division of love's labor continues to this day. Our sons now learn that while girls now have the *option* to pay, boys still have the *expectation* to pay. For starters, our sons are still expected to pay for the "Six D's": dinners, drinks, dates, dances, diamonds, and driving expenses. Of course, not all his expenses start with D; no one would want him to forget the flowers, or the tickets, whether to a rock concert, movie, or play. And our daughters are still internalizing that the more desirable they are, the more boys will pay for them.

People often object, "It had less to do with socialization than biology." But that's a false distinction. A woman socialized to choose a strong man also made a biological choice—a husband whose children had different genes than if she had been socialized to marry a starving, sensitive artist—a Vincent van Gogh. If beautiful women were competing to marry Vincent van Goghs, we'd have more irises and sunflowers, and fewer beautiful homes (or ugly nuclear weapons!).

All of this is to say that men's and women's work choices are rooted far more deeply than in mere rational work decisions. Understanding the power of these roots helps us understand where our freedom to choose may be undermined not by the other sex but by our own biology and socialization. However, there is a dynamic between the sexes that is leading men to feel more threatened than is healthy for men, which is also affecting the health of women.

If Women Contribute So Much to the Workplace, Why Do Some Men Seem So Threatened?

When I ask this question in corporate workshops, among the common answers—with men and women still turned away from each other—are:

> "Because the better women are, the more men are afraid of losing their jobs."
> "Because men are easily threatened."
> "Because men can't get used to women being their equals."
> "Because men are dumb."

Although the last three comments are usually made half-facetiously, it is only *half* so. And interestingly, when they are made, they draw laughter, not lawsuits. (If men were asked, "Why are so few women at the heads of corporations?" and answered, "Because women are dumb," the lawsuits might exceed the laughter.)

The anger many women feel toward men in the workplace—often reinforced by HR seminars characterizing the white man as a "racist, sexist, easily threatened, patriarchal oppressor"—often does leave men feeling threatened, thus creating a self-fulfilling prophecy ("men are easily threatened").

But such contempt of men belies an understanding of them. If men were so easily threatened, why did they adjust to each wave of cheaper immigrant laborers who threatened to do their jobs for less? Why do men keep inventing computers and robots they know will take their jobs away? The truth is that growing up male, participating in and watching team sports, unconsciously teaches boys that everyone is a replaceable part—we wear uniform #7 until someone better comes along. We may not like it, we fight to remain valuable and valued, we exaggerate our good points and cover up our flaws (if we can!), but we are socialized to accept the reality of "the best wins," and, as legislators, men facilitate it. So as legislators, men passed the Equal Pay Act in 1963 to guarantee equal opportunity for women in the workplace—a half decade before the new women's movement asked for it.

So if men could adapt to new workplace immigrants, invent their own replacements, and pass an Equal Pay Act in 1963, why do many men still seem so threatened by women as workplace immigrants?

Prior to the 1960s, if a society was industrialized, both its moms and its dads might be said to have lived in the Era of Focused Responsibilities: Moms raised children and dads raised money. When the divorces of the 1960s ushered women into the workplace, only women—millions of them—made a transition to the Era of Divided Responsibilities. Only women's responsibilities were *divided* between work and home.

Immigrants had not entered the workplace with divided responsibilities. The cabdriver from Iran was working 70 hours a week in his role as breadwinner. Women were the first "workplace immigrants" with divided responsibilities.

Women became *more* threatening to men than immigrants in part because affirmative action laws required executives to promote women with divided responsibilities more quickly than men with focused responsibilities. Laws had never given that advantage to the mostly-men immigrants.

Women-plus-government also threatened many CEOs as they felt forced to be sexist and to undermine basic business economics by being forced to pay men less even if they worked more, and to promote men more slowly even if they were more productive.

The average male worker—who witnessed his company go from a motto of "productivity equals promotions" to "productivity equals promotions *unless* we have fewer women than men, in which case promoting you will mean discrimination against women . . ."—was left feeling that the core credo by which he had learned to earn money, attract love and respect, and protect those he loved were all undermined.

The minor distinction about immigrants and the workplace was that immigrants adapted to the workplace, while women got the workplace to adapt to them.

The major distinction was that many men felt women used their power to alter the law and have it both ways: to respect male-female differences when it worked for them (on sexual harassment, flextime, maternity leave, and separate women's sports teams), but to ignore these differences when it worked against them. That is, despite the differences between women's divided and men's focused responsibilities, women insisted they should be represented in equal numbers, except when they were already represented in greater than equal numbers (as nurses, elementary school teachers, in most departments at Wal-Marts), which then should be ignored. It was not women's power to legally change the workplace that left men more threatened by women than by immigrants, but the way that power was used.

On the home front women are still marrying men who they expect will earn more, and when a man fails to do so, it often sows the seeds for divorce. Thus a man can feel threatened that his wife's success may catalyze love's failure, the breakup of the family, and the loss of his children and the family home. He can fear that friends and family will see him as a failure at both marriage and work.

Other than losing his wife, children, and home, and disappointing his family and friends, he has no reason to feel threatened!

We can get a clearer picture of men's feelings if we reverse roles: If affirmative action gave divorced fathers more-than-equal access to the children, imagine how threatened many mothers would feel.

Some feminists still protest, though, that when women are mothers, bosses assume "mother track" in a way that they wouldn't for a father, and that this discriminates against "career track" women. It's a possibility worth checking out.

Do "Mother Track" Women Create a Stereotype That Affects "Career Track" Women?

It appears that the workplace makes clear distinctions among people who do and do not contribute. For example, even among men who all received their MBAs from the same universities, the salaries of the men who were the sole breadwinners increased at a 50% faster rate than those of the other men with the same MBAs, the same number of children, and the same amount of time in the workplace.[12] Overall, these sole-breadwinner men earned 31% more. The 31% pay gap between these two groups of men is greater than the 20% gap between men and women. While this is not a study of women, it is a study of the ability of the workplace to make distinctions based on the type of contribution made to the workplace. And it gives us clear data that the workplace makes these distinctions among men—that similar distinctions among women are not a sign of gender discrimination.

I believe this encourages those mothers who wish to pursue a career track to do so—as long as Dad is devoting the time to the children. Is this, though, realistic? When a mom earns more, do dads work more at home? Contrary to popular belief, yes. The more women *earn* in the workplace, the more their husbands participate in housework and child care—to the point that, among women who earn more, the men do more of the housework and child care.[13] (Interestingly, this is not true for women who earn less, usually working more like 35-hour weeks, commuting less, and doing more fulfilling work.)

In brief, there is not just a mommy track, but also a daddy track. Men who divide obligations between work and home earn less, just like women. But this brings us full circle: If women do pursue the career track either as employee or employer, how can they apply this understanding of the underlying male-female dynamic to everyday situations like paying for help? I promised an answer.

Paying for Help

Let's take a closer look at the finding that women-owned small businesses hire fewer employees. And that their employees are twice as likely to be part-time and paid less.

I would not think much of these differences if I did not see many women who begin their own businesses, or who work outside the home, hesitant to "invest in themselves" by hiring someone to clean their home, do repairs, run errands, and do their books. I frequently hear, "Why should I pay someone when I can do it myself for free?" They don't calculate what they could make by investing that time in perfecting their own expertise. I believe this resistance is part of what leads to women-owned businesses earning only 49% of what men-owned businesses earn—the part that can be changed without sacrificing quality of life.[14]

For example, a woman friend of mine with a lot of clients and a child was being paid a fixed amount to do a project. She realized it required her to travel to Santa Barbara, which is about four hours from where we both lived in San Diego. She checked out the airfare, and was understandably outraged at the cost. She decided to save money and drive.

Here's what was missed: She didn't calculate what she could make during the extra five-to-six hours of work she could get done both via the time saved and the ability to work on the plane and in the airport, but not in the car. Nor did she consider intangible costs like a loss of time with her son.

Some women object, "Well, okay, in the future I'll hire someone; but right now, I'm not making enough to afford that." Hopefully, this book has made it clear that those extra hours worked are the hours that pay disproportionately more, and that paying for others frees us to excel in our chosen field, without which there will be no future in which we can afford the help.

I believe this male-female difference in willingness to pay for others reinforced when we teach only our sons to figure out how to pay for girls from the moment they begin to desire them; and it does not help our daughters to learn that the more desirable they are, the more boys will pay for them. This is the opposite message to boys that "the more successful you are, the more you have to learn to pay for others."

Schools need to expand discussions about women being paid equally to women paying equally.

How Technology Is Making Women and Divided Responsibilities Viable in the Twenty-first Century

Divided responsibilities are the wave of the future—not just for women, but for many men, too. Not for all workers, but for some. Why? Technology. Cellular phones allow a mom to pick up an important call from a home-office-on-the-soccer-field while watching her daughter kick a goal past the Running Devils (not necessarily a boys' team!). Laptop computers allow Dad to retrieve a file while his son is retrieving a fly. Instead of "home, home, on the range," it's "office, office, in the home . . . where our sons and daughters roam." Ironically, the same technologies that facilitated independence and the option of divorce and therefore the destruction of families is now also creating opportunities to reunite families.

My projection is that by 2020, approximately 70% of dads will have responsibilities that are significantly divided between work and home. Making use of the gift of working women, then, involves treating women as pioneers in helping companies adapt to the divided responsibilities that will be a twenty-first-century reality. It also involves helping employees understand why someone with divided responsibilities cannot be paid as much as someone whose responsibilities are more fully focused on work.

CHAPTER 9

The Myths That Prevent Women from Knowing Why Men Earn More

It isn't right that women should get paid 59 cents on the dollar for the same work as men.
—GERALDINE FERRARO; VICE PRESIDENTIAL
NOMINATION ACCEPTANCE SPEECH, 1984[1]

As should be apparent by now, it is unlikely women ever earned 59 cents to the dollar for the *same* work as men—for work that involved 25 differences, yes, but not the same work. Yet the 59 cent statistic is perhaps the only statistic on which George Bush, Sr., Michael Dukakis, Geraldine Ferraro, and Ronald Reagan all agreed. And as we have seen by 2004, George W. Bush Jr. made no objection when John Kerry claimed affirmative action was still needed since "women earn 76 cents to the dollar for the same work as men."[2] This was months after the Census Bureau reported the gap to be 80 cents to the dollar in both the first and second quarters of 2004—a gap the Census Bureau never claimed was for the same work.[3] Politicians' jobs are often dependent on making people feel like victims so they can become the victim's savior. So we can expect "victim" power to be kindled by politicians.

But the job of the university is truth-seeking and empowerment. So it is more surprising that the belief that men earn more for the same work is also reinforced in the universities. I bought a T-shirt from the American Association of University Women in 1991 based on the 59-cents calculation that said, "For a woman to make as much in a day as a man, she'd have to work until 10:30 at night . . . then who'd make dinner?"[4]

Is this issue of great concern to women? Indeed. In an AFL-CIO survey of employed women, 94% identified equal pay as *the* most important workplace issue.[5]

The credibility of the pay gap is so embedded that few seem to question the point behind cartoons such as this:

If we believe this cartoon's message—that being born a girl means being sentenced to a lifetime of wage discrimination—we cannot help but feel a deep-seated anger toward men. This anger is reinforced by the media nationwide quoting magazines such as *Ms.*, which concluded, "The average woman is cheated out of about $250,000 in wages over a lifetime."[6] This creates a feeling that men have created a system "run by men, for men, to the detriment of women," and which devalues women. This doesn't just make women angry at men. It also makes many men angry at other men. And some men angry at themselves for being a man. Telling one group that it is being cheated out of a quarter of a million dollars by another group is the politics of victim power—it can lead to not only the most dangerous racism of the twentieth century, but also to a dangerous sexism.

This belief not only objectifies men, but also damages women's careers.

How the Belief in the Discrimination Against Women Hurts Women's Careers

Men and women alike might question why it should be the mother who considers leaving her job—but as a practical matter, working women earn 68 cents to every dollar men earn and are, therefore, the obvious candidates for child care, another poorly paid job.

—*New York Times*, 1991[7]

The belief that women are discriminated against in the workplace reinforces a couple's tendency to have the woman stay at home. It is the tendency for women to stay at home that makes the workplace value her less. Then, shortly after she is married, it begins to make sense for her to move for her husband's career, not for her husband to move for her career. Conversely, it makes sense for them to invest in his medical, law, or engineering degree—rather than hers. Soon the mother is out of the workplace, her skills are outdated, and she fears reentry. For some women, fear of reentry leads to having more children in order to keep her life meaningful. Children become her career. The problem is not children-as-career per se, but the belief that she would face discrimination at work, which adds to her fear of returning to work.

Ironically, then, a reality has been created from a false reality. And, ironically, women's careers are hurt via comments meant to prod a society into helping women's careers. The road to hell is paved . . .

I saw this thinking radically alter the life path of Karla and Chuck. When I first met them, they were deeply in love, and she soon became pregnant. They wanted to get married, but Karla couldn't follow through: "He has just a master's degree in sociology and no real career plans." Although Karla had just graduated from college and been elected to Phi Beta Kappa, she saw the work world as biased against women and feared she would never be able to do well in it. She struggled with what to do about her pregnancy until her second trimester; then, in enormous mental anguish, she had an abortion and broke up with Chuck, whose heart was also broken.

About a year later, Karla married an attorney. I attended their wedding. Even on their wedding day I didn't see the love in her eyes for her husband that I had seen repeatedly for Chuck. When Karla spoke of Chuck it was with such affection she had to make sure her husband wasn't within earshot. When Karla and her husband had a child, Karla didn't think twice about who should take care of it—she had chosen a husband who was earning more, and who wasn't that into children anyway. When their son was five, Karla and her husband separated. Karla raised her son as a single mom. It took years for Chuck to get over the breakup, and maybe he never did, but he eventually got married, has children, and is a wonderful dad.

What saddened me most about Karla's fear of discrimination was how it persuaded her to pursue what she thought would be an easier life that turned out to be a lonelier life. I will never know the child-to-be who was aborted, but Karla's son viewed his dad much more as a wallet and much less as a dad than would have been the experience of any son of Karla with Chuck.

Karla's decision also led her to never really develop a career, and led to her choice of a husband who was strongly career-oriented and therefore prone to earn even more when their son was born. Karla's decision was encouraged by the belief that men earn more and reinforced the statistic that men earn more.

How the Belief in the Discrimination Against Women Poisons Love and Divides Families

A woman who believes she cannot earn equal money to a man feels justified having a man pay for dinner on their first encounters. Not so significant? Who pays for the first dinners out is as clear a message about the roles each person expects as who cooks the first dinners in. Their actual behavior is their most powerful statement of their real expectations. The man responds by earning more, and the woman responds by cooking more. By the time children come, they are serving as role models of limited flexibility.

Both sexes have an enormous investment in giving a woman a fair shake in the workplace. When women get a fair shake, the woman doesn't have to "marry up," and the man doesn't feel he has to compete to be the "up" in order to earn her love. He feels less chained to the workplace jail and, therefore, less attracted to the bars outside the jail; less pressure to deny his feelings and "tough it out" because "what's the use of complaining—I can't do anything to change it." When he denies his feelings, there is no possibility for real intimacy. In fact, when either sex denies feelings, there is no possibility for real intimacy.

In brief, the belief that men unfairly earn more creates confusion in dating, stereotyped and inflexible roles, and loss of intimacy. Other than that, no problem.

Protecting Women vs. Helping Women

In the past, the belief in discrimination at least created the power of affirmative action. In the future, female-as-victim will become increasingly disempowering. Women who received protection as employees will increasingly pay for that protection as employers.

As an employee, she may have favored government regulations designed to address the security concerns of women: health benefits, overtime pay, paid vacations, and employer contributions to social security. As an employer, she may figure out all these additional costs will make the difference between making money versus losing money. So she decides not to hire anyone. Now, the very government regulations that used to make her feel secure are making her feel insecure. She becomes resentful that she and an employee are not free from government interference to create a contract that feels good to both of them.

As these women's small businesses grow in size, a woman entrepreneur might increasingly resent being told she will be sued if her women employees feel insulted by a "dirty" joke. Or resent government demands to hire a certain percentage of women, rather than be allowed to use her own judgment about whom she wishes to hire; she may wish to use flextime when her judgment dictates and her employees need it, not when the government's judgment dictates and passes a law in response to political pressure.

In brief, women's new roles increasingly make female victim power dysfunctional for women; portrayals of women employees as potential victims takes on a different twist as women become the employers.

For women managers, there's a related problem that backfires against women: the belief that women make better managers.

The "Women Make Better Managers" Trap

It is currently in vogue to say that women make better managers than men, because they are less hierarchical, more collaborative, more connected between their left and right brains and therefore better able to juggle, and so on. Books with titles like *The Female Advantage* to books predicting the future like *Megatrends for Women,* as well as many of the human resources development officers in government agencies and corporations, tell our daughters that women make better managers because they have a more interactive style, a greater tolerance for ambiguity, are more people-oriented, and more into networking or working with everyone as equals.[8] They are also supposedly less into punishment and more into reward; less into closed information systems and more into open information systems; less into issuing orders and more into teaching and facilitating; and less into imposing discipline and more into valuing creativity.[9] All of these may have some truth. But each misses the whole truth.

If we say that what women derive from women's socialization and biology creates many characteristics that can be helpful to the workplace, I agree—and have spent much of my life communicating that to women. But when we say that as a result women make better managers than men, then that's an assertion that begs for proof. And there is none.

If we measure better managers by how employees feel when they work for women versus men around the world, well, worldwide, in each of the 22 countries polled, both sexes who have experience working for men and women bosses prefer working for men bosses. Women prefer men bosses by a ratio of more than two to one, and men prefer them by a ratio of more than three to one.[10]

Do countries that have the most experience with women bosses feel better about women-as-bosses? Unfortunately, no. In countries such as the former republics of the Soviet Union (Latvia, Lithuania, Estonia) that have had the most experience with women as bosses, and in which Communist ideology strongly supported women in management, both sexes were 6 to 10 times as likely to prefer men bosses.[11] There is an exception. Among women in the United States, the gap narrowed in Gallup's most recent poll: 23% of U.S. women now prefer a woman boss, and 32% prefer a man boss.[12] The good news is that in the U.S. at least, almost half of women, and men, express no preference.

So competitive statements like "women make better managers than men" take the focus away from the positive contributions of many women—as we just did here! And they exude self-righteousness, something that makes a bad manager.

There's another problem with the assertions of women-are-better-because-they-are-less-competitive, more collaborative, and more win-win. These assertions are awfully competitive and win-lose. Similarly, when we say women are less hierarchical than men, isn't that awfully hierarchical? Beyond that, is it accurate? And should the very word "hierarchy" be used pejoratively?

I believe expecting women to enter business management without understanding the positive values of hierarchies is like expecting the former Soviet Union to be successful sending Marxists to manage U.S. companies. Here's why . . .

What the Belief That "Men Are Hierarchical, Women Are Collaborative" Misses

Hierarchies definitely have their downside: They often encourage rigidity, intimidation, and the belief that those who have more status know more about everything (merely because they usually know more about many things). When a person is at the top of a hierarchy, we tend to think of him or her as more competent as a human being, not just more effective at the job.

Both sexes participate in hierarchies in different ways. Men's desire to climb to the top of a hierarchy is direct; women's indirect. Traditionally, men competed to be the doctor; women competed to marry the doctor. Women competed to marry the officer and the gentleman, not the private and the gentleman. (There are few movies titled *Swept Away by a Private!*)

When someone says "hierarchy," and especially "corporate hierarchy," their voice usually reflects dislike or disgust. But let's not turn the hierarchy into a devil too quickly.

Hierarchies were and still are men's way of creating standards, of holding each other accountable. Of "bribing" each other to better provide for their families. In comparison to a private, a four-star general had to successfully meet higher standards for longer, successfully handle more responsibility, and be more accountable for more people.

Mothers' standards and accountability are more voluntary, less mandatory, more private, less public. In mothering, there is no licensing. Mothers usually mothered well, but they didn't lose pay if they did it badly, or gain pay if they did it well. A mom's standards were more self-imposed, voluntary, and optional.

The male-dominated hierarchy was not a strategy designed to benefit men at the expense of women; it was a strategy to get men to pay the expenses of women! Or, more accurately, to pay the expenses of the entire family. The strategy included men giving each other constant "report cards,"—called promotions, demotions, or being "downsized." The results of these report cards were announced on business cards.

While report cards in school could give most of the class A's and B's, business "report cards" could give only a few men promotions, thus forcing more introspection. Most every man who wanted to be loved and respected had to climb this hierarchy, and therefore had to learn to receive criticism, give criticism, and receive criticism for the criticism he gave. It was not a strategy to benefit either sex exclusively; it was a survival strategy for both.

When we suggest that men are at the top because men discriminate, we miss the point. Men are at the top of the work hierarchy because work has been primarily men's responsibility.

We think of hierarchies as creating only external values like the pursuit of money, rank, and status. That stereotype falls short of how hierarchies also create introspection. A man who wasn't promoted as quickly as another had to look hard at what he was doing wrong. Hierarchies were men's ways of forcing themselves to introspect. Without the help of a therapist. Rugged introspection. The evidence of the introspection was not introspective talking, but the outcome of introspection: improved performance and promotion.

The mottoes of men ladder-climbers were "Talk's cheap" and "Just Do It." But these mottoes shortchanged the *process* a man went through to "just do it"—"Just meet your sales quota" translates into rethinking his relationship with every client, the way he is presenting himself, his product, the way he is organizing his time . . .

Paradoxically, nonhierarchical arrangements are often the most hierarchical. People who argue for a group or meeting to have no facilitators because facilitators are "hierarchical" are almost always the people who dominate the decision-making. They know that rules and structure will limit their power.

When I first began speaking on these issues in the late 1960s and early 1970s, almost all of the men's movement that existed at that time, and most of the women's movement, was opposed to hierarchy. Yet, when I needed to change a plane schedule, I was not told to see any member of the collective at random, I was told, "See Jim." Room change? "See Jim." It only took two or three "who can get this done?" questions to find out who in the "collective" (politically correct word) was in reality "in charge" (politically incorrect words).

Robert Michels developed a theory almost a century ago called "the iron rule of oligarchy"—that every organization turns into an oligarchy because none of us have time to do everything; we must therefore allow people to specialize in what they do best and then hold them accountable.[13]

In brief, hierarchy is ubiquitous, engaged in by both sexes, and its positive side—creating standards, accountability, the requirement to handle criticism, be introspective, and the incentives to produce—should not be tossed out with the bathwater of its shadow side.

The myths about hierarchy are not nearly as insidious as the belief that women are better managers because they're better jugglers—a belief that makes men feel misunderstood by their women colleagues.

The Bias That "Women Are Better Managers Because Women Are Better Jugglers"

When a mother works, we call her a "working mom." This acknowledges the duality of her role—her juggling act. When a dad works, we don't call him a "working dad," and so we fail to acknowledge his juggling act. Most dads also juggle their desire to provide for their families both economically and emotionally—to work late to provide for the orthodontist, yet to take off early to attend his daughter's soccer game.

Thousands of articles and cartoons such as the accompanying "Doonesbury" focus only on the women's juggling act. Note how this Doonesbury plays upon and reinforces society's failure to have equal compassion for men; in the process, it helps make us vulnerable to a second bias—that "women are better managers because women are better jugglers" of their dual roles as mothers and workers.

In reality, women and men juggle in different ways. As a rule, moms do more juggling at home and dads do more at work.

Mom's juggling at home is well recognized: While the laundry and dinner are on, she's nursing her infant, answering a cell phone, and using eye contact and six fingers to give her seven-year-old permission to visit a friend next door but to be back by six for dinner. Men are more likely to contribute to the home in some 50 different ways that are less predictable, more as-needed: repairing, assembling, remodeling; driving under dangerous conditions when everyone is tired; working outdoors shoveling snow, raking leaves, mowing lawns, coaching kids; climbing ladders to paint or put up screens, check out a roof, or get something from the attic.[14] These kinds of contribution go largely unrecognized because many of them, like driving, coaching, and assembling, are not measured by "housework" studies, so they don't make headlines and we think of only women as having a "second shift."

Men's juggling, though, is more likely to occur at work than at home. For example, although women today are as likely as men to win public office when they seek it, men are still much more likely to seek it. Yet every politician is a walking, talking juggling act—expected to juggle hundreds of conflicting interests yet avoid conflict-of-interest. Governors, for example, juggle the taxpayers' demand for lower taxes with the same taxpayers' demand for the best education systems and highways; they try to attract companies to their state to pay those taxes by keeping down the taxes the companies pay. They juggle the interests of largely wealthy contributors, who are mostly Republican, often to provide programs for poor constituents, who mostly vote Democratic. They juggle the concerns of environmental-

Doonesbury. Copyright 1985, G. B. Trudeau.

ists to protect the environment with the concerns of their constituents to protect the jobs of lumberjacks and miners who in turn produce homes and energy that harm the environment. They cannot stay elected unless they speak and listen most every night to another constituency, yet are accused by their family of spending every night taking care of everyone except the family. If they don't juggle well, they soon find themselves praising family values and watching their own family fall apart. They juggle winning with losing-even-if-they-win.

In an era of mergers and downsizing, every merger has meant mostly men top executives merging diverse corporate cultures, often previously competitive ones with different accountants, retirement plans, PR strategies, images, and names. Simultaneously, they are juggling stockholders' desires for profit, with employees' desires for job security and pay increases, with consumers' desires for cheaper yet better goods. All of this within the constraints of tax laws, labor laws, permits, and codes, in languages and cultural nuances foreign to the company. In each country, they juggle the adaptation of the product to the culture, its consumers, its laws, its competition. One mistake can cost millions. (When Osco Drugs moved into San Diego, near the Mexican border, it soon discovered that osco meant "repugnance, as in wanting to vomit" in Spanish—not the best marketing draw for the thousands of Mexicans living in San Diego!)

Boys' training for their juggling act is considerably different from girls' training for theirs. The quarterback needs to juggle the ambitions of his potential sackers with the second-by-second progress of the play. He has to project the speed at which each play's pattern will be executed and where each of the 21 other boys will be by the time a ball can get there. He has to determine whether he should pass for a small possibility of a large gain or pass-off for a greater possibility of a small gain. As he is looking at how clear it is to the first down, an unanticipated hole might open up. He knows that he has a bigger chance of making it if he runs it himself, but that also increases the possibility of cleats puncturing his throwing hand as he's crushed under a pile of 250-pound guys.

These decisions are made in a few seconds, by a 15- to 17-year-old boy who is also juggling pleasing his parents in the bleachers, his buddies in the stands, the cheerleader he hopes to ask out, his coach, and his judgment of himself. Failure can mean a smashed face or loss of face.

Both sexes, then, learn their juggling acts, but in slightly different ways. What has been unequal is the attention we've paid only to women's and the assumption this means women have a brain for juggling that makes them better managers.

The Bias That "Women Are Better Managers Because Women Stress Cooperation, Not Competition"

Since cooperation implies better people skills than competition, this statement has a corollary: "Women are better managers because women have better people skills."

What's true is that women's people skills have been honed over the millennia to be applied to the family and social networks, men's to the workplace. Most women bring many of their people skills to the workplace, and men often lack good people skills in social settings; but if, as we saw previously, both sexes worldwide say they would prefer working for male managers, then we might just have something to learn from the sex that refrains from the competitiveness of calling itself less competitive.

Sports: Cooperation or Competition?

Perhaps the major route by which boys develop both people skills and cooperation is via team sports. But because team sports are thought of as competition, we often miss the nuanced ways they develop cooperativeness in the male psyche. More about that in a moment. First, one might object, "Girls and boys both participate in team sports now, so what's the point . . . ?"

Fortunately, women are increasingly involved in team sports, but there are still three huge differences between women's and men's involvement that affect their workplace differences. First, most women's involvement is during school years; men's is more often for life (from grammar school to heart attack). Second, pickup team sports (e.g., picking up a game by wandering over to the school playground and practicing hoops until someone else shows up), the most radical team sport teacher, are still almost exclusively a male activity. Third, team sports are far more likely to bring love into a boy's life than into a girl's, which is only one of many reasons he is motivated to make team sports play a far more prominent role during his developmental years.

When we think of team sports, we usually think of organized team sports. But pickup team sports are an even more important contributor to people-skill development than organized team sports.

If organized team sports develop managerial skills for a corporate setting, pickup team sports are more like training to be an entrepreneur. For example, pickup team sports require participants to set the rules anew. ("Okay, who's gonna be the captain? Which captain gets first choice? Do we play half court or full court? What are the boundaries? Winner-out or loser-out?")

Once the rules are theoretically agreed upon, they have to deal with when the agreement just made is subject to misinterpretation. When it is, the differences have to be negotiated in an emotional setting with self-interest involved. Immature boys argue for their immediate self-interest, only to see that a rule operating in their favor one minute can be used against them the next minute. Bullies try to have it both ways.

The key here is that negotiating the difference in an emotional setting is done without the possible intervention of a supervisor: if a fight breaks out, they must settle it; if the emotions lead to someone slugging someone else, they have to deal with how they can avoid that next time, but again without relying on an adult. If they begin to lose, pickup sports require each person or team finding its own source of motivation without a coach.

Pickup team sports are still about 99% male. That is, this form of preparation to be an entrepreneur is about 99% male socialization. I believe this is one of many contributors to why men who run their own business earn twice what their female counterparts earn.[15] Both parents and the school system would help our daughters by encouraging pickup team sports more among girls or mixed-sex groups. Cell phones to call a parent or a security guard can give our daughters an extra layer of security when needed.

Organized team sports prepare girls and boys for virtually every managerial skill, especially in a corporate setting. For example, as Derek is dribbling toward the basket, he is constantly assessing and reassessing whether to keep the ball or pass it off. His decisions are informed by who is in the best position to move the ball toward a successful shot. He considers someone who is signaling to him for the ball; he assesses his chances; within a few seconds that opportunity disappears; as a new situation emerges, he assesses every possible play the coach has taught to take advantage of that new situation; he assesses mistakes the other team is making, mistakes they could be seduced into making, and who would be in the best position to take advantage of a mistake. Then he considers mistakes he could make if he gets too fancy. Each time he goes up and down the court, he is experiencing a new variation on the theme, rehearsing, learning from his mistakes, alternating what's logical with what will take the other team by surprise exactly because it isn't what would normally make the most sense to do.

Derek's people skills are honed by handling people under high pressure and high rejection situations. He's experienced being "bribed" into showing off by the presence of his parents or girlfriend watching from the stands. He's learned to whom he should delegate by learning whom he can trust—Ted, who always says "me," or Barry who never says "me" but is more likely to score, or Jim who seems "on" today . . .

Team sports are often considered the quintessential example of men's preoccupation with competition. Yet the irony of team sports-as-competitive is that it is competition to see which team can be the most cooperative. Cooperation is not the goal, but the method to the goal.

Do team sports teach that cooperation means equality? Yes and no. Team sports teach that everyone has an equal opportunity to be more than equal—that is, that everyone has an equal opportunity to be first string for a given role for a given play. Cooperation means that each team member cooperates with the best judgment about who plays a standout role and who plays a supportive role during the execution of the next play. Team sports, then, develop the skill of striking the balance between the self and the other by confronting players with constant temptation to think only of self, but rewarding players when they resist the temptation and instead strike the perfect balance between self and other.

What's the "evidence" that the best level of cooperation was achieved? Victory. What's the reward? Victory. And with victory comes the bigger reward of family approval and love.

For men—and for women who have treated team sports seriously—the words "competition" and "victory" imply "cooperation."

If that's true, why don't men say so? Well, suppose you are on vacation and you meet a retired professional football coach and ask him how successful he was as a coach. He responds that all his teams were very cooperative. As you walk back to your hotel, do you imagine the coach had a lot of winning teams? Correct. You'd guess his teams had never won a Super Bowl and he had mostly losing teams. Why?

Because although winning implies cooperation, cooperation does not imply winning. People who only cooperate are usually losers. So a coach who only discusses cooperation is usually a losing coach.

And again, men's methods almost always are attached to consequences: If concussions are biofeedback, hazing, criticism, and ostracism are socio-feedback. It's only a game, but . . .

Less socialization in team sports manifested itself for a woman friend of mine. She had just begun doing PR work for a company that was worried if it would survive the year. It had hired three PR firms, each assigned a different function. One evening, the CEO called her, delighted that the company had some interest from the *New York Times* in doing a story.

Upon hearing the details, my woman friend was upset—no, furious—because another PR company had placed the story in an area that was her jurisdiction. She thought that being a team player meant that each PR firm should stay within its limits. It took her a while to understand that the CEO did not care which PR firm got the *New York Times* story, that its survival was dependent upon anyone getting the story—that being a team player meant caring about the outcome for the team, not about whether you made the basket. In fact, my woman friend had assisted, and the CEO had acknowledged her assistance.

Team sports incorporate many qualities often considered female.

We consider cheerleading, inspiration, and nurturance female qualities. Yet a team member who inspires is called a team leader. And inspiration is one of the prerequisites of good coaching. Inspiration and nurturance are built into the male role, but because of the primary expectation that they will be in the right balance to produce victory, the importance of inspiration and nurturance is often lost.

It is important for men executives to understand how their own skills incorporate "female" qualities; it makes them more open to seeing how motherhood develops skills that might be associated with men. For example, every full-time mother has had managerial experience and negotiating experience ("Mommy, you just gave Gail more bacon than me," "She used all the syrup on her pancakes!"). Granted, mom might not be able to be fired . . . just tortured!

The Limits of Sports to Men's Managerial Skills

A woman may wonder, "If male socialization for team play is so good, how is it that the mostly-male FBI, CIA, and DEA (Drug Enforcement Agency) seem more often to be fighting turf wars than drug wars, and how did the FBI and CIA allow homeland security to become homeland insecurity?" Here's one reason . . .

Male socialization for team play defines the FBI as "their team"—to cooperate within the FBI, but to compete against the "other teams"—the CIA and DEA. So the woman employee sees teamwork one minute, turf war the next, and it makes no sense, which is one reason women are needed—to provide vision in men's blind spots.

When a woman understands male socialization she also understands its limits. For example, the pressure on men to be a hero creates considerable resistance to teamwork. For a single man, being a hero means the choice of cheerleaders and the respect of peer leaders; for a married man, it means security for his family, and therefore their respect—even if he dies in the process. In no industrialized country is the pressure to be a hero greater than in the United States—exactly because the reward is the greatest.

Because the pressure on men to be a hero is so great, men have to rely on team play as a counterpressure to a greater degree than women do. While in law enforcement, or any bureaucracy with overlapping responsibilities, it doesn't always work, but in many venues it works remarkably well. Given the potential ramification of a corporate merger that we discussed previously, it is remarkable that men can overcome the insecurity to, sometimes, merge their company with its previous enemy, forfeit its name, and move to a strange location.

Team sports is a constant teacher of making one's own interests subservient to the interests of the team and to the best final outcome. The failure of our school system and our parenting to encourage our daughters to understand male socialization's best influences as much as it encourages boys to understand girls' sensitivities leads to one of our deepest areas of discrimination against women.

Women and Cooperation

The belief that women make inherently better managers is also limited by the way our similar behaviors are often judged differently. A man might see two women talking about office politics and call it gossip even though he talks with another man over lunch and calls it tax-deductible. Conversely, two women managers at a party might refer to their conversation as networking even as they might disparagingly refer to a conversation between two men managers as "the old boy network."

What a woman might call intuition because she feels it in her gut, a man might call a logical conclusion based on a lifetime of experience. As for the feeling in his gut, he's more likely to call it a Maalox moment.

On the other side of the coin of men being less cooperative is the belief that women are inherently more cooperative. Since our framework is the workplace, and not competition for men (in which any soap opera would critique the "women-are-inherently-cooperative" belief), one of the best ways of testing the belief is looking at a women-dominated profession and seeing how women in this profession feel. A 2004 survey of nurses by the Australian Nurses Federation received these responses.[16]

- 84% experienced intimidating behavior
- 73% had an oppressive and unhappy workplace

- 65% had a fear of speaking up
- 38% had experienced hurtful teasing and jokes
- 23% experienced physically threatening behavior
- 15% experienced assault

In brief, both cooperation and competition are survival instincts, and both sexes have developed both—or none of us would be here.

The attitude that women are inherently better managers is just the tip of the "Men are the enemy" iceberg, and a setup for litigation rather than communication, and for a fear of hiring women. A better solution is to encourage our daughters to be involved with organized team sports and pickup sports and to encourage both sexes to see the crossover qualities contained within each sex's socialization.

None of this should discourage us from attentiveness to actual discrimination against women that also inhibits women from earning more.

CHAPTER 10

Discrimination Against Women

Is *Why Men Earn More* implying there is no discrimination in the workplace? No. The workplace is like every place—filled with unfairness and discrimination. But it occurs for women and against women. And is by both sexes. Here are some forms of discrimination that still work against women.

Guilt-Trippin' Mom

We have many ways of making a working mom feel more guilty than a working dad. It starts with the very phrase "working mom."

The Census Bureau reflects this bias by concerning itself only with how working moms leave their children, but not with how working dads leave their children.[1] The result? Census Bureau press releases become headlines in newspapers that read, "Half of Working Moms Leave Preschoolers with Relatives."[2] It turns out that the largest single group of those relatives is the dads.[3]

The bias against the working mom is that even when the children are with dad, we guilt trip mom by saying she just left them with a relative. (We would never say a child in mom's care was "left.")

The "Old-Boy Network"

As long as the top echelons of corporations and government are men, there will be "old-boy networks." And because male socialization includes male-style joking, emphasizes "doing" rather than process, and uses metaphors of sports that register more with men, most top-level men will be more comfortable with male-to-male communication when discussing work issues. Similarly, because top-level men's everyday personal lives are not as focused on flextime, health care, child care, sexual harassment, hazing, teasing, and criticism, male-male communication allows for more direct focus on the bottom-line. Top-level men are more comfortable with that.

Of course, in female-dominated professions the old-girl network works in a parallel way for women. In both cases, the effect is both to leave out the other sex, and to leave the other sex feeling left out.

The bad news about the old-boy network is that it exists, has bad effects, and is being replicated by the government! That is, the U.S. government now sponsors hundreds of formal old-girl network programs, without a single parallel for men.[4] This is bad news because combating informal behavior that isolates the other sex with formal programs that isolate the other sex is a lose-lose "solution." Even worse news is that many of the women's networking programs are sponsored by government agencies that are already female-dominated, such as the Social Security Administration. I'll look at these in greater depth in the next chapter on discrimination *for* women, but in this section I want to stick with the "old-boy network's" future and its intent.

Will these same-sex networks phase out? The more that employers are gagged by job interview restrictions enforced by the fear of lawsuits, the more informal networking becomes vital. They'll phase out only in professions not dominated by one sex, but not even there if the government continues to subsidize them.

The intent of the informal same-sex networks is not to discriminate—even if that is the effect. Then what is the intent? The old-boy network is to men-and-jobs what reputation checking is to women-and-dating. If you are a woman, you may be familiar with reputation checking: A man asks you out; you call another woman to check out his reputation.

Your intent? You don't quite feel you're likely to get from a man who wants to be involved with you a valid reference from his former woman friend—that is, a reference that says, "John's a charmer, a female disarmer, but once you've had sex, he's a goner." So you call a different woman to check out his reputation. You know that a good network, like a good vacuum cleaner, will pick up more dirt.

Just as reputation-checking's intent is to keep you from getting stuck in the mud, its effect is to discriminate against some men without checking back with them on the claims against them. The men end up feeling like you would if you couldn't get a bank loan but also couldn't see your credit report. Conversely, the old-boy network's effect is to similarly discriminate against women—even if its intent is just to get the skinny.

Discrimination Against Women Bosses

I've already introduced the Gallup poll of both sexes' attitudes toward men and women bosses.[5] The fact that in all 22 surveyed countries, both sexes prefer men-as-bosses means that a woman who wishes to be a boss is more likely to face discrimination and more psychological barriers.

Unfortunately, this bias is significant: People in the 22 countries, with a total population of over 3 billion, were asked:

"If you were taking a new job and had your choice of a boss (supervisor), would you prefer to work for a man or a woman?"

- Worldwide, 47% of men preferred men as bosses and 14% preferred women as bosses;
- Worldwide, 47% of women also preferred men as bosses, while 21% preferred women as bosses.[6]

Unfortunately, this discrimination can contribute to a self-fulfilling prophecy, or to applying a valid stereotype to the wrong person. We tend to see what we look for.

Valid Stereotype, Wrong Person

Although women are, on average, less likely to make any of the 25 sacrifices-to-the-company that lead to higher pay, this can work against an individual woman even when she might be one of many exceptions. For example, a woman seeking employment with a moving company faces skepticism about her ability to maneuver a refrigerator up a flight of stairs to a second-story apartment with no elevator. Although some of these "stereotypes" are accurate on average, the woman who is the exception can nevertheless fall victim to the rule.

Of course both sexes suffer discrimination in those areas in which members of their sex tend to do worse. A man applying to be a nursery school teacher suffers the skepticism born from men's greater likelihood to sexually molest children.

Voice Credibility

Women have historically suffered discrimination via the lesser credibility attached to a higher-pitched voice. Fortunately, this is changing. Women are increasingly being used to sell products that women tend to buy, while men are still selling most, but not all, of the machinery and technical products (when the product's technical qualities are the focus of the ad). And moms as Dr. Mom are seen as having more credibility than Dr. Dad, or sometimes even the doctor! Nevertheless, mom's credibility is role-based; and she still has to deal with less credibility from a higher voice in areas outside of relationships, family, and family health.

Humor's Risky Waters

Look at any personals column, and we find sense of humor one of the most-requested qualities sought by women in men; eavesdrop on a conversation among women about their bosses, and it is hard to miss that sense of humor is also appreciated at work. Yet those same women are unlikely to have "sense of humor" on their own resumes, so to speak.

A survey of Fortune 1000 women executives by Catalyst, a woman's career advocacy organization, found that maintaining a sense of humor and being a team player were crucial to women's success.[7] Although women intellectually know the importance of humor, they are less likely to have been brought up playing in male humor's *risky* waters, and especially not in its riptides. And this leads to men feeling less comfortable with women, which creates at best an unwitting form of discrimination.

Unfortunately, the differences in men's and women's senses of humor reflect the differences in their historic roles. Men have learned to test whether a colleague was humble enough to know how to handle criticism without becoming defensive or taking it personally. The sense of humor that emanated from this—especially among high-performing men—is the trading of wit-covered put-downs. Roughhousing and horseplay are just extensions of this sense of humor, with similar purposes.

When a woman in a mostly-male environment is confronted with the "team-player test" of wit-covered put-downs, she usually fails the test—just as a man in a mostly-female environment fails by giving the test.

A woman hearing a wit-covered put-down, then, may be more likely to feel hurt by the put-down than appreciative of the wit; and more likely to become defensive because she hasn't been socialized to playfully take the offensive. She sees her colleague as having already concluded he dislikes her rather than playfully testing to see if they trust and understand each other.

Ironically, human resource divisions' training programs in companies and government agencies are not teaching women the positive functions of humor and teasing—only its insensitivities. The negative excesses of ill-chosen humor have been stressed more than the value of humor, such as relaxing the atmosphere and increasing each person's oxygen and, therefore, energy level. Humor's sweet baby has been thrown out with humor's dirty bathwater.

Because these HR divisions can end a man's career, a new woman in the workforce often scares men. And this discriminates against women.

As HR divisions expand their functions to help each sex understand each other's sense of humor, men will understand what feels like a riptide to a woman, and women will see the riptide as an opportunity to develop their skills of "going with the flow."

Male Socialization Layered onto Male Biology

Since men dominate the upper echelons of the workplace, male socialization layered onto male biology creates the social glue. And that's going to feel as strange to most women as it would to a full-time dad sitting midweek in a park with infants, among moms who are speaking of how they had their hair colored.

Without the male social glue coursing through her veins, a woman may wonder why everything male has to be either a sport or a war (e.g., the "War on Drugs"). Male socialization and biology have taught men to be willing to die fighting the enemy. The clearer the enemy, the greater the ability to inspire opposition. So among men, it is more effective to call it the "War on Drugs" than the "Just Say 'No' Plan."

Male socialization and biology, though, are even more alienating to women than women's are to men. The sexuality and put-downs in male humor are more alienating to women than references to celebrities, weddings, divorces, affairs, children, and shopping are to men.

The problem with the alienation is the isolation. And women's isolation from men is magnified by men's tendency to not explain themselves. Few men explain, for example, "My off-color jokes are my way of breaking tension at the office . . . of pumping oxygen into the air so we can all work better and have more fun." Or, "I'm attracted to you, and my dirty jokes are a 'trial balloon' to see if you have an interest—I was afraid of being rejected directly."

Unexplained, men's defense mechanisms seem only like crude humor; the men appear immature, disrespectful, sometimes cruel, and almost always dysfunctional. When these same guys are strutting around saying "How 'bout them Yankees!" it leaves many women angry that people so immature are the ones they call "boss."

Without the male socialization toward sports discussed in the previous chapter (on myths), "How 'bout them Yankees!" does not appear like a summary statement of appreciation for a team's tangible and intangible strategies that finally accumulate to success. Women understand this as poorly as men understand, in women-dominated environments, how an excited, "I lost five pounds and kept them off" is a summary statement of ecstasy over her tangible and intangible strategies, which finally accumulated in a success that she feels will lead to feeling more valued in her life.

As men feel this contempt from women, they become uncomfortable around women, especially peers, and, with political correctness reinforcing their already repressed ability to express the discomfort, become passive-aggressive in their discrimination against women.

How Protecting Women Creates Discrimination Against Women

Special protection for any group almost always leads to discrimination against that group. Why? Because special protection costs employers money, forces them to hire additional employees to administer the special protection, and, perhaps most importantly, makes other employees feel like siblings feel when dad is giving special attention to one favorite child.

Companies are now preventing women who could become pregnant from taking jobs exposing them to poisons that could create birth defects. The companies feared women would sue if their children had birth defects.[8] They faced a dilemma: They would be sued if they allowed the women to take the jobs, and sued if they didn't.

Couldn't a company solve this by having these women sign contracts saying they would not sue? Normally, such a contract would hold up in court under contract law. However, when a woman signs away protection and later changes her mind, as with a prenuptial contract, she often is able to claim she signed it "under duress" even when she is entering such a voluntary association like marriage. If a prenuptial contract can be said to be signed "under duress," then certainly a contract she signed so she could make enough income to feed her family could also be said to be signed "under duress."

By trying to protect women from being hurt when they sign a contract, companies become fearful of signing contracts with women because the contract protects only the woman, not the company. We make women's contracts meaningless—as we would with a child.

Each time we require companies to hire women and then require them to protect women more than men, we tempt companies to develop a defense against legalized self-destructiveness. The most likely defense is "corporate passive-aggressive discrimination": to say they believe in equality for women even as they discriminate against women.

In a sense, the passive-aggressive companies are the only ones that do believe in equality for women. Their message to us is, "When you stop forcing us to discriminate in favor of women, we'll stop discriminating against women." Of course, the corporate attorneys would not appreciate their saying this at a press conference!

The Future of Mentorship Discrimination

As the gift of mentorship evolves into the minefield of mentorship, mentorship's discrimination in favor of women is evolving into discrimination against women. Here's why . . .

Although approximately half of American managers are women, women on the way up are five times as likely to have a man mentor.[9] That is, when women executives were asked if they had women mentors, only 15% said "yes." In contrast, when asked if they had a man mentor, over 74% said "yes."[10] The instinct of men to protect women—and of women to seek men's protection—currently makes men mentorship of women an area of discrimination in favor of women. But this is, I believe, likely to change. Why?

That mentorship study was published in 1993. Recently, though, I have heard more and more men executives quietly talk about becoming fearful of mentoring a woman. One became a client of mine in a sex discrimination case. He had mentored a woman by advising her that if she moved, he thought she would have a better chance at promotion. So she moved. But the company ended up downsizing. Although she kept her job, she was not promoted. My client felt she should have thanked him for keeping her employed. Instead, she sued the company, naming him in the lawsuit. His advice was interpreted as a false promise. This man had a history of mentoring women, but it is doubtful he will do it again.

One married executive told me that when he was mentoring a woman during office hours he was accused of being unfair for using office time disproportionately for her. Rumors circulated that he was having an affair. So they met after-hours. Then people were *convinced* they were having an affair! He feared that suddenly the tabs he had picked up for drinks or dinner would be evidence of sexual harassment, or that people who had seen him in a restaurant could become witnesses against him. When he read in the newspapers of colleagues whose careers had ended and marriages had shattered with lesser evidence, he shuddered.

Mentorship often involves sharing secrets, becoming relaxed, letting one's hair down, and worrying less about boundaries due to a growth in trust and respect. It creates an atmosphere where male humor—including dirty jokes—can be shared with less fear. Yet I also hear from some men a fear of doing this in today's atmosphere. They are reading in the news stories like the one of Captain Blanchard of the U.S. Coast Guard, whose dirty joke led to pressure to remove him despite his extraordinary popularity. Apologies were not enough—feminists insisted on Blanchard's removal. Captain Blanchard soon found his career, pension, mortgage, family's security, and reputation in jeopardy. That led to a marriage in jeopardy, which would mean his wife would have the children. With no escape in sight, Captain Blanchard committed suicide.[11]

When a man reads of a quasi-dirty joke (in Captain Blanchard's case), leading to the end of a reputable man's life, it makes him as fearful of mentoring as it might make a woman feel of Internet dating after reading about how a first date resulted in a rape.

Mentorship's Rebellion Process

Just as a teenager is prone to rebel when seeking identity, so is a woman or man who is being mentored likely to rebel against the mentor, to prove to both themselves and others they are not just a puppet. And just as adolescence is a dangerous stage for parents, so it is a dangerous stage for mentors. It always was. But now, with sexual harassment legislation, it can take as little as one angry outburst to end the career of a mentor. Even if he is acquitted, the blemish is on his record, in the company's psyche, and in his spirit. Soon someone who is less generous gets promoted over someone about whom there is doubt.

The gift of mentorship is becoming, then, the minefield of mentorship. As men see these connections, it may be turning men's mentorship of younger women into a dinosaur.

Men Have "a Wife"; Women Don't

We all know that a married male executive is far more likely to have a support system called "wife" than a married female executive is to have a support system called "husband."

Ironically, men are more willing to alter this discrimination against women than women are. That is, when I ask on radio shows for men to call in who are willing to play the traditional role of a wife—to be supported financially in exchange for caring for the home, family, and social life—I get many calls from men. However, when I ask women the parallel question, it is rare for a woman to call in saying she'd support a man financially in exchange for him supporting her as would a "wife." Not even one call. The pattern held in my book tours throughout the industrialized world.

Financially supporting a "wife" makes good economic sense. As we saw in Chapter 4, "Doing Time," a person who works 45 hours a week earns 44% more than a person working 40 hours per week.[12] If a spouse is running errands, cooking, shopping, and cleaning, it allows the breadwinner to work extra hours without eliminating quality time with the family, and to bring home 44% more pay. (Of course, the extra pay can also be used to hire someone to do the cleaning and errand running while the at-home parent runs an at-home business.)

The real discrimination against women here might be called "Princess Di socialization," illustrated by two and a half billion people glued to their TVs worldwide, creating the highest-rated wedding in history—a wedding of a woman they didn't know to a prince they didn't care for. When women marry supportive men homemakers, the ratings are a little lower!

The solution? Let's start with giving our daughters more encouragement to marry men who support them differently, so more will become women executives who have both a "wife" and a life.

CHAPTER 11

Discrimination in Favor of Women: Why Women Are Now Paid *More* Than Men for the Same Work

A careful review of each of the 25 ways makes us wonder whether *women* are now paid *more* than men for the same work. While the answer is not 100% clear, I believe that ultimately economists who measure all twenty-five ways will conclude that while men still earn more for different work, women now earn more for the same work. What is less clear is how much more. (To determine the precise gender pay gap by objectively measuring all these overlapping differences would take a genius in economic statistics, so that will have to wait awhile!) This chapter first looks at *why* women now earn more. Then I'll look beyond facts—to women's feelings. And finally we'll look at forms of discrimination in favor of women (or against men) that to my knowledge have never been previously discussed.

Do Women Earn *More* for the Same Work?

We saw in the Introduction that never-married men who never had children earn only 85% of their female counterparts—even when both groups worked full-time, were college-educated, and in the same age group.[1] This helps us see that men who don't have to support families don't make the trade-offs it takes to get higher pay, and that family decisions may determine pay far more than workplace discrimination.

I discussed how a nationwide study found men and women professional, administrative, technical, and clerical workers made the same pay when their titles were the same, and their responsibilities were both the same and of equal size.[2] Had this study also taken into account factors like the number of hours worked, years in the field, absences from the workplace, or willingness to move, all of which tend to lead to men earning more pay, it is probable the study would have revealed that had the women worked equal hours, and so on, they would have earned more than the men. And this was two decades ago.

As we looked at individual fields, the same pattern holds. Among engineers, when women and men started at the same time, worked in the same settings, with equal professional experience, training, family status, and absences, the women engineers received the same pay.[3] Among physicians, when men and women worked the same hours, and factors like the specialty and practice settings were the same, there was no difference in pay.[4]

Thirty-nine large fields have more than a 5% pay advantage for women—with women sales engineers (engineers who sell their employer's products) earning 143% of their male counterparts.[5] This is only the larger fields. In somewhat smaller fields, such as modeling, we will see that top female models earn about five times more than their male "equivalent."[6] Modeling is only a fraction of what we will explore in the next chapter on the genetic celebrity pay gap.

Since pay equity can hardly be mentioned without hearing "glass ceiling," or that a woman has to work twice as hard to get half as far, let's recall how prior to the age of 40, women are 15 times more likely than their male counterparts to become top executives at major corporations.[7] We saw that 21% of top women executives at major companies are under 40, while only 1.4% of the men executives are under 40.[8] We asked whether the women reach executive levels sooner because these women work twice as hard. We found that wasn't the case—that, in fact, the men executives work more hours, travel more, move more, earn more MBAs, have more job continuity, and make more of almost all of the sacrifices discussed in this book.[9]

TABLE 17 Responses of Women Executives as to Whose Career Has . . .[10]	Yours	Husband's
Progressed better?	65%	9%
Progressed faster?	67%	12%
Been financially more rewarding?	70%	15%
Been more rewarding in other ways?	43%	22%

Nevertheless, facts can be different from feelings. How do women executives feel about their progress?

Women-First Club Merges with Women-Quality-of-Life Club

When women executives were surveyed nationwide to see if their career or their husband's had progressed better (Table 17), the women executives were more than seven times as likely to feel their own careers had progressed better than their husband's. The women executives were also almost six times as likely to feel their careers progressed faster than their husband's, four-and-a-half times as likely to feel their careers had been financially more rewarding than their husband's, and almost twice as likely to feel their careers had also been more rewarding in other ways.

These findings are quite astonishing since the husbands of executive women are no slouches (executive women tend to "marry up" or not marry at all).[11] The survey results are indicators of the efforts of companies to make women's careers better than men's, promote women faster than men, make women's careers psychologically more rewarding than men's, and even financially more rewarding than men's.

What's Changed? "The Law of Profitable Inefficiency"

When I introduced this book, I said that any company that pays a man a dollar to do work a woman would do for less would soon be put out of business by a company that hires all women. So wouldn't the reverse hold true? Yes. Unless . . .

Unless a business is paid more for being inefficient than for being efficient. For example, in the 1950s, a law firm knew that a corporate client would feel more confident with a man than a woman attorney. So even if it knew the woman attorney was better, it also knew it would be more profitable to hire the man. It was guided by "The Law of Profitable Inefficiency": If a business is subject to laws or attitudes that make it more profitable to be inefficient, then the business will adopt the profitable inefficiencies until those laws and attitudes change.[12]

Fortunately, by the early 1970s the feminist movement led to an attitude adjustment that in turn catalyzed legal changes. This transition soon made it profitable for a business to be efficient and hire a woman attorney if she was equally competent. (On a personal level, my desire to change those attitudes and laws motivated my involvement on the Board of the National Organization for Women in New York City during the early 1970s.)

If women now earn more for the same work, then what created this reversal? For starters, "the big four" all changed simultaneously: both laws and attitudes positively affected women and laws and attitudes negatively affected men. This pushed the pendulum so far in the opposite direction that many businesses are now faced with a new profitable inefficiency: hiring the government-subsidized woman (e.g., by contracting with a woman-owned construction company even if it doesn't have the lowest bid or best quality). Here is some of what has changed to make the hiring of government-subsidized women the latest profitable inefficiency.

Let's start with the laws discriminating in favor of women. The federal government's listing of *Federal Programs Benefiting Women* is more than a hundred pages thick.[13] No equivalent list is available for men. We're most familiar with affirmative action laws and laws requiring corporations, universities, and the government to give preferences for contracts to women-owned businesses. Obviously this discriminates against men-owned businesses.

We're less familiar with hundreds of other federal programs. For example, all the government's social service agencies are women-dominated, yet women are given special advantages as if they were still the minority group. The Social Security Administration is typical.

Its workforce consists of 70% women. Yet there are "special executive development training programs specifically for women candidates" but nothing specifically for the men.[14] And of its employees who have received special counseling for career advancement, 90% are women.[15]

I promised in the last chapter some concrete examples of the hundreds of government programs teaching only women to network (vs. none for only men): NASA has women's networking teas; the Department of Energy and the Minority Business Development Agencies are among those with women's networking breakfasts; and the Small Business Administration, theoretically designed to help both sexes, has only a Women's Networking Roundtable.[16] Ironically, the government sponsors for women what it condemns for men: The buddy-boy network is called discrimination; the buddy-girl network is called the law.

Underlying these legal changes is an about-face in attitudes. A corporation in the 1950s would have hesitated to hire women attorneys for fear of losing prestige. Today women-as-partners add to a law firm's prestige, women ob-gyns and surgeons add to a hospital's status, and a woman CEO has publicity value.

Emerging simultaneously are the attitudes working against men. Now, hiring a man ob-gyn comes with the fear of women suing for sexual assault, or women just plain being uncomfortable. School systems contemplating hiring elementary and nursery school teachers fear men inappropriately touching children or being too rough with children. For example, the male method of coaching is often deemed too tough.

These attitude and legal reversals are the rudders that give direction to the "Law of Profitable Inefficiency." But the engine of this law is the "Affirmative Action Tax," and its lubricant is "Psychological Affirmative Action."

The Affirmative Action Tax and Psychological Affirmative Action

Companies have been able to pay women more than men and stay in business because affirmative action is like a tax imposed somewhat equally on all large companies. This might be called an affirmative action tax. Because all major companies bear about equally the burden of the affirmative action tax, they don't lose to domestic competition. The affirmative action tax, by equitably distributing "profitable inefficiency," hurts few companies domestically, but hurts most companies globally (see the Conclusion).

This affirmative action tax is a legal requirement for any company that wants a federal contract, a loan from the Small Business Administration, or virtually anything else to do with the federal government. But every major company understands that when push comes to lawsuit, their best defense will be their ability to demonstrate how they have psychologically prepared their employees for affirmative action.

The affirmative action tax, then, includes a quasi-legal requirement for what might be called "psychological affirmative action." The government understands that psychological affirmative action is to affirmative action as oil is to an engine: It keeps it running.

Psychological affirmative action, the province of the human resources (HR) division, focuses on teaching, for example, a hospital to place a positive psychological value on the special qualities a woman doctor might have to offer. Which is wonderful. But it is rare for the HR division to teach a hospital to value the special qualities men nurses might offer. Or for a school to have a special division to hire more men teachers and develop special programs to prevent boys from being the sex more likely to drop out and do worse in reading and in all their subjects except math and science, and be less likely to go to college. This lack of balance replaces the old sexism with a new sexism.

Psychological affirmative action goes beyond teaching the company to value what the woman employee might offer. It also extends to educating the company as to what she needs, whether it is maternity leave, flextime, health care, or sensitivity to what one or more women might consider sexual harassment. But even in women-dominated companies, it neglects the special concerns of the men employees for an atmosphere that allows greater freedom to joke, play, touch, tease, haze, take risks, establish standards and quotas, and exact consequences without excuses.

Each issue, such as sexual harassment, is in need of male-female dialogue, but many men silently feel that when only women's perspectives are aired, it creates the paradox of a company being told women are men's equals or superiors even as it is flooding the company with her needs for special protection.

The lack of dialogue, particularly on male-female sexuality, has left almost no one able to compassionately articulate the reasons for both sexes' differing perspectives. It is not the function of this book to do that—that is already done in my *The Myth of Male Power*—but to look primarily at the consequence of that ignorance in the workplace: a fear of male sexuality that leads to discrimination against men.

How the Fear of Male Sexuality Leads to Discrimination Against Men

Most every woman loves a massage, but many are hesitant to use a man massage therapist; most every man loves a massage, especially by a beautiful woman. If a stranger is going to touch us intimately, both sexes prefer a woman. Two men massage therapists who worked at the same place said they both often sat with no one to massage while the women massage therapists had people waiting in the lobby to see them.

Similarly, women are increasingly seeking out women ob-gyns. The combination of women's fear of male sexuality and men's desire for female sexuality leads to discrimination against hiring men—not only as massage therapists and ob-gyns, but as nurses, dental hygienists, nursery school teachers, and, apparently, even as elementary school teachers. Discrimination against men as elementary school teachers is the most damaging of all workplace discrimination because it also deprives our daughters and sons of male role models and mentors early in life.

Discrimination Against Men as Nursery School and Elementary School Teachers

Education has often been at odds with masculinity: Education stresses theory and caution; masculinity stresses doing and risk-taking. Yet when I did research for *Father and Child Reunion,* I was astonished to see the degree of psychological damage our children experience from the combined absence of men in the family and in the elementary schools.

This absence is most problematic in the inner city, where boys are most likely to grow up only with mothers, and then go from full-time mother to women elementary school teachers and back to mother. By age 11 some of these boys have never had a positive male role model either at home or at school—and then we express surprise when they are seduced by gangs or celluloid superstars.

Yet something prevents us from even considering potential solutions. For example, no one even debates the possibility that, if 80% of the children in a school district are brought up by mothers, perhaps 80% of the elementary school teachers in that school district should be men. This would provide both our sons and daughters male role models exactly where they are most needed.

The fear of men as sexual molesters has added to our inhibition about hiring them as nursery and elementary school teachers, especially the type of man who might be uninhibited about sitting a third grader on his lap, or wrestling with a fifth-grade girl. When an article about men working with children appeared in a London newspaper, here were some of the responses of professionals in the field:

> *. . . all men who seek careers in nursery education should be regarded with the deepest suspicion.*[17]
> —MARGARET TAYLOR, THERAPIST WHO
> COUNSELS SEXUALLY ABUSED WOMEN.

> *If men do work with children they should always work with a woman as well.*[18]
> —MICHELE ELLIOTT, DIRECTOR OF KIDSCAPE
> (A CHILD PROTECTION SERVICE IN ENGLAND)

Does the shortage of men elementary school teachers overcome our inhibitions about hiring men? When I broached the question during a National Public Radio interview, Patrick Hart, a man in Washington State answered:

After encouragement from my wife and other female teachers that I would be a wonderful teacher, I left my job as a state grain inspector, got a college degree and a state teaching credential (K–8) and began applying for teaching jobs. I and the other male members of my cohort could not get so much as an interview, while the females all got teaching positions immediately. Three-and-a-half years later, I and the other males are still subbing. I'm constantly asked by teachers if I wouldn't prefer a full-time job. They look incredulous when I tell them that I can't get an interview.[19]

Men who attempt to enter elementary education often feel they get "used" as subs—a sort of "back-of-the-bus" second-class citizen hiring status.

Isn't it true, though, that sexual crimes are more the province of men? Yes, definitely. Men and women commit different types of crimes against children. Mothers are twice as likely to murder their children, and almost nine times as likely to seriously injure and abuse children as are dads, but we don't use that statistical average as an excuse to keep mothers from being alone with children after divorce.[20] We have laws against refusing to hire an individual member of a given group because the average member is more prone to a crime.

Our suspicions of male sexuality are magnified by an unconscious double standard: When a woman at work touches a man on his rear, he is likely to say, "Thank you"; when a man at work touches a woman on her rear, she is likely to say, "Sue you!" Her touch begets a coy smile; his begets a criminal sentence. Only his violation makes the media, thus our distrust of only male sexuality is reinforced.

The fear of male sexuality creates a caste system in which we unconsciously treat some men as more "untouchable" than others.

The Caste System: Making the Transition from Untouchable to Touchable Male

When I addressed the American Assembly for Men in Nursing, one man nurse after another told me how hospitals often refused to assign him to women patients, whereas women nurses were freely assigned to men patients. Since women constitute most of the patients, the degree of discrimination is significant. Obviously, this attitude leads hospitals to hire women nurses since women give the hospital flexibility.

Although most hospitals prohibit men who are "just nurses" from seeing or touching a woman's fully naked body, if he earns an MD those restrictions go away; a woman nurse can generally see or touch either sex. Only by proving himself in a way not required of a woman can he transcend from the caste of "untouchable" to "touchable."

Similarly, both sexes allow men dentists inside our mouths, but, well, have you ever let a man who is a dental *hygienist* inside your mouth? The man must earn his way to our private places in a way not required of a woman—he must become the doctor or the dentist, or forget it.

You may protest, "I've never seen a man dental hygienist, so I can't say whether I'd let one in my mouth." That's the point. The caste system between men dentists and men hygienists runs so deep that a patient doesn't think of asking for a male hygienist, a dentist doesn't think of hiring one, and therefore a man doesn't think about becoming one.

It is not that there are no males qualified to be dental hygienists. Almost 5% of people who receive dental hygienist degrees are men, but less than 1% of people hired as dental hygienists are men.[21] When I ran this by a friend who is a dentist, his response was, "Oh, yes; when a man calls to apply to be a dental hygienist, I just say, 'sorry.' "

Discrimination against one sex often becomes discrimination against the other. The nonassignment of men nurses to women patients can discriminate against a woman patient should the most competent person on duty be a man nurse.

Ironically, the underutilization of men nurses violates the very standards by which hospitals are being evaluated. The main evaluator of hospitals, the Joint Commission on the Accreditation of Healthcare Organizations (JCAHO), is making patient safety and medical errors a high priority. If women are being endangered by the nonassignment of men to them, is this not endangering patient safety?

The underutilization of men nurses also increases hospital costs. By allowing only a portion of the nurses to be effectively used, it increases the wages hospitals need to pay nurses, who are already in short supply.

This discrimination is a bit ironic because it is based in part on the women patients' discomfort with a male nurse, whereas the women's movement during the 1960s had to confront many employers who did not want to hire women because their men customers would feel less comfortable with a woman.

The response of the women's movement leaders was, "Tough. Get used to it." Now, though, no one is willing to say to the woman patient, "Tough. You let a man doctor see you and touch you—why are you discriminating against a man nurse? Get used to it."

It would seem that a recent outreach toward men nurses is addressing this problem. Yes and no. The "yes" part is that men nurses are being sought out more, and in some cases, being given special scholarships. The "no" part is that almost no one is addressing the issue of assigning men to women patients. Instead, men nurses are often used by hospitals to double as weightlifter—to lift equipment and patients. The result? Back problems and herniated disks.

That's among professionals. In the working class, men must also compensate for inequality by developing special skills.

How Working-Class Men Compensate for Inequality by Developing Skills Fewer Women Possess

Working-class women have the option of invading our privacy; working-class men do not. For example, among the too many nights I've spent in the world's 3-H clubs (the Hiltons, Hyatts, and Holiday Inns), at least a half dozen times as I was getting out of a shower, drying off, and still in my birthday suit, a housekeeper knocked and entered as if in one motion (like the restaurant waiter who asks if you are finished and removes your plate before you answer).

Now it's not that the Hiltons, Hyatts, and Holiday Inns don't hire males in positions in which they are required to enter a guest's room—almost all of their engineers and bell persons are men. The difference is that they knock-and-wait. Sometimes, it seems, they knock-and-leave, but they don't knock-and-enter in one motion. The hotels and social custom make that differentiation.

What these housekeepers had in common was that they were all female. In positions requiring no skills or heavy lifting, especially in which encountering the customer is customary, working class men are almost always passed over for working class women. And this creates an ironic outcome: **by discriminating against men in**

unskilled positions like housekeeper, we unwittingly pressure men to develop skills to compensate for the hiring discrimination against them. Thus the men develop the mechanical skills of the hotel engineer, or reinforce upper body strength to make themselves more eligible for jobs requiring lifting, like a bellman. As with the male nurse in the hospital, the bellman in the hotel learns he can give himself an equal hiring opportunity by risking lower back injuries and hernias.

These special skills may then command higher wages which we call discrimination in favor of men. What lies beneath this dynamic? Female comfort power.

"Female Comfort Power" and Its Hiring Bias

Almost every corporation hires a woman receptionist. Apparently we get more pleasure from a woman greeting us than a man, and the company expects that our happiness at their front line will make them happier with their bottom line. Ditto for the restaurant hostess and cocktail waitress. But it doesn't stop there.

We can understand that Wal-Mart would hire 99% women in its ladies' sportswear and hosiery departments, as long as Wal-Mart's men's wear department hires about 99% men. But it doesn't. **In Wal-Mart, men's wear is 93% women.**[22]

Approximately 145,000 Wal-Mart employees are in departments in which 91%–99% of employees are women.[23] With the exception of one department requiring the expertise of auto mechanics—TBO Service (Time Between Overhauls [men love acronyms!])—no department had 90% or more men. Thus, when a department did have disproportionately men, it was usually because of either specific skills needed (maintenance, 80% men) or the risk of personal safety and willingness to use physical strength (security, 88% men).[24]

Whether in women's wear or men's wear, at Wal-Mart or anywhere, women are more likely to be hired when skills aren't required. Why? Female comfort power. The comfort of the customer. The result? Being a human being is sufficient cause to hire a woman; men are more likely to have to prove themselves as a human doing.

Now here's the irony. Wal-Mart is being sued, for discrimination against women—fewer are promoted to top management.[25] Yet no one is asking about the degree to which the discrimination against women is accounted for by the discrimination for women—hiring almost all women in positions requiring few or no skills. It seems obvious that an assessment of discrimination should begin by asking, "What percentage of equally skilled men versus women get promoted?" Once that is controlled for, there are 24 more assessments to measure before we can conclude discrimination as a probable cause.

Meantime, there's a deeper issue. Why are we not asking for affirmative action programs to prevent companies from hiring 91%–99% women in departments requiring virtually no skills, or to prevent companies from hiring 93% women in men's wear! No form of discrimination is easier to measure than entry-level discrimination in jobs requiring no specific skills.

If the government is to dictate that companies cannot discriminate based on gender, the Fourteenth Amendment's equal protection clause would require that this apply when the discrimination cuts against men. If the government is not going to worry about discrimination against men, it should allow companies to hire and promote as they see fit. Or as its customers dictate. Or as the biases of its customers dictate!

Discrimination for Women in College and University Teaching—Especially in the Social Sciences

Economics majors in top universities outnumber women's studies majors by roughly 10 to 1. Nevertheless, 54 out of 55 leading universities offer more courses in women's studies than in economics.[26] What does this reflect?

It reflects the priorities and attitudes of university cultures in the liberal arts throughout the industrialized world, especially the United States, Canada, England, Australia, New Zealand, northwestern Europe, and Scandinavia. The headline is "Men are the oppressors, and women the oppressed." Anyone who would object to that ratio of economics to women's studies classes is under suspicion—and besides, the objection would be to no end.

The atmosphere was built on the well-meaning rationalizations of people like myself in the late 1960s and early 1970s. (At the time I was doing my doctorate at New York University and was on the Board of the National Organization for Women in New York City.) We saw that "men earned a dollar for each 59 cents earned by women," assumed that meant for the same work, and believed that reflected a world created by men at the expense of women. We set out to change that. Leading the mission was more compelling than understanding statistics.

With alacrity that amazed even those aware of the instinct of men to protect women, the university community in the liberal arts became one in its belief that women were powerless, men powerful, and that almost any offense a woman felt by something a man did or said was to be taken seriously. The reverse, however, was to be understood as an act of the powerless asserting themselves against the powerful. The double standard resulted in speech codes, political correctness, scholarships for women-as-minorities (even though women in the liberal arts had long been in the majority), and a deeply anti-male atmosphere.

The atmosphere became so anti-male that although what I am saying in this book about the pay gap could have been said at its core decades ago, professors of economics could not get funding to ask the probing questions. Few tried, knowing their survival in the academic community would be threatened if they published results that confronted the thesis of women-as-victim. The pioneer or two who made him- or herself an exception, like Thomas Sowell, could survive academically only if she or he was not a Caucasian male (Sowell is African American).[27]

As more than 30,000 women's studies courses[28] offered only the men-have-the-power perspective—versus two or three courses nationwide that tried to add some balance to that perspective—the graduates entered every part of society, but especially the human resource divisions in governments and in corporations, and the portions of the media that dealt with male-female issues. This made in-depth research questioning the pay gap almost impossible to be funded; thus a nonacademic (yours truly) who is not an economist is writing something (the book you are holding) that should have been written two decades ago.

While the anti-male attitude in universities is damaging, it is perhaps most damaging when it infects all the programs that train professionals who help families. The dynamic has led to psychology moving from a men-dominated field to a women-dominated field, to seminaries making that same transition, and to a misunderstanding of men among nurses and marriage and family therapists. Perhaps the field that is most anti-male, though, is social work. The anti-male attitude makes it difficult for a man to feel comfortable working in the field, and, even more importantly, affects the work lives of economically poor men and women.

Discrimination for Women in Family Services

Social workers learn to think of men as more powerful than women in the same way one class is more powerful than the other. The comparison misunderstands the essence of the male-female relationship, especially the instinct to protect women that is at the core of masculinity, and the intricate male-female dance that often leaves both sexes feeling powerless in its own way. The irony of schools of social work treating men as all-powerful is that such an attitude reinforces problems in family communication among the very professionals whose job it is to solve those problems. Solving family problems starts with treating both sexes' vulnerabilities with deep and impartial respect.

How does the social work bias affect men and women at work? The perception of men as more powerful leaves men feeling misunderstood, therefore even more resistant to the social workers' help than his male socialization already provides for. This leaves the couple vulnerable to divorce. The divorces lead to economically poor women having custody of children. This in turn leaves dads without children and no reason to work hard (the dad feels the more he makes the more he just has to give to an ex who feels he's the enemy, and to children he feels have been turned against him). Women are then given economic boosts not available to men via programs such as W.I.C. (Women, Infants and Children), and guidance by social workers to enter the workforce. The women are overworked, and the men become self-destructive in their purposelessness.

That's but the tip of a large iceberg. The dynamic is better understood by seeing how it plays out in the training of social workers in the field of domestic violence. In the past quarter century, more than 100 domestic violence studies have documented the equal likelihood of men and women to be subject to domestic violence at every level of severity.[29] Yet in social work schools, this two-sex approach to domestic violence is rarely taught. This establishes an educator bias against providing shelters for men who are abused (there are thousands of shelters for women only, and at best one or two for men only who are abused), so men are not hired to staff the nonexistent men's shelters, and rarely hired to staff the for-women domestic violence shelters. Cecil County, Maryland, is a good example of how that bias gets translated into everyday life.

Cecil County claims it doesn't need to worry about men since it gets few calls from them. But the name of their center is Domestic Violence Rape Crisis Center.[30] Most men sense that the people staffing a rape crisis center are feminists who see women as victims of men. Male victims of domestic violence are jeopardized not only by the domestic violence itself, but by the double jeopardy of male socialization to not ask for help. If a man overcomes that socialization, begins to pick up the phone and imagines asking for help from someone who may see him as the likely perpetrator, well, that's triple jeopardy.

Is this, though, an accurate portrayal of the domestic violence social worker? And if so, why? Well, in 2003, after ABC's *20/20* finally introduced the country to the two-sex nature of domestic violence (more than a quarter century after it had been well-documented as an equal opportunity tragedy) and produced a segment that included interviews with male victims, it was about to be shown to the Cecil County Family Violence Coordinating Council, which included judges and people able to influence policy. But Karen Dunne, who oversees the county's women's shelter, read a prepared statement objecting to it even being shown and led a walkout of her colleagues. Her colleagues joined her.[31]

This attitude toward men creates "solutions" that reinforce the problem. Social worker training to see domestic violence as part of the male role discourages looking at it as part of the male role *broken-*

down; seeing it as an extension of male power discourages examining the possibility of seeing it as a momentary act of power designed to compensate for a deeper experience of powerlessness. (Which is why it is most common among the poor, less well educated, elderly, unemployed, and by mothers toward children.) Between the sexes, both sexes are violent because both sexes experience powerlessness in relation to each other.

All of these attitudes in combination create what has begun to be called "the woman industry": women professionals and administrators hired to help mostly women who are poor—giving middle-class and wealthy women opportunities and scholarships not available to men. In this atmosphere, no one thinks of public service ads reaching out to abused men, hiring male counselors to staff hotlines or to speak to groups of the elderly where domestic violence against men is most prevalent.[32] All of these outreach programs would make it clear that thousands of shelters for abused men are needed, and that there is a need for males to be hired to staff them.

In these "family fields" dominated by women, many men feel closed out, just as many women do in male-dominated fields. There is, though, a big difference: in these female-dominated fields, an anti-male attitude is embedded into the curriculum (the litmus test is that people emerge more angry at men than when they enter); while in men-dominated fields, human resource and diversity programs sensitize men to women, and men frequently mentor women to make their involvement more welcome and successful.

Women, Men, and the "Mentorship Gene"

> *Marshall [Goldsmith] helps me recognize my power,*
> *but also to treat life like a game. Marion Baker helps*
> *me push the Pause button . . . to ask myself, Is there*
> *enough white space in my life?*
> —BEVERLY KAYE, CEO, CAREER SYSTEMS
> INTERNATIONAL, LOS ANGELES[33]

> *I had different mentors for different purposes. One*
> *invested a quarter million that kept my company from*

going under; another got me onto boards of other com-
panies; another taught me the complexities of finance.
—KAY HAMMER, CEO OF EVOLUTIONARY
TECHNOLOGIES INT'L, AUSTIN, TX[34]

My mentors have been white males. The mentor who
taught me how to sell had more chutzpah than anybody
I ever knew! He would ask people for things that I
thought he'd be thrown out of the room for. But people
would say yes—some said no, but it was no big deal.
He taught me how much I could accomplish if I wasn't
afraid of rejection.

Another mentor was a VC [venture capitalist] who
backed up his investment with introducing me to some
of the most successful CEOs in the country—they
would meet with me, talk with me, be available to me
over the phone to answer my questions. Some became
my friends, some were like coaches.

Yet a third was my seeing-eye dog into the corporate
world. He was like a translator who helped me read
between-the-lines.
—MARCIA RADOSEVICH, FORMER CEO, HPR
(HEALTH PAYMENT REVIEW), CAMBRIDGE, MA[35]

The male protector instinct gives men, in effect, a "mentorship gene." If a woman is smart enough to ask for help, men will compete to give it. It's in their genes.

In this respect, women have deep instinctual advantages over a man: Men's facade of strength is their weakness, and this discourages men from asking for help; women's facade of weakness is their strength, and this encourages women to ask for help. Whether she breaks down in tears, needs something repaired, needs a bug killed (or captured but not killed), needs a noise in the house checked out at 3 a.m., or is stranded on the side of the road, she asks, he responds.

In the world outside the home, women asking for help and men giving it is nature's dance. And to procure a mentor, asking for help works. But keeping a mentor is best done via the fuel of appreciation.

Yet to this day, while I've seen thousands of greeting cards putting men down, I have yet to see one thanking a man for being a mentor.

Lack of appreciation seems especially acute in the United States, where women are almost twice as likely as women in Europe to have mentors. (About 77% of U.S. women executives have had mentors versus 40% of European women executives.[36]) Despite this, U.S. women are more likely to feel they are deprived of mentoring. In fact, in comparison to European women, U.S. women executives perceive themselves as more likely to face barriers to success in every aspect asked.[37]

Mentorship's slippery slope is when Jack is mentor and Jill is beautiful. Too often, after Jack leads Jill up the hill, they come tumbling down . . . usually together. Jack and Jill's trip up and down the hill is even faster if Jill is what I call a "genetic celebrity."

CHAPTER 12

The Genetic Celebrity Pay Gap

Until now I have focused on what a woman can do to increase her pay inside the workplace. This chapter (probably my personal favorite) will look at the pay opportunities for women outside the workplace.

Women's greater social desirability and beauty power afford opportunities for creating both measurable and invisible income. While the opportunities are available to almost all women and some men, they are available in abundance to the "genetic celebrity."

And What, Pray Tell, Is a "Genetic Celebrity"?

A genetic celebrity is a woman so beautiful that men do more than look and talk—they follow her. We see a genetic celebrity when we see a woman surrounded by men doing most anything to get her attention. Though they know nothing about her, they aspire to be valued by her. Both sexes do this with celebrities, but only men go this far for beauty alone. Since this exceptionally beautiful woman has celebrity status based largely on her genes, I call her a "genetic celebrity."

While height and good looks are a big advantage for any man, virtually no man is a genetic celebrity. That is, a woman doesn't start stalking a man who is good-looking unless she knows something about him—he's a football player, famous actor, respected and famous politician. . . . This makes him an earned celebrity—his good looks are his genes, but he can only reach the celebrity status of making her follow him if she knows he used his good looks to a good end.

Because her genetic celebrity status is not earned, but inherited, she rarely appreciates it, until it fades. Genetic celebrity power is the only universal passport to other cultures and any economic class.[1] But like all passports, it expires. Because it arrives on her doorstep before the call of maturity and before mortality beckons, it is likely to be used as recklessly as the new BMW given to a teenage boy in a society requiring no driver's license.

When a man sees a genetic celebrity, he feels like a groupie. After explaining this to an audience, a woman shared this story of "Andrea." Whether apocryphal or not, it's a great laugh and can help a woman understand how a man approaching a genetic celebrity might feel . . .

Andrea opened the door of a Baskin-Robbins off of the main plaza in Santa Fe. There was Robert Redford, sitting across from where the ice cream was being scooped. She wanted desperately to approach Robert, er, Mr. Redford, to get an autograph. Her stomach in knots, her heartbeats stumbling over themselves, and her mind playing A.D.D., she gets MTV glimpses of her strategies . . . "I know, I'll ask him for an autograph 'for the children'—no, no, probably everyone asks that. . . . I'll tell him what a big fan of his I am—bummer, my mind is frozen on the names of his movies. I know, I'll just casually wander by him, and say, um . . . um, let's see, what can I say that he hasn't heard a thousand times before? This is ridiculous; I'm acting so immature. I'll just get my ice cream and leave. No, I can't do that . . . what will I tell my friends?"

Andrea gets to the counter before she gets up her nerve.

"One scoop of anything on a cone" Andrea mutters as she contemplates how to catch his eye. "Oh, dear. If I do catch his eye, I don't want him to see this hair-as-mop. There's got to be a lady's room . . . No, he could walk out."

Andrea pays but can't get it together to approach Robert, er, Mr.

Redford. As soon as she gets outside she feels immense relief but also thorough disappointment in herself. Then she realizes . . . she forgot the ice cream!

Her body reignites like that of a soldier who's just arrived home only to be called back to battle. She reenters, reviewing every option, every anxiety. "I'll get the ice cream first."

"Excuse me, I forgot my ice cream."

"Excuse me, ma'am," she hears Robert, er, Mr. Redford say, as he stands up and walks directly toward her. "I believe you put your keys and your ice cream in your purse."

A woman who can identify with that scenario has a little glimpse of the inner dialogue of virtually every heterosexual male who encounters a genetic celebrity. The main difference is that his inner dialogue is considerably longer and all his past rejections come flashing back like post-traumatic stress syndrome.

Genetic Celebrity Power's Invisible Income

A genetic celebrity's visible beauty creates invisible income. How?

A man who feels like a genetic groupie next to a genetic celebrity feels that he must in some way "pay" to earn his way to equality with her: to buy her drinks before the first date, then dinner on the date; buy flowers for no occasion, jewelry for a small occasion, and a diamond for the big occasion. Whatever the income on a genetic celebrity's pay stub, genetic groupies compete to increase it. Between the genetic celebrity and the rest of the world, there is a "genetic celebrity pay gap."

Let's start at a baseball game . . .

The Genetic Celebrity as Tip Magnet

I am at a San Diego Padres home baseball game. I signal for a beer and a bag of peanuts. The vendor pitches the peanuts, then deftly hands off the beer to the fans that convey it to me to complete the "double play." The process must have triggered the memory of the woman behind me . . .

"There's great tips in being a vendor," she recalls to her boyfriend. "Especially for a girl. I used to make up to $200 per hour."

The "$200 per hour" stopped my first peanut dead on my tongue. I try to be discreet about turning my head to steal a fuller picture. I see a woman who looks like an actress playing a doctor on ER. Fortunately her boyfriend, as riveted as I, encourages her to explain.

"I was in junior high, maybe about 12 or 13, and our school was near Fresno State. So before their ballgames I'd get myself a ride to Fresno State. We'd buy soft drinks and junk foods from a supplier and sell them during the games. We just put down the upfront money. The profit and tips were ours. The games would be over in 2–3 hours and I'd sometimes have about $500 profit."

"$500. No way!" her boyfriend exclaimed. "You couldn't have sold that many drinks!" Before he could do the math, she clarified . . .

"Most of the profits were tips."

"From guys, I'll bet," her boyfriend adds. I sense his jealousy alleviated a tad by the likelihood his prediction is right-on.

"Yeah, mostly men—it wasn't unusual to get a $5 or occasionally even a $10 tip."

"And that was for just a few minutes' worth of work?"

"And a smile," she responded—with a smile.

"So you flirted . . . you sold your beautiful, innocent smile?" her boyfriend teases, laughing (to camouflage his quasi-jealous touch of envy).

"Oh, come on. I was only 12 or 13, so there weren't any come-ons. But maybe I did sell my innocence."

"How's that?"

"I got that as a girl I could earn a lot just by being me—plus a smile. And in some ways that spoiled me. When I know I have that option, it makes it harder for me to be motivated to do the work med school will require, knowing that with HMOs and taxes I may not earn much more than I did with my smile."

The genetic celebrity is a tip magnet. The more of a genetic celebrity she is, the more he pays: His money is his equalizer. Money is the man's toll road to equality.

At what age do girls become aware of their power? They experience it before they become conscious of it. Girls experience it as infants when they are touched more frequently than boys, and touched if they are beautiful even more frequently than if they are not.

When my wife and I were on vacation in the summer of 2004, I had just completed a draft of this chapter on the genetic celebrity and, would you believe, the young teenage girl sitting in front of us on the plane was making this translation of her genetic celebrity power about as succinct as I could hope for. We told her of my book-in-process, and she graciously agreed to pose for the accompanying photograph. . . .

The Genetic Celebrity's Free-Serve Stations

When I was pumping my own gas at the Texaco station near my home in Carlsbad, California (where, to paraphrase Garrison Keillor, all the gas pumps are self-serve and all the women pumping gas are more beautiful than average), a beautiful 16- or 17-year-old young woman, whose clothes were carefully designed to make her beauty visible, pulled up to the self-serve pump next to me.

Within seconds, two mechanics who were on break were quick-stepping toward her, each trying to outcompete the other to get "permission" to transform her self-serve station into a full-serve station.

They escaped making fools of themselves by divvying up the labor: One pumped her gas; the other cleaned her front window. The one who pumped her gas also did her back window while the gas was pumping. (Who said men can't do more than one thing at a time—and he was simultaneously looking at her!) Yes, they had successfully turned their self-serve station into a full-serve station.

A genetic celebrity unconsciously learns that she can get full service at self-serve prices.

Genetic celebrity power creates not only invisible income in the form of tipping and services, but also in the form of free gifts. An attractive research assistant of mine who was completing her law degree while working for me was technically in debt, but had a new car paid for by her dad, and rent paid for by her boyfriend. When she was reading some of my sections on the hidden income of genetic celebrities, she good-naturedly laughed in agreement, and shared with me how often in her life men she barely knew had spent weekends doing things like painting the rooms she was living in, repairing her old car, or helping her move.

As we were laughing, she was eating her lunch. Suddenly she looked like she had just found a diamond in her burrito. Tucking a half bite to the side of her mouth, she pointed to the burrito, blushed, and said, "When I bought a Coke at Roberto's, the guy asked me if I like burritos. I said yeah, he put this in a bag, rang up the price of the Coke, and smiled."

"Has this happened before?"

Now she looked like the cat that had swallowed the burrito. "Well, actually, I've been buying Cokes there for quite a while now, and he always does something like that."

"Wow!" I said, astonished. "You have sort of a deal going, then—you and the price of a Coke equals lunch. Couldn't he lose his job?"

"I guess. I never thought of that."

"Has this happened all your life?"

"Well, since I was in high school. In high school, I used to love pizza (still do), and all throughout my junior year, every day, this guy would give me one or two free slices, whatever he could sneak to me."

"What happened in your senior year?"

She smiled. "I got a boyfriend, and. . . ."

Together we laughed, "And *he* paid for the pizza—and the Coke, too!"

"Other examples like this?"

"This is embarrassing, but you've got me on a roll. Let's see, well. . . . You know how quickly I drive. I've been stopped a *lot*, but only gotten one ticket. So I guess that's a freebie of sorts."

"I'd say so. At about $150 a ticket plus avoiding an increase in your insurance, yes, I'd say that's a freebie! I'm afraid to ask how many times you've gotten a flat tire."

"Oh, my God, you'll love this one. Twice. But once a guy stopped with his girlfriend in the car. I thought she would kill him. He was real nice to me, but then she got out of the car, and he became very matter-of-fact. When she got back in the car, he was more helpful again. Then she opened the window, and he went back to being matter-of-fact. There was so much tension, I was ready to give the tire a stress test!"

All of this happened in the 1990s, to a woman who in a couple of years later would be earning about $100,000 annually as an attorney (she was number one in her class).

What was most astonishing about our conversation was that this had happened so often, so routinely, and for so long that she mostly took it for granted. It was unconscious. And, of course, if she were asked how much she earned during the year, she would never have added up the value of her free rent, rooms painted for free, car repairs, speeding tickets that never got filled out, insurance rates that therefore never increased, free burritos, pizzas, or the thousands of dollars spent on her for more formal dates: from ski weekends to Hawaii vacations.

The Genetic Celebrity Pay Gap

Top women models earn about five times more, that is, about 400% more, than their male "equivalent."[2] Put another way, men models earn about 20% of the pay for the same work (even when we compare, say, a top male model to a top female model).

How much are we talking about? For the top women supermodels, that's about $50,000 a day for women versus about $10,000 for men. Among the top 10%, the average woman earns $10,000 to $15,000 per day. About three-quarters of the models are women.

Why don't we hear about this genetic celebrity pay gap—why is it under our radar? Because no National Organization for Men or National Organization for Male Models protests men being worth only 20% of their female colleagues. We don't see men models with placards demanding, "Equal Pay for Equal Pose," or "Same Position, Same Pay." Why? First, men sense the market value of men's looks is about 20% of women's—that women's fashion and cosmetics generate more money than men's. Men are generally more accepting of the marketplace determining value rather than their values dictating value.

All this said, there is no pay gap that is clearer or greater than the invisible pay gap of the genetic celebrity.

Genetic Celebrity Hiring Discrimination

When I was doing a book tour in Japan for *Why Men Are the Way They Are,* I was told of an institution called the "snack." The "snack" works like this: A man is coming home from work, and has had a bad day. He doesn't feel that his wife wants to hear about it, so he pays between $50 and $80 for a "snack"—a sandwich and a drink and an attractive woman who will listen empathetically to him—sort of a beautiful psychologist with refreshments. No men need apply.

In all the jobs in which female comfort power (you'll recall from Chapter 11) gives women an advantage, the more she is a genetic celebrity, the greater her advantage. This is true for both jobs and careers (e.g., in jobs such as cocktail waitress, receptionist, restaurant hostess, or waitress; or in selling clothing, cosmetics, or jewelry in a department store).

As for careers, genetic celebrity discrimination works for hundreds of thousands of women sales reps who meet men clients in person, and in professions from corporate PR rep to women flight attendants and dental hygienist. (We discussed how most people prefer a woman's fingers in their mouth rather than a man's, but even more prefer the fingers to be those of a genetic celebrity.)

A genetic celebrity harvests the greatest power when most of us wouldn't want to even think of hiring anyone else: Even if a male cheerleader in college were the best in the country, how many Dallas Cowboy fans would want to see him as a cheerleader during an NFL game? Or after the game at Hooters? Does this mean there will never be a man as a Dallas Cowboy cheerleader? No. If a man can do something no woman cheerleader can do that makes the women look better—such as tossing a woman cheerleader higher into the air—then he serves a purpose: enhancing her genetic celebrity power.

If your son applies for a job as a cocktail server, his only chance of being hired is as a comedian. Two hundred dollars a night is not unheard of for tips alone in the top-quality, urban-area cocktail lounges and oyster bars. Five nights per week, fifty weeks per year, that's $52,000 per year in tips—plus minimum wage of about another $12,000, plus benefits.

When we see figures that only a tiny fraction of women earn as much as $64,000 per year, we don't see even one cocktail waitress listed among them. So the gap between men's and women's income needs to be reduced by that portion of genetic celebrity-based tipping that never gets declared as income.

In the meantime, the previously male-dominated field of bartending is now attracting women who are neither being laughed at nor discriminated against, but smiled at and tipped more.

Often, though, the people we tip are not the ones we take seriously—not the ones we'd hire as a VP for our company or an attorney to sue our company.

Doesn't Beauty Work against Women Who Want to Be Taken Seriously?

We often hear that although a beautiful woman gets our attention, no one takes her seriously—especially in more serious work settings. We are now discovering that while there's definitely some truth to that, the net effect may be the opposite: Beauty pays.

For starters, a study of attorneys found that the attorneys whose pictures were judged independently to be the better-looking ones earned about 12% more per year than the less good-looking ones.

The better-looking attorneys worked longer hours, but even when that and dozens of other variables were controlled for, the better-looking attorneys were able to bill significantly more per hour.[3]

Needless to say, the men attorneys were ranked as much less attractive than the women, increasing the gap in women's pay over men's. The bigger the gap in looks, the bigger was the gap in pay. The more time passed, the more the gap widened. Sometimes life isn't fair.

The *American Bar Association Journal* did a story of one of its members who also put the "beauty pays" theory to the test—in a slightly different way. Rosalie Osias ran ads with the accompanying seductive picture of her lying across a desk.

The result? Her real estate and banking law practice experienced an increase in closed loans of between 400% and 800%.[4] Now that's being taken seriously.

The fact that beauty pays and leads to a woman being taken seriously can be different from a woman being taken seriously at the outset. Being taken seriously for a beautiful woman is often a process, a process set into motion by her genetic celebrity power. The process starts with "access discrimination."

"Access Discrimination"

Access to a potential client is so important to sales reps that entire conferences are held on "getting access." Sam, a sales rep for security systems, gives an example:

> I walk into a bank to try to sell a new security system. I know I have a good one, but the male bank VP responsible for security says, "Sorry, I'm busy." Susan, though, walks into the bank lobby and makes a request to see the VP in charge of security; the VP looks through his glass barrier to the lobby, gets one look at Susan and suddenly he "has a minute." Susan comes out an hour later with a commitment for a second meeting with potential users at the bank.

Sam has just been the victim of "access discrimination" via the glass preview—the tendency of men to preview someone who wants access to them, whether via the glass in their office window or their picture on a Web site, or via the "old-boy network," and to give more access to a genetic celebrity.

The Savior Syndrome

Once a woman has access, her femininity triggers his "savior syndrome"—a male biological desire to help a woman (remember the mentor gene?), whether a woman wants to escape a fire, or is in his office asking him if he knows people he can call to lay the foundation for her to develop a new account. I've seen some men make a jerk of themselves proving they can "clear all the paths" and get an attractive woman access to whomever she wants.

The savior syndrome is most likely to work in women's favor in men-dominated environments where more men are competing for women's favor, either consciously or unconsciously.

The greater the cries of "discrimination against women" the more men's savior syndrome is triggered and the men compete to be the heroes who save women from being victims of that discrimination. The men compete to "prove themselves," to be in the elite of the "enlightened men," to be the biggest jock in the sensitivity group.

Men's savior syndrome is the dance partner to women's desire to be saved. It transforms a woman's cry of victim into female victim power. Sometimes, of course, she is genuinely a victim. But the trigger is pulled merely by her expressing the feeling.

"Marrying Up": Reality Haunts Expectation

Women "marrying up" is so much a part of our fantasy life that a pretty, homeless female prostitute marrying a millionaire makes it as a popular movie (*Pretty Woman*), while a movie with the roles reversed—a handsome homeless gigolo marrying a female millionaire (let's say, *Handsome Man*) never gets made. In real life, even when wealthy women who don't need the money nevertheless "marry up," be they Princess Di or Jackie Kennedy, they remain etched in our memories and our fantasy lives. Ask a man if he remembers the name of one man who's "married up."

Is "marrying up" something of the past? Here's how I update my answer to that question via my presentations and workshops (which tend to select for educated men and women, both of whom work).[5]

Since the question is *marrying* up—not which sex earns more—I first ask women and men to close their eyes and recall their wedding day. (In California I allow for a random selection of wedding days!)

I begin by asking the women, "Pretend I asked you just prior to your wedding, even though this is the last thing on your mind, to predict whether your husband-to-be was likely to earn as much or more than you during the course of your life together. Would you have predicted 'yes' or 'no'?" About 95% of women raise their hand to "Yes," that their husband would earn as much or more.

I then ask the men if they would have predicted they would earn as much or more than their wives during their lives together. About 98% of men say "yes."

"Marrying up" as expectation is different from "marrying up" as reality. In reality, only 77% of husbands earn more than their wives.[6] So there's a gap between expectation and reality. And that creates problems.

When a man believes he is expected to earn more, and downsizing leads to a man earning less, it can lead to a marriage becoming a mess. It *can;* whether or not it does generally depends on whether the woman believes the man will eventually return to making a good living. If so, no problem. If not, it's a big test analogous to the type of test he faces if she gets a mastectomy. She discovers whether she is genuinely okay with him earning less. He discovers the conditions of her love.

If she is genuinely okay with it (usually because she loves her career and because his earnings were not a significant factor in her desire to marry him), then he usually adjusts because he still feels respected and valued. If she is not accepting of his earning less, the criticism seeps out, his disappointment in himself expands into major insecurity; his insecurity magnifies her loss of respect, and the result is a marriage-in-trouble.

"Marrying Up" as Invisible Income

"Marrying up" is one reason that, although men earn more money, women often have more, spend more, and have it longer.

We frequently hear that men executives are more likely than women executives to have a "wife." True. We also hear that these wives do unpaid labor. Not true.

The men executive's income is also his wife's income. The fact that we say she does unpaid labor is evidence that her income is invisible. In many respects, the income is hers more than his: The wife of the executive man has more time to spend it and usually makes more of the spending decisions (which is why she is more the target of marketing people). She lives longer, and once he dies, her time to spend it is significantly greater than his!

"Marrying Up's" Invisible Income Creates Women's Options for Less Workplace Income

Her invisible income gives her freedom from the workplace-as-obligation, and therefore creates the option of taking a job she enjoys more that pays her less.

"Marrying up" allows women social options, which in turn create financial options. Socially, marrying up allows her to:

    a. marry a doctor
    b. become a doctor
    c. marry a doctor and become a doctor

Reprinted with special permission of King Features Syndicate.

If she chooses either of the two marry-a-doctor options (as a metaphor for marrying any man who earns well), she gains three other options when children arrive:

a. career full-time
b. children full-time
c. some combination of the above

Her successful husband has three "slightly different" options:

a. work full-time
b. work full-time
c. work full-time

A successful husband is rarely offered the full-time dad option, and rarely offers it to himself. He may fleetingly consider the option, but usually discounts it as unrealistic—fearing that his wife, children, parents, and friends would look down upon him for "quitting his job" and abandoning his career to become a full-time dad.

Would he want it if offered? Only if his wife wanted to advance her career and she made it clear she would value him even more if he were a full-time dad. Under those circumstances, about 70%–80% of educated men would like the full-time dad option; most of the remainder would prefer a blend of part-time work and part-time child care.[7]

Sometimes the freedom to invest in oneself and take risks that marrying up creates can have monetary returns. Arianna Huffington married a multimillionaire and used the security created by their divorce to write creative and risk-taking columns and books—and run for governor of California.

"Marrying Up" as "Career Flashdancing"

In the movie *Flashdance*, Jennifer Beal's character's genetic celebrity power and talent entices an influential man to help advance her career "in a flash," past hundreds of talented women who had danced harder for longer for the same position. I call this "career flashdancing." When this happens via marriage, it might be thought of as marrying up as career flashdancing. For example, you've heard of the sex researchers, Masters and Johnson. Which is the man, which the woman?

Chances are if you are not in the social sciences, you won't know— or will have to think, because you think of Masters and Johnson as equals. The one who had an MD and was a famous sex researcher prior to their marriage is William Masters. Virginia Johnson had no advanced degree. They got married and became professional equals, Masters and Johnson.

Many women who marry established psychologists or authors, but who themselves have far fewer credentials, follow the Masters and Johnson model. After the marriage, the woman appears as a coauthor on his next book, or as a cofacilitator in the next workshop brochure. While the process creates opportunities for talented women, it cannot be called equal opportunity—either in relation to men or to other women who didn't marry the right man.

Many women artists and writers I know devote full-time to their writing. Yet marrying up is often what enables them to do that. Their husband's income creates the freedom for them to be a full-time writer or artist. Her success is hoped for, but not required. Generally, for a man who receives the full-time support of his traditional wife in order to write, success is either already achieved, or expected, not just hoped for.

In the business world, the pattern is similar. Bill Agee and Mary Cunningham promised the world there was "nothing between them" when she was rocketed through the ranks to working just under Bill at the top of Bendix. Yet soon after saying there was nothing between them, they were married. (Who knows, maybe there was nothing between them!)

She Marries Up, He Dies Off, She Moves Up

Worldwide, men who lead their country and lose their lives are commonly succeeded by their wives.

In Sri Lanka, both candidates for president were women whose husbands had been slain.[8] In Bangladesh, Khaleda Zia became prime minister after her husband was assassinated.[9] In India, Sonia Gandhi became the head of the Congress Party when her husband, former Prime Minister Rajiv Gandhi, was assassinated.[10] Both Benazir Bhutto of Pakistan and Indira Gandhi became prime ministers when their fathers died.[11] And, of course, Eva Peron succeeded her husband Juan Peron in Argentina. Occasionally it happens in reverse, as when Rajiv Gandhi took over from his mother, Indira, when she was assassinated.

In the United States prior to the early 1980s, a majority of women who had served in the U.S. Senate were initially elected or appointed upon the deaths of their husbands.[12] Similarly, the death of Katherine Graham's husband flashdanced the much less-experienced, yet very competent, Katherine Graham to the head of the *Washington Post;* and Ray Kroc's death left his wife, Joan Kroc, with McDonald's and ownership of the San Diego Padres. Georgia Frontier's ownership of the Los Angeles Rams occurred when her husband Carroll Rosenbloom died. Anna Nicole Smith married a famous elderly billionaire and soon used her inherited fame and fortune to become a TV star and artist whose name recognition allows her to sell one painting for doubtless more income than Van Gogh made in his lifetime. (Van Gogh never sold a painting to a nonrelative.)

Some of this is coming full-circle. Teresa Heinz inherits a fortune when her husband dies, and at least a small portion of that fortune is able to be used to support Senator John Kerry to become president of the United States in 2005.

Career flashdancing via marrying up—like nepotism and passing on a company to the oldest son—works in favor of a few and against equal opportunity. There are laws against gender wage discrimination, but not if it comes in the form of marrying up.

In Conclusion

Women's genetic celebrity power magnifies men's protector instinct. It inspires the government-as-substitute-husband. Men's addiction to the genetic celebrity is either invisible or in the denial stage—thus we either don't see it, or when confronted, deny it. That is, we either don't see or deny genetic celebrity hiring discrimination, access discrimination, the savior syndrome, and "career flashdancing." We rarely see and often deny the power of "marrying up," and marrying up as a facilitator of career flashdancing and promotions-by-death. And we either don't see or deny the genetic celebrity's invisible income as tip magnet, or as inspirer of free gift-giving and service-providing by genetic celebrity groupies (virtually every heterosexual male).

Perhaps men models earning about 20% of what women models earn gives us the best clue as to the genetic celebrity pay gap. If unmarried men who have never had children earn only 85% of what their female counterparts earn inside the workplace, it is likely they earn more like 20% of what their female counterparts earn outside the workplace. While few of us are models, the degree to which our physical attractiveness creates income or services from the other sex takes off from that advantage or handicap.

While almost every woman suffers psychological damage as she compares herself to the genetic celebrity (using makeup to make up the gap between the power she has and the power she'd like to have), almost every woman also benefits from the billions of dollars spent reinforcing men's addiction to an image that is far more like hers than like his. This will remain unchanged as long as we acknowledge our addiction to the genetic celebrity the way an addict acknowledges an addiction to a drug—looking for a place to pay for more.

CHAPTER 13

Two Nagging Questions . . .

Two questions are so embedded in the public consciousness that they nag at us even when we understand the differences between men's and women's work patterns. The questions linger because they suggest two injustices that have not directly been addressed. Before I get into the more complex question of comparable worth, let's dispose of the question with the simpler answer . . .

When Women Enter Men's Occupations, Doesn't the Pay Go Down?

Usually yes. We've already seen 25 reasons why. But these reasons don't make a few other dynamics apparent . . . Prior to the 1960s, when psychology was the province of men, men prevented other men who had less than an MD or Ph.D. from practicing, and certainly from getting the insurance to make a practice viable.

When women entered, mostly male legislators and insurance executives responded by reducing the credentials necessary to get insurance coverage. This made private practice viable for people with only MA's since potential clients could get reimbursed for the cost of therapy. This also increased the respect for and pay of psychologists with only master's degrees.

The pay of these women therapists definitely averages less than for men psychologists with Ph.D.'s and psychiatrists (with medical degrees), but not due to discrimination against women, but due to discrimination in favor of women. How so? Women (and men) are now allowed to practice with much less education and can therefore afford to work fewer hours to make their investment pay off. If she chooses, she can work the longer work weeks and make $50,000 to $100,000 or more per year, but it is a choice, not a necessity for return on investment.

Sometimes pay goes down when women enter because women enter when technology has made the field female-friendly, and that both increases the supply in the field and its desirability. For example, when technology makes the occupation safer and cleaner, as it did with typesetting; or safer and more convenient, as it did with mail delivery. Mail carriers are now protected by covered trucks with heat rather than attacked by unleashed dogs in heat. As a result, both sexes want to be typesetters or mail carriers and the increased supply allows pay to go down.

Still other times, after women enter, technology allows the occupation to require fewer skills, as was true in baking.[1] Or technology makes the skills of all people in the profession less needed, as ATMs and computerization did to bank tellers.[2]

It gets trickier. Once the pay goes down, men who are supporting families are forced out, as are men who want to increase their attractiveness to women as top wage earners. Soon the field is dominated by women, but we don't focus on how the men felt that the expectations on them forced them out—especially the moment the occupation became desirable. We act as if the profession's pay went down because women came in. We don't see headlines saying, "Men Forced Out of Clean, Safe Occupations," or, more accurately, "Men Make Occupations Cleaner and Safer So Women Can Replace Them."

"Isn't the Issue More Than Equal Pay—Isn't It Comparable Worth?"

As economists found pay was a lot more equal than feminists publicized, feminists redefined equality. They said the issue was more than equal pay, it was comparable worth.[3] For example, a woman with a

BA in education or French literature should be paid equally to someone with a BS in engineering or physics, since comparable bachelor's degrees indicated the preparation for their work was comparable; or, that the person with a college education should be paid more than someone without a college education, such as a truck driver, mechanic, or coal miner.

The problem with comparable worth is that it creates higher pay for higher fulfillment positions that everyone wants and lower pay for lower fulfillment positions that are hard to fill unless we pay more. Thus it leaves us with few people to build our highways, bridges, or homes; pick up our garbage, clean up our sewers, mine our coal; or do most any job that employs almost all men. Why?

Test this out yourself. Imagine that for a month you have neither had your garbage picked up nor an opportunity to read about new anthropological discoveries. Which would you pay more money to remedy? **A society that functions effectively adjusts the pay until the supply matches the need.** Failure to make these adjustments not only creates streets filled with garbage, but also leaves unemployment lines filled with anthropologists.

As the economist June O'Neill points out, "One need only consider the economies of Eastern Europe to observe the results of replacing the market with administered and planned systems."[4] In Germany, the high cost of German workers relative to productivity has led to unemployment as high as 15%. However, even after considering those economies, the states of Washington, Minnesota, Iowa, New York, Oregon, and Wisconsin implemented comparable worth, as did Canada.[5]

In real life, comparable worth was usually a method of increasing the pay for "women's" jobs versus men's. Problem is, women's jobs fit the low-pay criteria because more people compete to do what is more fulfilling, indoor, flexible, people-oriented, and so on. **The results of comparable worth? Women were hurt. There was reduced employment in women-dominated fields because women became too expensive given the abundant supply.**[6] And the states themselves (as well as Canada) reported administrative and budgetary nightmares, reduced competitiveness, and shortages in some fields.[7]

Unemployment, of course, sends the economy into a recession, creating more unemployment. Ironically, unemployment hurts women more than men. Feminists argue that's because of sex discrimination: "Women are the last to be hired and the first to be fired." Correct on the outcome; wrong on the reason. We hire first what we need most, and we fire first what we need least. That's why you hire the garbage collector first, and fire him last. **Men may be hired first and fired last because more men are willing to do society's dirty work and hazardous work for a lower price.**

Were comparable worth to be applied to both sexes, it would affect thousands of individual women like singer-songwriter Alanis Morissette who, at age 23, made $22 million.[8] Comparable worth would reduce her salary to about $22,000. Where is her Ph.D.? In this respect, comparable worth is socialist because it takes away the ability of the consumer to determine value. If we buy more records by Alanis Morissette, she receives more money. No one tells us that she is worth less than an elementary school teacher and therefore reduces her pay.

I do not personally agree with values that lead to real U.S. presidents making $400,000 while Bill Pullman makes $2.5 million for "acting" president (in *Independence Day*), but I appreciate a system in which we can make a political decision to pay the president the amount we feel will bring us a good president, and make millions of small consumer decisions that lead to it being worthwhile for a studio to pay Bill Pullman his $2.5 million.[9] As long as we have the freedom to change those priorities when we feel we need to.

If I were to judge comparable worth by my personal self-interest in it, I would vote in favor. After all, I would love my Ph.D. to earn me as much as a Ph.D. in engineering. Or, as a gender specialist, I would love my Ph.D. to earn me more-than-equal pay to women like Gloria Steinem, who has equal work experience, but no Ph.D. But if "gender specialists" got a comparable worth bill passed that forced universities to pay more for me than for Gloria Steinem, no one would hire me. So, what would seem to be a victory for my higher pay would really signal a victory for my greater unemployment.

Comparable worth would not just replace the economics of capitalism, but also replace the underlying democracy of capitalism. Here's why.

The shopping mall is capitalism's voting booth. Every purchase we make is a "vote." Only 50% of U.S. adults vote politically, and they vote politically only about once every year or two. Yet virtually 100% vote economically, and they vote that way almost every day. That's capitalism's real democracy. Comparable worth would replace your vote with its vote.

Comparable worth is a unique economic blend of classism and sexism. It is classist because it systematically downgrades the jobs taken by non-degreed, working-class men to support their families. Simultaneously, it systematically upgrades jobs to which feminists are drawn—jobs of highly educated professors and teachers specializing in arts, literature, education, and social sciences, usually from highly educated, middle- and upper-class families. The argument that the art historian should be paid more, because she has "worked harder" to get a higher degree and therefore is worth more, discounts the hard work of the working class.

Comparable worth is also sexist, because it rarely if ever suggests increasing the pay of jobs held mostly by men, making, for example, jobs with a high risk of death comparable to a Ph.D. That would mean increasing men's pay more than 90% of the time. And of course, it never advocates even equal pay for any group of women who are paid more than their male counterparts, such as women cocktail waitresses, models, porn stars, or prostitutes. They focus only on making sure the jobs that men tend to take pay less in comparison to the jobs that women tend to take.

The easiest way to see the sexism of comparable worth is by doing a role reversal and imagining a male version of it.

The Male Version of Comparable Worth

If a men's movement persuaded us to define "comparable worth" as paying men what it would cost for that job to be done if 50% of the people doing it were women, imagine the increased costs of buying a home. That is, imagine home costs if we had to pay what it would cost to have half the construction workers be women—walking on beams to construct roofs in high winds, digging pipelines through frozen dirt, repairing backed up sewers. If you are a woman, think of how much pay you would require before you committed to spending every working day of your life that way.

Now add to that housing cost the cost of hiring 50% women as the lumberjacks to create those beams. Add to that the cost of 50% women truckers to transport the logs to make the beams.

Truckers who are owner-operators often work 12- to 14-hour days to support their families. A neighbor of mine is such a trucker. He is still recovering from falling asleep at the wheel at two in the morning and finding his head embedded in a telephone pole. It is 8 years later, and he tells me he has never spent an hour without pain. Think of what building supplies would cost if we had to pay to have half our truckers be women.

And this is just the beginning of the increased costs of a male version of comparable worth. For example, if home construction costs doubled, the portion of our property tax that reflects home value would double. And to replace half of the volunteer men firefighters with women would doubtless require the virtual elimination of communities' abilities to rely on volunteer firefighters. This would at least triple the cost of our protection from fires. But wait . . . because the homes they are protecting now cost twice as much, making their replacement value twice as high, fire insurance could easily cost six times what it currently costs.

The increase in the cost of homes would be nothing compared to the increase in the cost of office buildings. Imagine the cost of hiring tens of thousands of women to spend their working lives on rafters outside the 40th story of buildings, feeling the cold wind destabilize the rafters, knowing, while trying to catch steel beams, that the rafters hadn't been double-checked for safety. Seven men died building the Empire State Building in New York City. Almost every major bridge is built at the cost of men's lives.

Why, then, is there no equivalent men's movement suggesting their version of comparable worth? It has to do with a boy's socialization.

He learns at an early age that it doesn't do any good to say that a lineman should have comparable worth to the quarterback, or the right fielder to a pitcher. Instead, he learns that if he wants the pay or the publicity of the quarterback, he's got to make himself the best at that position. On the other hand, he learns that if he is willing to sacrifice his body to be a lineman, he'll have a better chance of making the team. Reality becomes a boy's reality; and his reality includes trade-offs. When he grows up, then, he wouldn't think of becoming a construction worker and then complaining his paycheck was less than Alanis Morissette's $22 million per year, despite more years on the job.

The deeper truth is that both sexes do certain jobs for less than the other sex would do them. If we began to require half of secretaries to be men, the chances are the costs of hiring a secretary would go up. For these reasons, comparable worth with a bias toward either sex would be an economic disaster.

The solution? Well, it has more to do with being an adult than being an economist. Being an adult involves taking responsibility for the trade-offs involved in each of our choices, as opposed to making a choice of entering lower-paying, fulfilling fields and then complaining we aren't paid more than those in the killing fields. The former is "adult" economics; the latter is "adolescent" economics.

To politically succeed in the quest for women having both more options and equal pay is not comparable worth, but is incomparably good politics. To expect that outcome is not comparable worth, but adolescent economics. To demand that outcome is not comparable worth, but spoiled brat economics. As every economist knows, we get more of what we pay for.

CHAPTER 14

Conclusion: Toward a New Vision of Men and Women

If I have a dream for *Why Men Earn More,* it is that it has indeed planted the seeds I identified in the Introduction. Seeds to grow a transition from female "victim power" to female earning power; from employee-versus-employer litigation to employee-and-employer communication; from diversity training as a monologue to diversity training as a dialogue; from the disappointed dreams of the "Have it all era" to the balanced dreams of the "Trade-offs era"; from responding to women passive-aggressively to responding to women honestly; from the "Era of the multi-option woman and no option man" to the "Era of the multi-option woman and multi-option man" (an era that features more women running companies with lots of input from men, and more dads caring for children with lots of input from moms); from the assumption that men have more power because men earn more money to the understanding that the traditional male definition of power—feeling obligated to earn money someone else spends while he dies sooner—is more akin to powerlessness; from the assumption that men-have-the-power-and-women-don't to the understanding that both sexes have areas of power and powerlessness.

If this book has set the stage for effective change, it has given enough specifics to make each of those transitions more than rhetoric, and enough direction to make it clear that anyone who follows all these ways to higher pay is probably not doing a careful evaluation of trade-offs. A woman following all 25 ways is in danger of becoming an imitation man. Just as women's socialization has inhibited higher pay at work, so men's socialization has inhibited greater fulfillment in life.

If this book is effective on a personal level, you will use it to make higher pay the servant of a better life, and never to become the servant to higher pay. This perspective has led most of my friends to assume that doing what I love and relationships have been my highest priority, so when I started this book on pay, one of my friends asked, "Okay, now you seem to be trying to put it all together. Any 'half dozen recommendations' on how to be at the top of a field you love, have a happy marriage and still have a nice home and all of that?"

Top Six Recommendations toward Doing What You Love, Being with Those You Love, and Still Being Economically Secure

First, put in the hours. The clearest revelation of my research that's a different take from the normal self-help book is that if you're going to march to the beat of your own drum and still be a success, you have to be willing to "do the time"—to put in long hours. However, long hours are worthless if you're neglecting family. So the deeper question is, How can you put in the hours without putting out your family?

Second, hire. My rule-of-thumb: Hire-out what would take you 20 to 30 hours a week to do and put those 20 to 30 hours into becoming among the best in your field. For example, hire out everything that is repetitive and unskilled that you do not enjoy doing (cleaning, laundry, shopping, errands, repairs, lawn-mowing, weeding). Repetitive, unskilled labor costs little, and you'll be employing someone who needs the money. Next . . .

Third, work from home. Then every day is "take your daughter to work day" and "take your son to work day." If you take frequent breaks but keep your door shut when not on break you can tune in to the ebb and flow of both family and work. Next . . .

Fourth, form community, but don't be imprisoned by the community you form. Social contact with other writers allows me to not personalize the loneliness of a writer or the critiques of editors. But becoming too enmeshed in the structure of your profession can lead you down the path of being the best at their values and priorities rather than creating your own. For example, in the medical field the funding for drug research becomes a Siren that seduces enmeshment in the value of drugs rather than the potential for yoga, meditation, water, and vegetables. In my field, an author who looks at what is being published overlooks what is not being published. For the last third of a century books on women's perspectives have been published and a "woman industry" has been formed, so an author too enmeshed in the values of the professions of writing, publishing, psychology, gender studies, human resources, literature, sociology, or social work will not even know what a men's issue is. Next . . .

Fifth, choose your partner carefully. Make sure your family commitments are not sending you down the money track if that's not right for you. Make sure your priorities and your partner's are on the same page. And as for the kids . . .

Sixth, help your children use their time and your time well. For example, when they ask for the gift of your time, consider turning that gift into three gifts: Tell them you'll do that as long as they do more reading, a chore, practice the piano, or do something for another family member (including you). What you ask of them should get them to stretch. Then you'll know each time you give, you will be giving three times: the gift of your time; the gift of their growth; the gift of modeling for them how a parent can do what she or he loves, provide for their family, and love their family.

It helps your family to have friends, and this book has a tough-to-absorb message, so how do you talk about it and keep your friends?

"How Do I Share the Pay Gap Info in This Book and Still Have Friends?"

There are three ways to keep friends and share the pay gap part of this book: the first, to listen; the second, to listen; the third, to listen. On the presentation side, think ahead about how to present what you now know vis-a-vis what they will still be hearing in the news.

Test yourself for a minute. The next time a friend reading a newspaper tells you, "You're wrong about men and women earning the same money for equal work. I'm reading a headline saying, 'Male Ph.D.'s Earn More Than Female Ph.D.'s,' " how would you respond? Which factors would you ask your friend to check?

Hopefully, you remembered to have your friend check whether the men had more Ph.D.'s in the sciences; the women, in the humanities. Now suppose you did, and your friend responds, "It says here that even women with Ph.D.'s in engineering earn less than men with Ph.D.'s in engineering." Did you remember to check subfields, remembering, for example, that chemical engineers of either sex get paid more than biomedical engineers of either sex, and that women are more likely to become biomedical engineers? And did you ask whether the study checked whether the men and women were working equal numbers of hours with the same number of years on the job and, especially, the same number of years of recent, uninterrupted experience with their current employer? Were equal percentages working for public as opposed to private firms? Were more of the men engineers working outdoors (e.g., on oil pipelines in Alaska vs. in a government office)? And did you ask if the study checked for whether the sexes had moved equally as often, traveled equally on the job, supervised the same number of employees, gone for equal advanced training and certificates? Just ask these questions gently.

Most important, you now know enough to not let your friend stay with the woman-as-victim argument, but to ask her or him to use that energy to help women focus on what they can do to earn more income. If your friend responds, "Suppose a woman doesn't want to work longer hours in more hazardous jobs?" You now know enough to explain that such a woman is exercising power—the power of choice—not the powerlessness of someone who has no choice but to drive a truck at two o'clock in the morning so his children will not have to do that when they get older.

If you've also been listening, you will have heard whether the friend with whom you are speaking took time off to raise the children, traveled more, worked later. Start them with their own lives. But plant the examples like seeds, otherwise they'll feel like a tree facing a hammer and nail.

Haven't Studies Similar to Those in This Book Still Found Women Earn Less?

Many other studies have controlled for a number of variables and still found women earn a little less than men. Why? In part, because only a few studies control for whether one is working in a public or private arena; exact number of hours worked; years both in the subfield and on the job; or advanced training in the subfield. But most important, no study that I know of controls for even close to all 25 factors, including any of the following five:

- Exposure to equally hazardous assignments in equally hazardous jobs;
- The extent of the job search;
- The degree to which the job has pleasant conditions;
- The willingness to move to undesirable locations at the company's behest;
- The job's exposure to wind, rain, sleet, cold, humidity, and heat.

While I know of no study controlling for any of those, I also know of none controlling for the other 20 combined.

Does This Book Prove Men Earn Less Than Women for the Same Work?

Why Men Earn More is far from the definitive study. With respect to the pay gap, the variables are too complex and overlapping for anyone to do a definitive study—perhaps ever.

I do believe, though, that when we fully weigh the 25 trade-offs men are more likely to make in the workplace, with income implications calculated and overlapping subtracted, five things will be clear:

- Women now make more money than men for the same work;
- Many other women make the same money men make for fewer sacrifices (e.g., in the armed services);
- Many unskilled women have jobs rarely made available to men (e.g., cocktail waiter; receptionist; housekeeper in a hotel; restaurant host; salesperson of women's—and often men's— clothing);

- Many skilled women have careers in which it is much more difficult for equally qualified men to find employment (e.g., dental hygienists; nurses; massage therapists; family law attorneys; gender studies teachers; nursery and first and second grade school teachers; domestic violence social workers);
- Some women professional athletes can make a living for achieving at a level not afforded to a man achieving at that same level (e.g., tennis, basketball, golf).

It is not necessarily desirable to change all these inequities, but it is disingenuous to cry victim without acknowledging any of them.

Male vs. Female Income Power

The focus on the pay gap is, in a sense, a sexist focus. It does not account for the full amount of each sex's income power, but especially neglects women's income power.

Writing the chapter on the Genetic Celebrity Pay Gap made me aware the degree to which "income power" is not just about money earned in the workplace. It is also about one's power to generate income outside the workplace, and one's spending expectations and obligations. In those two areas, women's income power becomes far more apparent.

While the genetic celebrity attracts income options without even knowing it (speeding tickets not received; the full-service at life's self-serve stations), even women who are not genetic celebrities generally benefit from at least a fraction of that during the first half century of their lives. And women who are married, while usually making less than their husbands at work, receive, in effect, half their husband's paycheck. Women pay much less into Social Security but choose less stressful careers and more balanced lives, which doubtless contributes to their longer lives and therefore receiving more from social security—plus more from virtually every government spending in which the government plays substitute husband.

Income power also cannot be measured without looking at each sex's spending expectations (what each sex is expected to spend if it is going to be valued by the other sex, parents, and peers). While I've discussed how men spend more on the six D's (dinners, drinks, dates, dances, diamonds, and driving expenses) and other direct expenses of courtship (and certainly spend more on child support, alimony, and house payments should a marriage result in divorce), women also have considerable spending expectations not incurred by men.

The most unacknowledged spending expectation among women is the amount of time spent by single mothers caring for children, not only physically, but psychologically. It is my feeling that **only a small percentage of a mother's time is normally compensated for by child support, given what a woman could make by adding these hours to workforce hours.** This time expenditure, no matter how fulfilling or valuable to mom, or no matter how costly to the dad, or dysfunctional for the children (in comparison to equal parenting), nevertheless hinders a woman's career. It is why women who have never been married and never had children earn so much more in the workplace than women who have had children.

Women's second spending expectation is "makeup." I'm defining "makeup" broadly here. Makeup is what women do to "make up" the gap between the power they have and the power they'd like to have. Men's obsession with the quasi-anorexic woman pressures women to choose between losing weight or losing men. And the pressure encourages not only more money for beauty care, but more time. Similarly, this pressure translates into some women taking more time to "get ready" for work.

This "makeup" spending expectation is tricky because a lot of women pay money for what impresses other women more than for what impresses men. That is, most men prefer kissing a woman's lips more than her lipstick, and looking in her eyes more than at her eye shadow. And while women still feel pressure to pay for the designer label, most men would pay more to see her without a stitch. Similarly, many women do still feel pressure to wear nylons and high heels, for example, feeling they need attractants to get a man to approach her to begin with, but the best men are secure enough to delight in a woman approaching them. Nevertheless, whether the outcomes are functional or dysfunctional, the woman still feels the pressure, which creates the spending expectation.

Toward a New Vision of Men and Women

In the past quarter century, men's work sacrifices were virtually invisible because we used the words "fulfillment" and "career" as if they followed each other: "fulfilling career." This inspired women to work, but by not seeing clearly the sacrifices men made to provide for their families via careers, we did a poor job preparing women for sacrifices in their careers. Therefore, the phrase "sacrificing a career" made sense because we didn't understand the sacrifices of careers.

If *Why Men Earn More* succeeds, it contributes to a new vision of men—not as a sex that used its power to develop a system that benefits men at the expense of women, but as a sex willing to die to support the wives and children they loved.

If *Why Men Earn More* succeeds, it creates a vision of men as a sex willing to establish a system so subtle yet bold in its persuasion that its sons would follow without question a definition of manhood that got boys to compete to be disposable to keep women, children, and other men alive. Men are willing to do this because they intuited that every society that survived persuaded its boys to call it "glory" to die, and labeled its boys "cowards" if a boy valued his own life when it was needed for potential sacrifice in war or in a coal mine.

Men unconsciously knew that teaching their sons to value their lives would have undermined their willingness to lose their lives. So to this day men who are called leaders still ignore their health until they are in the hospital—as with Bill Clinton's quadruple bypass heart surgery and Dick Cheney's heart attacks. And to this day, we reinforce this outcome as our leaders compete to show us who had the courage to risk death in Vietnam—a competition that could not occur were the 2004 presidential candidates Teresa Kerry and Laura Bush rather than John Kerry and George Bush.

In reality, of course, men did not develop this system. All human systems are developed by both sexes, and both sexes developed what they felt would best help their children to survive. The result of this two-sex system, though, is that, to this day, men's weakness is their facade of strength, and women's strength is their facade of weakness.

Just as women developed a role as mother that defined them so fully that to this day a mom often fails to allow a dad as equal participant, so men developed a pride in their ability to support a family that sometimes made them blind to women's capacities to be equal participants. The difference is that men passed laws to prevent themselves from doing what had once supported women as soon as women complained it was no longer supporting them. Those laws, like the Equal Pay Act of 1963, preceded the modern women's movement. Men's efforts were successful enough to quickly facilitate women having at least as much income power as men in the workplace, and more outside the workplace. Men were, paradoxically, both strong enough to keep their mouths shut about it, and too weak to open their mouths about it.

Throughout the world, wherever there is a division of labor between the sexes, both sexes reinforce it in three ways: First, both sexes discriminate against "deviants" (e.g., homosexuals); second, both sexes compete among themselves to be best (e.g., cheerleaders and football players competing among themselves to become the best cheerleaders and football players); and third, both sexes fall in love with the most successful role players—be they football player with cheerleader, or Diana Spencer with a prince.

The division of labor has meant both sexes had monopolies in their areas of responsibilities: Men's monopoly of the workplace might be called a "manopoly"; mothers' monopoly of the children might be called a "momopoly."

Despite this division of labor, when it came to the workplace, we have seen that male-dominated occupations now discriminate in favor of women; and female-dominated occupations discriminate in favor of women. By not understanding this, many female-dominated occupations emanating from the universities' liberal arts majors (sociology, literature, psychology, social work) developed an ideology of men as women's oppressors. Other female-dominated occupations have fears of male sexuality that tend to discriminate against men (e.g., nursing, nursery school teaching, and elementary school teaching), or a tendency toward protectiveness that makes men feel their greater propensity for encouraging risk-taking is not appreciated (psychology, teaching K–12 and college, government in the social services). Still other female-dominated occupations seem to have a "men need not apply" sign (the dozen or so skilled and unskilled ones discussed previously).

The new vision is not of a women's movement blaming men, or a men's movement blaming women. We need a gender transition movement helping both sexes make the transition from the rigid roles of survival to the more flexible roles that allow a balance between survival and fulfillment.

Both Sexes' Genetic Investment in the Belief That Women Earn Less

When we systematically avoid questioning a belief, it is generally because we possess a need to believe it. Could it be that most men don't question the myth that women earn about 80% of what men earn for the same work because, underneath it all, they're still into taking care of a woman? Could it be that women don't question it because, underneath it all, they are still into men's taking care of them? By blaming the system or blaming men, women will tap into men's protector instinct—and the men will either protect them to success (affirmative action, mentorship), protect them from barriers (sexual harassment), or rescue them if they fail (Women, Infant and Children programs)?

In one way or the other, men's protector instinct makes it easier for women to succeed, and easier for women if they fail. This makes women less desperate to succeed, which makes it harder for women to succeed.

"Helping" women this way is no more progressive than welfare. It is just an extension of men competing to be loved by being protectors and women defining a man's love by the degree to which he takes care of her.

The implications of these findings extend well beyond the workplace. They pose questions about our psychology, global economics, personal economics, our "sexual economics" and about our families—from getting men more involved in fathering, to reducing anger about housework, to helping women have hope for escaping abusive relationships.

In the "Genes" of a Bureaucracy

Would a movement such as the women's movement perpetuate victim power if it were dysfunctional to women? Not consciously. But unconsciously, the perpetuation of victim power is in the "genes" of any bureaucracy. A once-upon-a-time story illustrates the dynamic:

Once upon a time, a group of boys at Equal Elementary School took a special course in which they discovered that the boys' grades were only 80% of the girls' grades. They were outraged. Their teacher, Mr. Wright, explained, "This is because 'the system' is against you: Your female teachers value female niceties, female obedient behavior, female writing style, female class contributions, even the way females ask questions rather than speak out." Mr. Wright called this matriarchy. He explained this was sexism. He encouraged the children to protest to the Board of Education.

At first the newspapers called them "jock strap burners," but within 10 years, the teacher had become famous and departments of boys' studies were in all the "progressive" schools around the country. No one even thought there should be departments of girls' studies—they

already had mostly female teachers, the girls were already doing better both academically and socially, more girls were already graduating from high school, going to college, and graduating from college.

One day, though, some of the teachers discovered that the boys' grades were now better than the girls' grades, if the boys attended class equally and put in equal hours of homework.

All the boys, girls, and even the teacher jumped up and down for joy when they saw the new findings. Then Billy spoke up, "If you publish these findings, Mr. Wright, will we still have a Department of Boys' Studies?" Mr. Wright hesitated. Then Johnny said, "I want to be a Boys' Studies teacher when I grow up, just like you, Mr. Wright."

All the boys and girls thought and thought and thought. Mr. Wright thought, too. Mr. Wright wanted his job. No one knew what to do.

Then Mr. Wright jumped for joy. He noticed that the boys only did better if they attended school more, but they didn't, so on average, they were still doing worse than the girls.

Mr. Wright and all the girls and boys agreed those would be the findings that should be published. No one ever mentioned the other findings again. And Mr. Wright and all the boys and girls, and the boys' studies department, lived happily ever after. The end.

When a group needs to be oppressed so its members can keep their jobs, it becomes "oppression-dependent." While all bureaucracies perpetuate the need for themselves, this propensity is especially strong for the women's movement because of thousands of years of female socialization to find a savior—to "drop the handkerchief" and discover who would pick it up. And it is especially dangerous for the women's movement because, **just as the Sirens tempted male sailors to crash into the rocks due to male dependence on female sexuality, so male saviors are really male Sirens who tempt women to crash into the rocks of dependence on the belief in discrimination.**

Toward Solutions to Improve Our Children's Lives

The Impact of These Findings on Affirmative Action

Affirmative action's positive contributions include encouraging women into the workforce and expanding sensitivity to virtually every level of women's economic and psychological needs. The result has been an extraordinary expansion of women's talents in an extraordinarily short historical period. Women now have concrete role models in virtually every field. We have enriched women's lives and enhanced corporations by diversifying the talent from which they can draw. It is difficult to overstate the positive values these affirmative action taxes have catalyzed.

Once we are clear that men do not get paid more than women for the same work, it becomes time to phase out the affirmative action tax and psychological affirmative action. This doesn't mean that affirmative action was necessarily a mistake, just that it has reached its historical point of diminishing returns.

If the subsidies to women participation are not phased out, I believe our children will inherit problems in four areas: foreign competition; domestic passive-aggressiveness; morality; and taxes.

Foreign Competition

Affirmative action effectively adds a tax to domestic labor that makes it more difficult to compete with foreign labor. This increases the cost of American products, leading to fewer sales. Or, it leads to "American" products being produced outside America. Thus fewer Americans are hired, including fewer American women. Whenever the government requires companies to pay workers more than the market would bear, to pay for long vacations and extraordinary health benefits, the unemployment rate soars and the country risks the political rebellion now happening in countries like France, Germany, and Sweden.

Domestic Passive-Aggressiveness

Now there's a term! When someone feels forced to do something that doesn't work for them, they often become passive-aggressive—they say "yes" overtly and do what works for them covertly. Men know what this means when women do it ("Oh, I'd love to make love, but I have a headache"), but men have their own version. Many men employers (and, increasingly, women employers) are beginning to fear hiring women. They fear that if a woman doesn't get promoted as quickly as affirmative action has led her to expect, they'll be sued. So they become passive-aggressive ("Oh, I'd love to hire her, but I have a special need for him"). Dozens of employers have shared with me—privately—their overt willingness to obey affirmative action mandates so they don't get into trouble with the government, but their fears of hiring women. As one executive put it, "In my experience, they're walking lawsuits." The 1.5 million women suing Wal-Mart for sex discrimination (even as men who are refused jobs in the many Wal-Mart departments that are 90%–100% female say nothing[1]) reinforces that fear.

Morality

Affirmative action leaves our children with a *morality* question. Worldwide, most people feel it is immoral to pay one person more than another for the same work. They are open to mandates to eliminate that, but are not open to mandates to eliminate that for one group only to institute it for another group. Even if it could be justified economically, and even if employers did not respond passive-aggressively when forced to pay equally for unequal work, they would still consider it immoral. I agree.

Taxes

Government agencies do not need to worry about competing, so they can do much more affirmative action hiring. The only restraint on government discrimination is the taxpayer-as-voter. Many taxpayers are sensing we have now passed the adolescent stage of woman-as-worker; it is time for the adult stage of woman-as-worker, in which the government can stop treating the woman as a child.

The Future of Affirmative Action: An Anti-Trust Tool to Break Up Gender Monopolies

None of this suggests that affirmative action needs to be wiped out of our political consciousness or that it is not an effective transition tool for a generation or two. But it should be used as a tool to break up monopoly hiring, just as the Justice Department would use anti-trust legislation to break up a monopoly. For example, when a profession is perhaps 80% or more one sex—such as welders, roofers, plumbers, coal miners, or, on the other hand, nurses, teachers of nursery schools, elementary schools, or gender studies, human resource personnel, social workers, receptionists, secretaries, flight attendants, cocktail servers, or men's wear clerks at Wal-Marts—then it is appropriate to begin checking the system for conscious or unconscious discrimination that reinforces a gender monopoly. We would check whether the schools are educating girls as much as boys to these options; whether the profession has adequate outreach to the other sex; and whether, once hired, the atmosphere is user-friendly to the other sex's different style and sensitivities.

Do feminists favor affirmative action because they are biased in favor of women or because they believe in helping people who are left out of the opportunity market? There is an easy litmus test. An adult feminist, one who genuinely cares about equal opportunity, would put no more emphasis on opportunities for women than on men becoming nurses, elementary school teachers, flight attendants, cocktail waiters; or opportunities for boys to not drop out of school, but attend college and graduate schools in equal numbers, get into social work programs, teacher education programs, and, now, even theological seminaries. An adult feminist favors affirmative action programs to assure that men are no longer dying 7 years sooner, or comprising 93% of the people who die at work, or becoming 85% of the homeless, the only ones required to register for the draft, and committing suicide 4 times as frequently.

Affirmative action will have more integrity when we make a transition from affirmative action that excludes men to affirmative action that includes men.

Affirmative Action vs. Alternative Medicines

Affirmative action is institutional surgery—it cuts open an institution and adds what is deemed needed: some women, some African Americans. . . . Sometimes surgery is necessary, but when we visit only the surgeon we skip past alternative cures.

Alternative cures begin with alternative questions: Suppose we ask, "How can we create high-level opportunities for women that will still allow them to be with their family, give children and dads more of each other, decrease corporate costs, and increase corporate benefits?"

One solution that potentially addresses all of these problems is worth considering as a second opinion prior to surgery. That alternative, team jobs, is suggested by Cambodia's two premiers. Here's how it might work in a corporation for the position of an executive vice president working about 80 hours per week and making, with stock options, salary and other benefits, between, let's say, $1 and $2 million per year. Coexecutive vice presidents would each work approximately 45 hours a week (35–40 hours separately, 5 to 10 hours overlapping, sharing the same office and phones).

Wouldn't a corporation lose money? Not if its package for the coexecutive vice presidents is negotiated to pay for both what they would normally pay for one. Unrealistic? As in, who would take an executive vice presidency for one-half the pay when she or he could perhaps be offered an executive vice presidency for full pay? The answer: Anyone who wants a life. Anyone who wants a role in her or his family. Balanced people. People other people might enjoy working with.

Obviously this won't work for every position. But I challenge the assumption that one exhausted mind in an exhausted body providing money for a seldom-seen family is always better than two minds in less-exhausted bodies each leading balanced lives. This will open up competition for jobs structured like this to thousands of competent women who wouldn't touch a 70–80 hour week and exhausting travel. As for men, traveling and 70–80 hour weeks are a setup for divorce. Men who are having trouble at home soon have more trouble at work—they're more vulnerable to affairs, sexual harassing, drinking, gambling, and drugs. It can make a corporation tipsy. And men who divorce are 10 times as likely to commit suicide as are women who divorce.[2]

Updating Divorce; Updating Dating

Two barriers to the goal of gender transition are divorce and dating. Divorce first . . .

During the last three decades, women have been less flexible at work than they might have become, because divorces have resulted in the mother's obtaining custody of the children about 90% of the time, so her flexibility has to be with them, not her job. (Deadlines at work are important; emergencies at home are vital.)

Assigning children of divorce to mothers has created a self-fulfilling prophecy of women-as-mothers and men-as-wallets. Divorce recreated the old division of labor even as it created the new division of family. To say nothing of turning millions of children of divorce into fatherless children.

The assumption that the workplace is biased in men's favor leads us to assume that any man who does not earn at least as much as a woman must not be very competent, either as a worker or as a father. After divorce, men are caught in a Catch-22: If they don't earn enough, they are deprived of the children because they are too irresponsible to be a father; if they earn a lot, they are deprived of the children because they are better as wallets. Our blindness to the man who is either successful or unsuccessful at work being successful as a father helps reinforce the myth that women are better mothers than men are fathers, which reinforces men earning more at work.

Dating second . . .

I gave many examples (for example, the Six D's) of how we socialize our sons to earn more at an early age by continuing to give our sons the expectation to pay for girls while giving our daughters the option of paying for boys. However, the economics of sex won't change until our attitude toward sex changes.

One part of our attitude won't easily change: Boys' desire for sex is stronger than girls' (most boys have one condition for sex: "I'm attracted"; girls prefer nine conditions be met: attraction, mutual respect, self-confidence . . .).[3] This creates a starting point of boys earning more to pay for the greater demand on the shorter supply.

We then magnify the gap between male demand and female supply by sending the message that sex is dirty and telling our sons to initiate the dirt. We send the sex-is-dirty message when we see our children watch violence on television, yet we leave the television on, but express outrage that we couldn't turn off the television as we see them watch Janet Jackson bare her breast.

With the message that sex is worse than killing, we tell our sons there's something worse about you than girls for wanting it more. Aside from making our sons feel shame, it makes them feel that paying is the least they can do. He becomes like a nation that is desperate for oil and can't get rid of its SUV drive; she becomes like an

OPEC nation wanting to make sure she keeps it in short enough supply to keep the value up.

Once our sons are paying more for the girls they value more, our daughters begin to think of themselves as valued more the more boys pay. And so the dance begins that leads to boys learning to be earning.

Men don't protest the financial inequality, in part because the person who initiates wants the period of time between eye contact and intercourse to be as short as possible to shorten the period of potential rejection. Protesting would be interpreted as whining, and whining would lengthen his period of potential rejection. Besides, earning money has not just been his source of female love, approval, and respect, but of his male friends', and his parents' love.

Even in private, few men will express their feelings about being taken for granted financially until another man brings it up and no one appears to be disagreeing. Then, well, Pandora found her match! In front of a woman, though, the tiger retreats to pussy cat, and he fears that even hesitating to pay makes him appear cheap, and it's all downhill from there. In brief, it's easier to earn more than be rejected more often.

While the women's movement helped women protest their unilateral services to men to the point that virtually every woman would be outraged if a law required her to clean house for her ex, no men's movement made men feel outraged at laws requiring them to pay for a home for their ex.

Meantime our daughters, largely unaware of this, are aware that men are the sex with less education that does worse in school, yet they end up earning more. All this seems like it must be the result of discrimination against women rather than the pressure on men.

Why men earn more at work cannot be separated from the lessons boys learn about why they need to earn more to pay for their first date, or what men learn about why they need to earn more after the birth of their first child. When men can earn less and be valued more, we will unlock our sons from being human doings and free them to become human beings. Our daughters deserve that.

Bibliography

Abramms, Bob, and George F. Simons, *Cultural Diversity Sourcebook* (Amherst, MA: HRD Press, 1996).

Alessandra, Tony, *10 Qualities of Charismatic People* (New York: Simon & Schuster, 2002).

Barnett, Rosalind C., and Caryl Rivers, *She Works/He Works* (San Francisco, CA: HarperCollins, 1996).

Bennis, Warren, *On Becoming a Leader*, rev. ed. (New York: Perseus, 2003).

Berkowitz, Robert, *What Men Won't Tell You But Women Need to Know* (New York: Morrow, 1990).

Blau, Francine, *The Economics of Women, Men, and Work*, 3rd ed. (New York: Prentice Hall, 1997).

Boaz, David, ed., *Toward Liberty* (Washington, D.C.: Cato Institute, 2002).

Bolles, Richard, *What Color Is Your Parachute?* (Berkeley, CA: Ten Speed Press, 2005).

Branden, Nathaniel, *The Six Pillars of Self-Esteem* (New York: Bantam Books, 1994).

Brodow, Ed, *Beating the Success Trap* (New York: HarperCollins, 2003).

Bruce, Tammy, *The New Thought Police* (New York: Crown, 2003).

Canfield, Jack, and Mark Victor Hansen, *Chicken Soup for the Unsinkable Soul* (Deerfield Beach, FL: HCI, 1999).

Cathcart, Jim, *The Acorn Principle* (New York: St. Martin's Press, 2000).

Chavez, Linda, and Daniel Gray, *Betrayal* (New York: Crown, 2004).

Chaykowski, Richard P., and Lisa M. Powell, ed., *Women and Work* (Ontario, Canada: McGill-Queen's University Press, 1999).

Cose, Ellis, *A Man's World* (New York: HarperCollins, 1995).

Edelston, Martin, and Marion Buhagiar, *"I" Power: The Secrets of Great Business in Bad Times* (Fort Lee, NJ: Barricade Books, 1992).

Farson, Richard, *Management of the Absurd* (New York: Simon & Schuster, 1996).

Friday, Nancy, *The Power of Beauty* (New York: HarperCollins, 1996).

Fripp, Patricia, *Make It So You Don't Have To Fake It* (Mechanicsburg, PA: Executive Books, 2000).

Furchtgott-Roth, Diana, and Christine Stolba, *The Feminist Dilemma* (Washington, D.C.: AEI Press, 2001).

Gilder, George, *Wealth and Poverty (ICS Series in Self-Governance)* (Oakland, CA: ICS Press, 1993).

Goldsmith, Marshall, ed, et al., *Coaching for Leadership* (San Francisco, CA: Pfeiffer, 2002).

Halpern, Howard, *Cutting Loose: An Adult's Guide to Coming to Terms with Your Parents* (New York: Fireside, 1990).

Hammer, Kay, *Workplace Warrior* (New York: AMACOM, 2000).

Helgesen, Sally, *Web of Inclusion* (New York: Doubleday, 1995).

Jeffers, Susan, *Feel the Fear and Do It Anyway* (New York: Ballantine Books, 1987).

Johnson, Spencer, *Who Moved My Cheese?* (New York: G.P. Putnam's Sons, 1999).

Kaye, Beverly, and Sharon Jordan-Evans, *Love It, Don't Leave It: 26 Ways to Get What You Want at Work* (San Francisco, CA: Berrett-Koehler, 2003).

Kiyosaki, Robert T., with Sharon L. Lechter, *Rich Dad, Poor Dad: What the Rich Teach Their Kids About Money—That the Poor and Middle Class Do Not!* (New York: Warner Books, in association with CASHFLOW Technologies, 1997).

Kofman, Fred, *The Spirit of Conscious Business* (Boston: Shambhala, 2004).

Loney, Martin, *The Pursuit of Division* (Canada: McGill-Queen's University Press, 1998).

Lynch, Frederick R., *The Diversity Machine* (New York: Simon & Schuster, 1997).

Minetor, Randi, *Breadwinner Wives and the Men They Marry* (Far Hills, New Jersey: New Horizon Press, 2002).

Morse, Jennifer Roback, *Love & Economics: Why the Laissez-Faire Family Doesn't Work* (Dallas, TX: Spence Publishing, 2001).

Mundis, Jerrold J., *Earn What You Deserve* (New York: Bantam Books, 1995).

Peters, Tom, *Thriving on Chaos: Handbook for a Management Revolution* (New York: Harper & Rowe, 1987).

Robbins, Tony, *Awaken the Giant Within*, reprint ed. (New York: Free Press, 1992).

Robinson, John P., and Geoffrey Godbey, *Time for Life* (University Park, PA: Pennsylvania State University Press, 1997).

Sowell, Thomas, *Civil Rights: Rhetoric or Reality* (New York: Perennial, 1985).

Stanny, Barbara, *Secrets of Six-Figure Women* (New York: HarperCollins, 2002).

Sukiennik, Diane et al., *The Career Fitness Program* (New York: Prentice Hall, 2003).

Vernon, Lillian, *An Eye For Winners* (New York: HarperCollins, 1996).

Wilber, Ken, *A Brief History of Everything*, 2nd ed. (Boston: Shambhala, 2001).

Young, Cathy, *Ceasefire* (New York: Free Press, 1999).

Youngs, Bettie B., *How to Develop Self-Esteem in Your Child* (New York: Ballantine, 1993).

Notes

INTRODUCTION   How the Journey Began, p. xiii–xxxiii

1. "Family" incorporates both straight and gay families. As a rule, gay men have had more freedom than heterosexual men to choose careers that are more fulfilling and pay less due to less obligation to support children. As gay couples marry and raise children, their choice of trade-offs will become similarly limited.

2. Based on raw data from the U.S. Bureau of the Census, *Survey of Program and Income Participation (SIPP)*, 2001 Panel, wave 6 (2003 data). Married men working full-time earned $47,467 per year on average, their never-married men counterparts $29,420.

   [80 cents to the dollar] U.S. Department of Labor, Bureau of Labor Statistics news release, "Usual Weekly Earnings of Wage and Salary Workers: Second Quarter 2004," July 20, 2004. Full-time workers who are female earned 80.1% of what their male counterparts earned. In the first quarter of 2004, the figure was 79.7% (U.S. Department of Labor, Bureau of Labor Statistics news release, "Usual Weekly Earnings of Wage and Salary Workers: First Quarter 2004," April 16, 2004).

3. Women actually would give their employer 69% more for the dollar: The $1 paid men divided by the original 59 cents paid women. (For example, if women were paid 50% of men's pay, the employer would get twice as much from women for the same money or 100% more, not 50% more.)

4. June O'Neill, "An Argument Against Comparable Worth," *Comparable Worth: Issue for the '80s,* a consultation of the U.S. Commission on Civil Rights, Vol. I, June 6–7, 1984, 179.

5. See Note 2. U.S. Department of Labor, Bureau of Labor Statistics news release, "Usual Weekly Earnings of Wage and Salary Workers: Second Quarter 2004", July 20, 2004.

6. U.S. Department of the Treasury, Internal Revenue Service, Statistics of Income Division. Unpublished Table E2-1, "Number of Male-Operated Sole Proprietorships by Six Broad Industry Categories, 1985–2000"; Table E2-3, "Business Net Income of Male-Operated Sole Proprietorships by Six Broad Industry Categories, 1985–2000"; Table E3-1, "Number of Female-Operated Sole Proprietorships by Six Broad Industry Categories, 1985–2000"; and Table E3-3 "Business Net Income of Female-Operated Sole Proprietorships by Six Broad Industry Categories, 1985–2000." In 2000, an estimated 12.2 million men-owned businesses had combined net incomes of $163.9 billion, or $13,460 on average. An estimated 7.4 million women-owned businesses had combined net incomes of $48.7 billion, or $6,566 on average.

7. Mark Sieling, *Monthly Labor Review,* June 1984, 32. His source is the U.S. Bureau of Labor Statistics, *1981 Survey of Professional, Administrative, Technical, and Clerical Pay (PATC sur-*

vey). The *Monthly Labor Review* is a publication of the Bureau of Labor Statistics. The USBLS did not record the gender of the workers, but Mark Sieling derived it from the raw data from those companies that did include the gender. The USBLS has updated this survey, calling it the Occupational Compensation Survey (OCS), but no one has repeated Mark Sieling's efforts.

8. Laurie A. Morgan, "Glass-Ceiling Effect or Cohort Effect? A Longitudinal Study of the Gender Earnings Gap for Engineers, 1982 to 1989," *American Sociological Review* 63 (August 1998); 479–493.

9. Jessie Bernard, *The Future of Marriage* (New York: World Publishing, 1972).

10. *U.S. Census of Population: 1960, Subject Reports: Marital Status* (Washington, DC: U.S. Department of Commerce), 112–113, Table 6.

11. *Economic Report of the President, Transmitted to the Congress January 1973* (Washington, DC: U.S. Government Printing Office, 1973), 105.

12. American Council on Education data, cited in Thomas Sowell, *Affirmative Action Reconsidered* (Washington, DC: American Enterprise Institute, 1975), 33. Table 7, "Academic Year Salaries by Sex and Marital Status, 1968–69." The never-married, unpublished women at teaching institutions earned $13,075; the men, $9,027. Never-married women with publications and without publications earned more than never-married men with and without publications at both the top research universities and the teaching universities. There was no category in which the never-married men earned equally to the never-married women.

13. Bernard, *The Future of Marriage*, unnumbered end page, Table 20, "Some Selected Socioeconomic Variables among Never-Married White Men and Women 45 to 54 Years of Age."

14. U.S. Census Bureau's Survey of Income and Program Participation, 2001 Panel, wave 2. The exact median earnings for the women are $46,896; for the men, $39,996. Latest available data as of 2004. I began investigating this in 1990. The gap was about the same then—**women earned 116% of what their male counterparts earned**—as the graph below indicates. Note that the graph has three different parameters from Figure 1 to the text: the graph says "no children present," which is a less perfect control than the "never had children" of Figure 1, since women between 45 and 54 who have "no children present" may nevertheless have had children, and therefore taken time away from the workforce to raise them; the graph also has higher education and work requirements. I relaxed these requirements for Figure 1 in the text to get larger numbers, to see if the gap still held when the numbers were larger. Here are the findings in graph form:

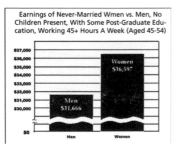

U.S. Bureau of the Census, "Current Population Survey, March, 1990." Data compiled on request by Bob Cohen of Mathematica Policy Research, March 10, 1991.

15. U.S. Bureau of the Census, unpublished data from *Employment and Earnings,* Table D-20, "Median Weekly Earnings of Part-time Wage and Salary Workers by Selected Characteristics." In the first quarter of 2004, the median weekly earnings of men, 16 and over, who were working part-time were $180; while for women the figure was $198, or 110% of the men's.

16. Based on raw data from the U.S. Census Bureau's Current Population Survey (CPS), January–March 2004. Hours worked are medians.

17. Lawrence C. Baker, "Differences in Earnings Between Male and Female Physicians," *The New England Journal of Medicine* 334, no. 15 (April 11, 1996): 960–964. Table 1. Dr. Baker is at the Department of Health Research and Policy, Stanford University Medical School.
18. Credit to Joyce McHugh for this conceptualization.
19. Tim McGuire, "Generosity Is an Elusive Quality in Schools, Workplaces," *St. Louis Post-Dispatch,* April 5, 2004, E2.
20. U.S. Department of Labor, Bureau of Labor Statistics, in cooperation with state and federal agencies, Table 4, "Fatal Occupational Injuries and Employment by Selected Worker Characteristics, 2002," *Census of Fatal Occupational Injuries.*

CHAPTER 1   Field of Dreams

1. See, for example, Marsha Sinctar, *Do What You Love, The Money Will Follow,* reissue edition, March 4, 1989.
2. Les Krantz, ed., *The Jobs Rated Almanac,* 6th ed. (New York: Ballantine Books, 2002), 3–6. The *Almanac* is done in conjunction with Careerjournal.com of the *Wall Street Journal.*
3. Ibid., 6.
4. U.S. Bureau of Labor Statistics, Table A-26, "Usual Weekly Earnings of Full-Time Wage and Salary Workers by Detailed Occupation and Sex, Annual Averages 2003" (unpublished table). Occupations marked n/a were not reported in the BLS table.
5. Ibid. It appears that the four with n/a are also predominantly male jobs.
6. Bureau of Labor Statistics, Table 39, "Median Weekly Earnings of Full-Time Wage and Salary Workers by Detailed Occupation and Sex," *Employment and Earnings* (Washington, DC: U.S. BLS, 2004), 249–253. Also, unpublished Table A-26, "Usual Weekly Earnings of Employed Full-Time Wage and Salary Workers by Detailed Occupation and Sex, Annual Averages 2003."
7. Ibid.
8. Ibid.
9. National Association of College and Employers (NACE), "Average Yearly Salary Offers—Bachelor's Degree Candidates," *Salary Survey: A Study of 2002–03 Beginning Offers. September 2003* 42, no. 4 (Fall 2003): 6–7, 10–11.
10. Bureau of Labor Statistics, *Employment and Earnings,* 249–253. Table 39.
11. Bureau of Labor Statistics, Table A-26. "Usual Weekly Earnings of Employed Full-Time Wage and Salary Workers by Detailed Occupation and Sex, Annual Averages 2003" (unpublished table). To be eligible for this table, the occupations listed had to have at least 3,000 male plus 3,000 female workers, increasing the probability that these wages' averages are statistically significant.
12. Engineers who sell their employer's product.
13. Matthew Barakat, "Women Narrow the Salary Gap: Male Workers Earn Less in Some Fields, Survey Finds," *Associated Press,* July 4, 2000. The *Working Women* survey also found that in occupational therapy, women average over $39,000, exceeding male occupational therapists by more than $7,000 per year; and women physicists earn over $65,000, about $400 more than their male counterparts.
14. National Association of Colleges and Employers (NACE), "Average Yearly Salary," Offers—Bachelor's Degree Candidates," Salary Survey: A Study of 2002–03 Beginning Offers. September 2003, Fall 2003, Vol. 42 No. 4, 8–11.
15. Ibid.

CHAPTER 2   The Field-with-Higher-Yield-Formula: One to Five

1. Peter McCarron, *Journal of the Royal Society of Medicine* (August 2003).
2. Karen Kaplan and Alex Pham, "Industry Downturn Hasn't Killed Tech's Big Appetite for Top Talent," *Los Angeles Times,* December 9, 2001, C1.

3. Michael Duffy, "How to Fix Our Intelligence," *Time,* April 26, 2004, 30.
4. Lisa Girion, "Wage Gap Continues to Vex Women," *The Los Angeles Times,* February 11, 2001, national edition, W1-2. Girion refers to a study by Heather Boushey of the Economic Policy Institute.
5. Arnaud Chevalier, "Motivation, Expectations, and the Gender Pay Gap for UK Graduates" (paper presented at the Royal Economic Society Annual Conference, Warwick, England, April 7–9, 2003).
6. R. McNabb, S. Pal, and P. Sloane, "Gender Differences in Educational Attainment: The Case of University Students in England and Wales," *Economica* 69 (2002): 481–503.
7. Girion, "Wage Gap Continues."
8. Josephine Mazzuca, "Teen Career Picks: The More Things Change," Gallup/Education and Youth, May 13, 2003.
9. Judith Kleinfeld, "Contrition Feminist-Style: The AAUW's 1998 Report, Gender Gaps," *The Women's Freedom Network Newsletter* (November/December 1998): 2, 14–15.
10. Telephone interview with Zoe Woodworth, Carnegie Mellon University student, February 23, 1998, by Sophia Ruiz.
11. Telephone interview with Sally Helgesen, February 24, 2003, by Warren Farrell.
12. Telephone interview with Cathey Cotton, founder of MetaSearch, February 27, 1998, by Sophia Ruiz and Warren Farrell.
13. California Healthline, "Boston Globe Examines Increase in Nursing School Applicants," August 12, 2004.
14. Eve Tahmincioglu, "Men Are Much in Sights of Nursing Recruiters," *New York Times,* April 13, 2002, national edition, sec. 10.
15. Sara Corbett, "The Last Shift," *New York Times Magazine,* March 16, 2003, 58–61.
16. Tahmincioglu, "Men Are Much in Sights of Nursing Recruiters."
17. Ibid.
18. Rebecca Vesely, "Rx for the Nursing Shortage," *Alameda-Star Times,* July 8, 2003.
19. U.S. Department of Education, National Center for Statistics, Table 255.
20. Bureau of Labor Statistics, Table A-7.
21. Bureau of Labor Statistics, 2003, cited in Les Christie, "The Top Ten Most Dangerous Jobs in America," *CNN/Money,* October 13, 2003.
22. Bureau of Labor Statistics, Table 39, "Median Weekly Earnings of Full-Time Wage and Salary Workers by Detailed Occupational Sex," *Employment and Earnings,* (Washington, DC: U.S. B.L.S., 2001), 210–215.
23. Bureau of Labor Statistics, "National Census of Fatal Occupational Injuries 2002" (press release, Sept. 17, 2003).
24. Christie, "The Top Ten Most Dangerous Jobs in America."
25. Ibid.
26. Ibid.
27. [Iraq] Defense Manpower Data Center, Sept. 30, 2003. Supplied by U.S. Navy Captain Lory Manning, director, "Women in the Military" project at the Women's Research and Education Institute (a policy think tank in Washington, DC).

    [female] Department of Defense, Directorate for Information Operations and Reports, as of July 24, 2004, from http://www.dior.whs.mil/mmid/casualty/castop.htm. Women accounted for 13 of 556 hostile deaths.
28. Department of Defense, Directorate for Information Operations and Reports, as of July 24, 2004, women accounted for 7 of 208 nonhostile deaths.
29. Ibid.
30. Ibid.
31. U.S. Department of Defense, Table B-38 FY Table B-29 FY 2002, "Active Component Enlisted Members by Occupational Area, Service, and Gender," http://www.defenselink.

mil/prhome/poprep2002/appendixb/b_29.htm (accessed August 16, 2004). Among the enlisted, 48% of women (vs. 18% of men) are in the safer areas of medical or administrative services.

32. Department of Defense, Directorate for Information Operations and Reports, as of July 24, 2004, from http://www.dior.whs.mil/mmid/casualty/castop.htm.

33. Ibid.

34. GlobalSecurity.org, May 15, 2004, http://www.globalsecurity.org/military/ops/iraq_orbat. htm.

35. Defense Finance and Accounting Service, 2004 Pay Table, "Basic Pay—Effective January 1, 2004." E-2 monthly basic pay for less than two cumulative years of service is $1,338. See http://www.dfas.mil/money/milpay/pay/2004paytable.pdf.

36. Military Pay Resources, "Combat Pay Varies, but It's Generally an Additional $150 a Month" (150 × 12 = 1800) April 3, 2003. Their source: Bureau of Labor Statistics, U.S. Department of Labor. See http://www.militarypay.com/US%20Military/Military%20Pay.html.

37. Military Pay Resources, "Annual Salaries for Sales Clerks at Clothing Stores ($26,780)" April 3, 2003. Their source: Bureau of Labor Statistics.

38. Defense Finance and Accounting Service, 2004 Pay Table.

39. Mohammed Al Rehaief's story was featured in a movie about Jessica Lynch on NBC called "Saving Jessica Lynch."

40. Shoshana Johnson is a single mother of a two-year-old girl.

41. Rena Singer, "S. African Women Gain Ground Below Surface," USA Today, May 17, 2002.

42. Telephone interview with Lance Hough, an Alaskan commercial canner in the 1990s, on April 11, 2004.

43. See also Kate O'Beirne, "An Army of Jessicas," National Review, May 19, 2003, 40.

44. Women are prohibited from Special Forces and in submarines, in infantry and artillery, as combat engineers, in some air defense units, and on attack helicopters.

45. O'Beirne, "An Army of Jessicas."

46. Ibid.

47. Ibid.

58. Ibid.

49. U.S. Drug Enforcement Agency, "Biographies of Agents and Employees Killed in Action," http://www.usdoj.gov/dea/agency/10bios.htm (accessed June 29, 2004).

50. The root of the word "hero" is ser-ow. In Greek, the connotation was "protector." The Latin root for "protector" is servare. From the same word family comes the word servire, meaning "slave," from which we get our word "serve." See Julius Pokorny, Indogermanishes Etymologisches Worterbuch (Bern: Francke, 1959); or, for slightly easier reading, The American Heritage Dictionary of the English Language (New York: American Heritage Publishing and Houghton Mifflin, 1969), 1538.

51. Emily Nelson and Matthew Rose, "Media Reassess Risks to Reporters in Iraq," Wall Street Journal, April 9, 2003.

52. Ibid. In the United States, 40% of the journalists are women.

53. ClariNews, "Women Journalists Share Experiences in War Reporting for Women's Day," March 7, 2003. http://quickstart.clari.net/qs_se/webnews/wed/bi/Qwomen-ilo-media.RJ7c_DM7.html.

54. Anthony Feinstein, "A Hazardous Profession: War, Journalists, and Psychopathology," American Journal of Psychiatry, 159, no. 9 (September 2002): 1570.

55. Ibid., 1572.

56. Ibid., 1570.

57. AlterNet.org, "Female Correspondents Changing War Coverage," November 4, 2002.

58. Associated Press, "Jacksonville Cab Driver Survives Barrage of Bullets," Palm Beach Post, June 25, 2003.

59. Interviews conducted by Alexa Deere or Warren Farrell from April 17–19, 1996 of Yellow Cab Companies in Manhattan, Brooklyn, Los Angeles and Philadelphia.

60. [Killed on the job] U.S. Department of Labor, Bureau of Labor Statistics, "Number, Percent, and Rate of Fatal Occupational Injuries by Select Worker Characteristics, Occupation, and Industry, 2002." (unpublished table). Taxi drivers and chauffeurs had a fatality rate of 15.4 per 100,000, while police officers and detectives had a fatality rate of 11.6 per 100,000. For homicide, the gap is much greater; Daniel E. Hacker, "Occupational Projections to 2012," *Monthly Labor Review* 127, no. 2, (February 2004), 83–97. Police officers and detectives had a 6.4 in 100,000 chance of being a homicide victim, while taxi drivers had a 50.0 in 100,000 chance (7.72 times as much).

    [Wealthier neighborhoods] In addition to the owners' agreement, homicide figures were provided by Guy Toscano, economist, the Office of Safety, Health, and Working Conditions, U.S. Department of Labor. In 1995, 68 men and 1 woman cabdrivers were victims of homicide.

61. Pat Tillman was an Arizona Cardinal National Football League player who lost his life as an Army Ranger in Afghanistan in 2004.

62. Tim Sullivan, "Playing with Pain the Name of the Game," *The San Diego Union-Tribune,* January 23, 2003, 3.

63. Ibid. Jenkins did this in the 2002 season.

64. Ibid.

65. Mark Zeigler and Ed Graney, "Supersizing the NFL," *San Diego Union-Tribune,* January 23, 2003, 1.

66. Sullivan, "Playing with Pain."

67. Pierce Scranton, former Seattle Seahawks team physician, cited in Sullivan, "Playing with Pain."

68. Tamara Lush, "He's a Soothing Force for Officers in Torment," *St. Petersburg Times (Florida),* August 25, 2003, 1B.

69. Stephen Barr, "Bureau of Mines' Sudden Demise," *Washington Post,* December 4, 1995, A12.

70. Telephone interview with Barbara Kavovit, founder and president, Anchor Construction, March 26, 1998, by Sophia Ruiz and Warren Farrell.

71. From *The Fifth and Far Finer Than the First Four 637 Best Things Anybody Ever Said* (New York: Ballantine, 1993).

72. Paul Muni's 1932 movie *I Am a Fugitive from the Chain Gang* sparked some of these protests.

73. Bureau of Labor Statistics, *Labor Force Statistics from the Current Population Survey.*

74. Bureau of Labor Statistics, *Employment and Earnings* (Washington, D.C.: BLS, 2004), 249–253, Table 39.

75. Sir Richard Doll and Richard Peto, Table 19, *The Causes of Cancer:* (New York: Oxford University Press, 1981), 1242.

76. Interview with Landscape architect Cindy Benoit, August 20, 2004.

77. Telephone interview with Cathey Cotten, managing principal of MetaSearch (a tech recruiting firm), February 27, 1998, by Sophia Ruiz and Warren Farrell.

78. Interview with Lillian Vernon, founder and CEO of Lillian Vernon Corporation, May 6, 1998, by Warren Farrell.

79. Interview with Theresa Metty, senior vice president and chief procurement officer of Motorola, March 31, 2003.

80. Jane R. Eisner, "Working Mom Chooses Home," *The Press Democrat,* March 25, 1998, B5.

81. Interview, February 23, 1998.

82. Deakin University, the Australian National University, the University of Sydney, and Australian Unity, a health care and insurance company, give an Australian Unity Wellbeing Index to 2,000 randomly selected Australians. For the full study, see www.australianunity.com.au/au/info/wellbeingindex/default.asp.

83. Ibid.

84. Chevalier, "Motivation, Expectations, and the Gender Pay Gap," for UK Graduates. Paper presented at the Royal Economic Society Annual Conference, Warwick, England, 7–9 April, 2003.
85. Ibid.
86. Amy Waldman, "Sonia Gandhi Declines to Serve as India Leader, Startling Party," *New York Times*, May 19, 2004, I, A6.
87. Ibid.
88. Robin Finn, "Graf, Still Near Top of Tennis, Leaves it Behind," *New York Times*, August 14, 1999, B1.
89. Bill Simons, "Chaos, Crisis and the Liberation of Steffi Graf," *Inside Tennis* (June 2004): 8–11.
90. Eisner, "Working Mom Chooses Home."
91. Ibid. Quote is from Eisner, not Ms. Shmavonian.
92. Brian Lavery, "Sinead O'Connor to Retire, but for How Long?" *New York Times*, April 29, 2003, B5.
93. Ibid.
94. See Rick Blizzard, "Healing the Gender Divide," Gallup/Healthcare, October 29, 2002 (http://www.gallup.com), for a University of Pennsylvania study saying 7.5% of men nurses drop out versus 4.1% of women.
95. Ibid.
96. Ibid.
97. U.S. Department of the Treasury, Internal Revenue Service, Statistics of Income Division. Unpublished Tables E2-1, "Number of Male-Operated Sole Proprietorships by Six Broad Industry Catagories, 1985–2000," E2-3, "Business Net Income of Male-Operated Sole Proprietorships by Six Broad Industry Catagories, 1985–2000," E3-1, "Number of Female-Operated Sole Proprietorships by Six Broad Industry Catagories, 1985–2000," E3-3, "Business Net Income of Female-Operated Sole Proprietorships by Six Broad Industry Catagories, 1985–2000."
98. Melinda Ligos, "From Ocean to Pond With More Room to Swim," *New York Times*, June 3, 2001.
99. Ibid.
100. Digest of Education Statistics, 2002, Table 78.
101. Ligos, "From Ocean to Pond."
102. Ibid.
103. Miranda Wood, "Males Quit Teaching in Droves," *The Sun-Herald* (Australia), September 22, 2002. For example, in New South Wales (Australia) more than 15% of public primary schools have neither a male teacher nor principal. In Italy, only 5% of the public primary school teachers are men.
104. Michael Lewis, "What a Coach Can Do to a Kid," *The New York Times Magazine*, March 28, 2004, 42–88.
105. See Warren Farrell, *Father and Child Reunion* (N.Y.: Tarcher/Putnam/Penguin, 2001), especially chapters 1 and 2.
106. Ibid.

CHAPTER 3   The Field-with-Higher-Yield Formula: Six to Ten

1. See Salary.com.
2. Kent Hoover, *Enterprise* (April 2, 2004).
3. Women comprise 58% of America's financial managers. Bureau of Labor Statistics, Table 39.
4. See Warren Farrell, *Why Men Are the Way They Are* (New York: Berkley, 1988).
5. Barbara Stanny, *Secrets of Six-Figure Women* (New York: Harper-Collins, 2002), 171–189.
6. Telephone interview with Cathey Cotten, managing principal of MetaSearch (a tech-recruiting firm), February 27, 1998, by Sophia Ruiz.

7. Telephone interview with Sue Buchanan, cofounder, Aurum Software, February 16, 1998, by Sophia Ruiz and Warren Farrell.

8. Hoover, "Venture-Capital Firms Becoming More Male-Dominated."

9. Erin Allday, "Fearless Sisters Run Three Stores," *The Press Democrat,* February 27, 2001, 1.

10. Dianne Solis and Charlene Oldham, *San Diego Union Tribune,* June 18, 2001, D.

11. That is the estimate of VentureOne, a research firm in San Francisco that tracks venture capital distribution, for the 2000 distribution of venture capital, as cited in Solis and Oldham, "Bypassing the Glass Ceiling."

12. Telephone interview with Theresa Metty, senior VP, Motorola, March 31, 2003, by Warren Farrell, referring to Motorola shift workers. Other estimates are about 84 cents an hour increase, plus time flexibility. See Cindy Krischer Goodman, "Working the Night Shift Leaves Time for Living," *Miami Herald,* October 29, 2003.

13. Goodman, "Working the Night Shift Leaves Time for Living." The 5½ hour figure comes from David Mitchell of Circadian Technologies, a business consulting firm specializing in shift work arrangements.

14. Bureau of Labor Statistics, "Workers on Flexible and Shift Schedules, 2001," news release, April 18, 2002. Table 4.

15. Ibid. Of the 56.1 million male full-time workers, 16.4% (9.2 million), work a shift schedule, compared with 12.1% of the 43.6 million women who work full-time (5.3 million).

16. Korn/Ferry International and UCLA Anderson Graduate School of Management, *Decade of the Executive Woman: Survey of Women in Senior Management Positions in the Fortune 1000 Industrial and 500 Service Companies* (Los Angeles: Korn/Ferry International, 1993).

17. Amy Gage, "Shift Work Leaves Many Feeling Disconnected," *Leader Telegram* (Eau Claire, WI), March 16, 1997, 2D.

18. Andrew Pollack, "Opportunity at a Price," *New York Times,* July 8, 1997, C1–C4. For example, women cabdrivers have been exempted from the prohibition on late night work since 1985, but still constitute only 2% of all drivers as of 1997.

19. Ibid.

20. Telephone interview with Theresa Metty.

21. Lexie Verdon, "Resident Doctors Asleep at the Wheel," *The Washington Post,* May 14, 1996, z05.

22. Ibid.

23. Suzanne Daley, "Hospital Interns' Long Hours to Be Reduced in New York," *New York Times,* June 9, 1988.

24. See the chapter on the death professions in Warren Farrell, *The Myth of Male Power* (New York: Berkley, 1993).

25. Telephone interview with Barbara Kavovit, founder and president, Anchor Construction, March 26, 1998, by Sophia Ruiz and Warren Farrell.

26. The mean wage for never-married men is $18,000; for married men, $38,000. U.S. Department of Labor, Bureau of Labor Statistics, *National Longitudinal Survey of Youth 1979* (*NLSY79*). Wages are for 1999. Marital status was in 2000. The information was collected in 2000.

27. Daniel Weintraub, "Rich Deal Likely for State's Prison Guards," *The Press-Democrat,* February 13, 2002, B7.

28. Bureau of Labor Statistics, Table 39, "Median Weekly Earnings of Full-Time Wage and Salary Workers by Detailed Occupation and Sex," *Employment and Earnings* (Washington, DC: U.S. Department of Labor Statistics, 2004), 249–253; and unpublished Table A-26, "Usual Weekly Earnings of Employed Full-Time Wage and Salary Workers by Detailed Occupation and Sex, Annual Averages 2003."

29. See Table 4 in Chapter One of *Why Men Earn More.* Engineer mechanics are part of the category for automotive service technicians and mechanics. The women make 129% of what the men make.

30. Robert Guy Matthews, "A Steelworker's Lonely Life," *Wall Street Journal,* June 30, 2003, B1, B4.
31. Clare Ansberry, "Workers Now Need More Skills But Get Less Job Security . . . ," *Wall Street Journal,* June 30, 2003, B1, B4.
32. Matthews, "A Steelworker's Lonely Life."
33. *Occupational Outlook Handbook, 2002–03,* cited in "A New Blue Collar World," *Wall Street Journal,* June 30, 2003, B1.
34. U.S. Department of Education, National Center for Education Statistics, Table 255, *2001/2002 Digest of Education Statistics* (Washington, DC: U.S. Department of Education, National Center for Education Statistics, 2002), 3047–3114.
35. Ibid.
36. Telephone interview with Cathey Cotton.
37. Pamela Bentley, "The 25 Hottest Careers," *Working Woman* (July 1990): 76.
38. James P. Gander, "Gender-Based Faculty-Pay Differences in Academe: A Reduced-Form Approach," *Journal of Labor Research* 18, no. 3 (Summer 1997): 451–461.
39. Les Krantz, ed., *The Jobs Rated Almanac,* 6th ed. (New Jersey: Barricade Books, 2002).
40. [$73,000] U.S. Department of Labor, Bureau of Labor Statistics, *Occupational Outlook Handbook, 2004–05 Edition,* Aerospace Engineers, http://www.bls.gov/oco/ocos028.htm.
    [$32,000] Transmitter engineers' median base pay is $31,651. as of August, 2004. See http://www.salary.com.
41. Tables 1.6 and 1.7, *Physician Characteristics and Distribution in the United States: 2004* (Chicago: Division of Survey and Data Resources, American Medical Association, 2004), 13–15. The table below summarizes the data:
42. See Lawrence C. Baker, "Differences in Earnings Between Male and Female Physicians," *The New England Journal of Medicine* 334, no. 15 (April 11, 1996): 960–964. Table 1. Dr. Baker is at the Department of Health Research and Policy, Stanford University Medical School.
43. Ibid. Data are from the 1991 Survey of Young Physicians.
44. The variables controlled for are the same as in Note 47.
45. See Note 47.
46. Besides hours, specialty, and practice setting, the other variables used were medical education (type of medical school, ranking of the school, graduate degrees other than an MD, and taking a leave of absence during medical school), experience, personal characteristics (age, race or ethnic group, marital status, and parenthood status), the community in which the physician practiced (urban or rural, income per capita, proportion of population over 65 years of age, percentage of patients who were Black or Hispanic, and the U.S. census region), AMA membership, specialty-board status, number of concurrent practices, and whether the physician had ever been subject to a claim of malpractice.
47. Baker, "Differences in Earnings Between Male and Female Physicians."
48. Ibid.

CHAPTER 4   Doing Time: People Who Get Higher Pay . . .

1. National Education Association, *Status of the American Public School Teacher, 2000–2001* (Washington, DC: NEA Research, 2003), 5–8.
2. National Education Association, *Status of the American Public School Teacher, 2000–2001* (Washington, DC: NEA Research, 2003), 17. Table 7, "Teachers with 20 or More Years of Full-Time Teaching Experience, by Selected Subgroups, 1961–2001."
3. National Education Association, *Status of the American Public School Teacher, 2000–2001* (Washington, DC: NEA Research, 2003), 40.
4. Ibid., 5–8.
5. U.S. Department of Labor, Bureau of Labor Statistics, *Current Population Survey,* March 2003. The average worker working 40 hours per week earns $634; the average worker working 45 hours per week earns $913.

6. October 13, 2004, at Arizona State University.

7. [80 cents] Bureau of Labor Statistics News Release, "Usual Weekly Earnings of Wage and Salary Workers: Second Quarter 2004," July 20, 2004. Full-time workers who are female earned 80.1% of what their male counterparts earned. In the first quarter of 2004, the figure was 79.7% (U.S. Department of Labor, Bureau of Labor Statistics News Release, "Usual Weekly Earnings of Wage and Salary Workers: First Quarter 2004," April 16, 2004)
  [42 hours per week] Bureau of Labor Statistics, *Current Population Survey,* March 2003.

8. Bureau of Labor Statistics, March 2003, *Current Population Survey.* The average worker working 45 hours per week earns $913; 42 hours $803, a difference of 14%.

9. This 70% doubtless overlaps with other variables such as choosing a higher-paying field, both of which would indicate taking the need or desire for money more seriously.

10. U.S. Bureau of the Census, *Current Population Survey,* Annual Demographic Survey, March 2003. The figures are medians.

11. American Association of University Women, "Equity Watch," *AAUW Outlook* (Spring/Summer 2002) 4.

12. U.S. Census Bureau, Current Population Survey, March Supplement, 2002. The median annual earnings for both men and women in this category was $31,000.

13. Malcolm Gladwell, "Big and Bad," *New Yorker,* January 12, 2004, 28.

14. See William C. Taylor, "How to Succeed in the Business News Business," *New York Times Book Review,* July 27, 1997, 8, reviewing Michael Bloomberg's *Bloomberg by Bloomberg* (New York: John Wiley & Sons, 1997).

15. William C. Taylor, "How to Succeed in the Business News Business," *New York Times Book Review,* July 27, 1997, 8.

16. Leslie Kaufman-Rosen with Claudia Kalb, "Holes in the Glass Ceiling Theory," *Newsweek* (March 27, 1995): 24–25.

17. U.S. Department of Labor, Bureau of Labor Statistics, *Current Population Survey,* April 2004. Of men working 35 or more hours per week, 26.7% worked 50 hours or more, and 0.5% worked 90 hours or more. Of women working 35 or more hours per week, 13.1% worked 50 hours or more per week, and 0.2% worked 90 hours or more per week.

18. Data from U.S. Bureau of Labor Statistics, *Current Population Survey,* March 2003.

19. Radcliffe Public Policy Center, "Life's Work: Generational Attitudes Toward Work and Life Integration," (Cambridge, MA: Radcliffe Public Policy Center, 2000). The Harris Interactive Poll was commissioned by the Radcliffe Public Policy Center.

20. Phyllis L. Carr, Karen C. Graeis, and Rosalind C. Barnett, "Characteristics and Outcomes for Women Physicians Who Work Reduced Hours," *Journal of Women's Health* 12, no. 4 (June 12, 2003): 399–405.

21. A Deakin University, the Australian National University, the University of Sydney, and Australian Unity, study of 2,000 Australians. For the full study, see www.australianunity.com.au/au/info/wellbeingindex/default.asp.

22. Janet Yellen, chair, Council of Economic Advisers, "Families and the Labor Market, 1969–1999: Analyzing the 'Time Crunch.'" Data from Census Bureau, as cited in John M. Berry, "Moms Spend More Hours On Paid Jobs," *Washington Post,* May 25, 1999.

23. Joan Ryan, "Careers in the Balance," *The San Francisco Chronicle,* March 21, 1999. The study included professionals and managers at 45 companies.

24. Joan Ryan, "Careers in the Balance," *The San Francisco Chronicle,* March 21, 1999.

25. Jason Fields, "Children's Living Arrangements and Characteristics: March 2002," *Current Population Reports* (U.S. Census Bureau, P20–547, 2003), 10. There are 105,000 stay-at-home dads; 5.2 million stay-at-home moms.

26. Amy Bach, "No Lo Contendere," *New York Magazine,* December 11, 1995, 49. This was based on a survey of listings in the industry directory of law firms, and included 719 associates. This article originated from a study funded by the W. M. Keck Foundation.

27. Jeff Madrick, "The Earning Power of Women Has Really Increased, Right? Take a Closer Look," *New York Times,* June 10, 2004, C2.
28. [current occupations] Based on raw data from the U.S. Census Bureau's Survey of Income and Program Participation (SIPP), 2001 panel wave 1, for full-time workers aged 21–64. On average, women have 10.5 years of work experience in their current occupation, compared to 12.0 years for men. The Census Bureau does not have income data for people with exactly 10.5 years of experience, but at 10 years of experience, workers earned an average of $37,426 per year, compared with $39,893 for workers with 12 years of experience in their current occupation. If you've graduated from college, and you're a guy, chances are you'll be in the workplace for 5 years more than your female counterpart; if you're a high school graduate, 6 extra years; but if you haven't graduated from high school, sorry guys, you'll average almost a decade longer (38%) than your female counterpart. The $2,467 difference corresponds to a 7% increase in earnings, or 5% for the one-and-a-half year male-female difference.

    [work lives] David L. Millimet, Michael Nieswiadomy, Hang Ryu, Daniel Slottje, "Estimating Worklife Expectancy: An Econometric Approach," *Journal of Econometrics,* 113 (2003): 83–113. See especially Table 2, "Updated 'BLS' Work Life Expectancy: by Gender and Education," 93.
29. See Note 28.
30. This study and its publicity illustrates the psychological barriers women in the mid-1980s faced as they entered the professions and were confronted with women-as-victim headlines: Vernon A. Stone, "News Directors Profiled," *RTNDA [Radio & Television News Directors' Association] Communicator* (June 1986), p. 23.
31. Author's calculation of years it takes men versus women to become news directors.
32. Korn/Ferry International and UCLA Anderson Graduate School of Management, *Decade of the Executive Woman: Survey of Women In Senior Management Positions in the Fortune 1000 Industrial and 500 Service Companies* (Los Angeles: Korn/Ferry International, 1993), 48, Table 86, "Age."
33. Ibid.
34. Marianne Bertrand and Kevin F. Hallock, "The Gender Gap in Top Corporate Jobs," *Industrial and Labor Relations Review* 55, no. 1 (2001): 7. Table 2, "Firm and Manager Characteristics."
35. Korn/Ferry International and UCLA Anderson Graduate School of Management. *Decade of the Executive Woman,* 22. Table 1.
36. Ibid.
37. *Physician Characteristics and Distribution in the United States: 2003–2004* (Chicago: Division of Survey and Data Resources, American Medical Association, 2003), 10–11. Tables 1.3 and 1.4, "Male Physicians by Age and Specialty, 2001" and "Female Physicians by Age and Specialty, 2001."
38. Telephone interview with V.J. Horgan, president, TXU Energy Trading, February 27, 2003, by Warren Farrell.
39. Marianne Bertrand and Kevin F. Hallock, "The Gender Gap in Top Corporate Jobs," *Industrial and Labor Relations Review* 55, no. 1 (2001): 7. Table 2, "Firm and Manager Characteristics." The study is of the top five executives at almost 3,000 of the country's largest firms. Seniority accounted for 67% of the gap.
40. Ibid.
41. U.S. Census Bureau, Survey of Income and Program Participation (SIPP), 2001 Wave 1. Men and women aged 22–62 who had worked full-time were asked if they had ever taken a break of 6 months or longer from work to care for a child or other relative. Of those who answered in the affirmative, 33.46% were women, compared to 3.77% of men.
42. Joyce P. Jacobsen and Laurence M. Levin, "Effects of Intermittent Labor Force Attachment on Women's Earnings," *Monthly Labor Review* (September 1995): 17. The study is of 2,426 U.S. women.

43. Ibid.
44. Bureau of the Census, "Male-Female Differences in Work Experience, Occupation, and Earnings: 1984," Series P-70, No. 10, Table 1,
45. U.S. Bureau of the Census, Survey of Income and Program Participation (SIPP), 2001 (wave 1). Of men and women aged 21–62 who had generally worked full-time, 32.09% of women had taken leave of 6 months or longer at least once in order to care for a child or other relative, compared with 3.64% of men.
46. Arnaud Chevalier, "Motivation, Expectations and the Gender Pay Gap for UK Graduates," Paper presented at the Royal Economic Society Annual Conference, Warwick, England, April 7–9, 2003.
47. [more money] Radcliffe Public Policy Center, "Life's Work"; see also Joyce Madelon Winslow, "Dads Can Learn from Moms."

    [expected to continue] Bureau of the Census, "Male-Female Differences in Work Experience, Occupation, and Earnings: 1984," Series P-70, No. 10, Table 1, "Workers with One or More Work Interruptions Lasting Six Months or Longer, by Reason for Interruption," *Current Population Reports* (Washington, DC: U.S. Government Printing Office, 1987). Of working men aged 21–64, 0.3% said they had experienced an interruption in work lasting 6 months or longer due to family reasons. Now, though, according to the U.S. Bureau of the Census, *Survey of Income and Program Participation (SIPP)*, 2001 (wave 1), it is 3.64% of men, a 12-fold increase.
48. In March 2002, 55.2 million men worked; in July, 55.1 million, a difference of 0.2%. In March, 40.7 million women worked; in July, 37.7 million women, a difference of 7.4%—almost 40 times greater than 0.2%. For March data, see U.S. Department of Labor, Bureau of Labor Statistics, Table A 26, "Persons at Work in Nonagricultural Industries by Age, Sex, Race, Marital Status, and Usual Full- or Part-Time Status," *Employment and Earnings* (Washington, DC: U.S. Government Printing Office, 2002), 32. For July data, see U.S. Department of Labor, Bureau of Labor Statistics, Table A 26, "Persons at Work in Nonagricultural Industries by Age, Sex, Race, Marital Status, and Usual Full- or Part-Time Status," *Employment and Earnings* (Washington, DC: U.S. Government Printing Office, 2002), 33.
49. Ibid.
50. Explained by Howard Hayghe, economist, U.S. Bureau of Labor Statistics.
51. Only 77–80% of full-time working women work 50 or more weeks per year (vs. 82–84% of men). December 10, 2002, the latest data available on weeks worked per year by each sex, is from the U.S. Department of Labor, Bureau of Labor Statistics, unpublished data for 2001, Table 1.
52. Telephone interview with Howard Hayghe, U.S. Department of Labor, Bureau of Labor Statistics, April 28, 2003. For the monthly survey, a woman's "usual" status will be considered full-time if the job she had when she took maternity leave was full-time, and she is still considered an employee by her employer while she is on maternity leave. For the yearly survey, the woman's "actual" status for that month would not be full-time, since she did not actually work 35+ hours during the reference week.
53. [temporary workers] Telephone interview with Howard Hayghe, U.S. Department of Labor, Bureau of Labor Statistics, April 28, 2003

    [women] Bruce Steinberg, National Association of Temporary Staffing Services (NATSS), "Profile of the Temporary Workforce," *Contemporary Times* (Spring 1994): 33.
54. U.S. Department of Labor, Bureau of Labor Statistics, Table 46, "Absences from Work of Employed, Full-Time Wage and Salary Workers by Age and Sex," *Employment and Earnings,* Volume 51, (Washington, DC: U.S. Department of Labor, 2004), 263. See also "Lost Worktime Rate" figures. The male-female ratio of hours lost is 1.3 for men; 2.4 for women.
55. National Center for Health Statistics, Table 82, "Ambulatory Care Visits to Physician Offices and Hospital Outpatient and Emergency Departments by Selected Characteristics: United

States, Selected Years 1995–2001," *Health, United States, 2003, With Chartbook on Trends in the Health of Americans* (Hyattsville, MD: National Center for Health Statistics, 2003), 260–261. In 2001, a male between the age of 18 and 44 was on average likely to visit a doctor 1.52 times a year (2.91 for females), or 91% more for women; between the age of 45 and 54 this was 2.73 times a year for men (3.97 for females) or 45% more for women; and between the age of 55 and 64 this was 4.85 visits a year for men (5.29 for females) or 10% more for women."

56. Interview with Carol Scott by Warren Farrell, April 30, 2003. The Medical Education Group is in Baltimore, MD.

57. Richard DeMartino and Robert Barbato, "Gender Differences Among MBA Entrepreneurs," presented at the United States Association for Small Business and Entrepreneurship/Small Business Institute Directors' Association Annual National Conference, Orlando, FL, February 7–10, 2001.

58. Data from the U.S. Census Bureau, *Survey of Income and Program Participation (SIPP)*, 2001 panel, wave 3. Full-time working men commute an average of 151.4 miles per week, while full-time working women commute an average of 110.7 miles per week.

59. Data from the U.S. Census Bureau, Survey of Income and Program Participation (SIPP), 2001 panel, wave 3. Full-time workers commuting 110 miles per week earned approximately $1,538 less than those commuting 150 miles per week. The figures for those who commute 110 and 150 miles per week were selected because no respondents commuted exactly 111 or 151 hours.

60. Clay Robison, "Hughes Still in the Oval Loop," *The San Diego Union Tribune*, May 27, 2003.

CHAPTER 5   On the Move: People . . . Are More Willing to . . .

1. Interview with Theresa Metty, by Warren Farrell, March 31, 2003.

2. Telephone interview with Robin Curle, director of strategic marketing, Evolutionary Technologies International, by Sophia Ruiz and Warren Farrell February 1, 1998.

3. Anne Hendershott, Table 2.1, "Percentage of Male vs. Female Relocated Employees," *Moving for Work* (Lanham, MD: University Press of America, 1995), 27.

4. U.S. Bureau of the Census, "Geographic Mobility: 2003," Table 32, *Current Population Reports* P20-549 (March 2004).

5. U.S. Bureau of the Census, *Current Population Survey,* March 2003 supplement.

6. [half of today's professionals] U.S. Department of Labor, Bureau of Labor Statistics, Table 39, "Median Weekly Earnings of Full-Time Wage and Salary Workers by Detailed Occupation and Sex: 2003," *Employment and Earnings* (Washington, DC: U.S. Department of Labor, 2004). As early as 1996, 52% of professionals were women. In 2003, the figure was 50.3%.

    [18% transferred] GMAC Global Relocation Services, *Global Relocation Trends, 2003/2004 Survey Reports* (GMAC: 2004), 15. See www.gmacglobalrelocation.com.

7. Interview with Theresa Metty, senior vice president and chief procurement officer of Motorola, by Warren Farrell on March 31, 2003.

8. Leslie Kaufman-Rosen with Claudia Kalb, "Holes in the Glass Ceiling Theory," *Newsweek,* March 27, 1995, 24–25.

9. Anne Hendershott, Table 2.1, "Percentage of Male vs. Female Relocated Employees," *Moving for Work* (Lanham, MD: University Press of America, 1995), 27.

10. Frank Edward Allen, "Work & Family: What Problem?" *Wall Street Journal,* June 21, 1993, R7, as cited in Anne Hendershott, *Moving for Work* (Lanham, MD: University Press of America, 1995), 29–30.

11. Catalyst, "Leaders in a Global Economy: A Study of Executive Women and Men" (2003), 9. Worldwide, 11% of men executives surveyed had a spouse who worked full-time, compared with 74% of the women, i.e., almost 7 times as likely. Catalyst is a women's advocacy group.

12. Richard Hader, "Salary Survey 2004," *Nursing Management* 35, no. 7, (July 2004) 28–32. The West Coast is California, Oregon, Washington, and Alaska.

13. Andrea Billups, "Teachers' Low Pay Likely Will Worsen School Shortages," *Washington Times*, July 5, 2000. Based on the AFT study, "Survey and Analysis of Teacher Salary Trends, 1999."

14. U.S. Bureau of the Census, Table p18. *Census of Population, Census 2000 Summary File 3* (SF 3), (Washington, DC: U.S. Bureau of the Census, 2000).

15. Rebecca Vesely, "A Traveler's Tale: Nursing Shortage Boosts Demand for "Gypsy" Nurses," *Alameda-Star Times* and Nurses.com., July 8, 2003.

16. Ibid.

17. See Chapter 2.

18. Warren Farrell, *Father and Child Reunion* (New York: Tarcher/Putnam/Penguin, 2001), 51–52.

19. Warren Farrell, *Father and Child Reunion* (New York: Tarcher/Putnam/Penguin, 2001), Ch. 1.

20. [half of today's professionals] U.S. Department of Labor, Bureau of Labor Statistics, Table 39, "Median Weekly Earnings of Full-Time Wage and Salary Workers by Detailed Occupation and Sex: 2003," *Employment and Earnings* (Washington, DC: U.S. Department of Labor, 2004). As early as 1996, 52% of professionals were women. In 2003, the figure was 50.3%.

    [16% of frequent flyers] According to a segmentation study conducted by United in 1995, 83.6% of the United frequent fliers defined as "Road Warriors" are male.

CHAPTER 6   Responsibility, Training, Ambition, and Productivity

1. Joanne Cleaver and Betty Spence, "All the Right Stuff: The National Association of Female Executives' Analysis of the 2004 Top 30 Companies for Executive Women," May 10, 2004, 1–5. Also see nafe.com/top30_04.shtml.

2. Ibid.

3. Ilene Lang, Catalyst president, says women fill less than 10% of the 6,428 corporate line positions at America's largest companies. Lang is cited in Joanne Cleaver and Betty Spence, "All the Right Stuff."

4. Stuart Silverstein, "Differing Views of the Executive Glass Ceiling," *Los Angeles Times*, February 28, 1996, D-1 and D-13. The polling organization was Catalyst, a women's advocacy group; 325 CEOs responded.

5. Mark Sieling, *Monthly Labor Review* (June 1984); 32. His source is the U.S. Bureau of Labor Statistics, *1981 Survey of Professional, Administrative, Technical, and Clerical Pay* (PATC survey). The *Monthly Labor Review* is a publication of the U.S. Bureau of Labor Statistics. The USBLS did not record the gender of the workers, but Mark Sieling derived it from the raw data from those companies that did include gender. The USBLS has updated this survey, calling it the Occupational Compensation Survey (OCS), and then the National Compensation Survey, but no one has funded Mark Sieling or anyone else to repeat his efforts.

6. Ibid.

7. Ibid.

8. Marianne Bertrand and Kevin F. Hallock, "The Gender Gap in Top Corporate Jobs," Table 2, "Firm and Manager Characteristics," *Industrial and Labor Relations Review*, 55, no. 1 (2001): 7. Bertrand is assistant professor of economics at the Graduate School of Business at the University of Chicago. Hallock is associate professor of economics and of labor and industrial relations at the University of Illinois at Urbana-Champaign.

9. Arnaud Chevalier, *Motivation, Expectations and the Gender Pay Gap for UK Graduates*, paper presented at the Royal Economic Society Annual Conference, Warwick, England, April 7–9, 2003.

10. Arnaud Chevalier, "Education, Motivation and Pay of UK Graduates: Is It Different for Girls?" Institute for Social Change, UCD, 2002, mimeographed.

11. Lawrence C. Baker, "Differences in Earnings between Male and Female Physicians," *New England Journal of Medicine*, 334, no. 15 (April 11, 1996), 960–964. Table 2. Dr. Baker is at the Department of Health Research and Policy, Stanford University Medical School.

12. *Physician Characteristics and Distribution in the United States: 2004* (Chicago: American Medical Association, 2004), 30–31. Tables 1.15 and 1.16.
13. Marilyn Bennett McLatchey, "Women's Work at Harvard," *The Women's Freedom Network Newsletter* 4, no. 2, (Spring 1997): 4.
14. Ibid.
15. In contrast, 19% of men aspire to be a CEO or managing partner according to Catalyst, "Leaders in a Global Economy: A Study of Executive Women and Men—A View from Western Europe and Asia-Pacific," June 17, 2003. See also Catalyst, "Women in U.S. Corporate Leadership: 2003," June 10, 2003.
16. M.A. Fasci and J. Valdez, "Performance Contrast of Male- and Female-Owned Small Accounting Practices," *Journal of Small Business Management* (July 1999): 1–7. Cited in Richard DeMartino and Robert Barbato, "Motivational Factors of Intending Female and Male Entrepreneurs," presented at the SBIDA 2002 Conference, San Diego, February 7–9, 2002.
17. Roper, "Virginia Slims American Women's Poll 1995." This is the latest poll posing this question as of 2004.
18. [Singapore] Ramin C. Maysami and Valerie P. Goby, "Female Business Owners in Singapore and Elsewhere: A Review of Studies," *Journal of Small Business Management* (April 1999): 96–105. Cited in Richard DeMartino and Robert Barbato, "Motivational Factors of Intending Female and Male Entrepreneurs," presented at the SBIDA 2002 Conference, San Diego, February 7–9, 2002.

    [Australia] L.V. Still and W. Timms, " 'I Want to Make a Difference' Women Small Business Owners: Their Businesses, Dreams, Lifestyles and Measure of Success," *Proceedings of the International Conference of Small Business,* 2000. Cited in Richard DeMartino and Robert Barbato, "Motivational Factors of Intending Female and Male Entrepreneurs."

    [Poland] A.M. Zapalska, "A Profile of Women Entrepreneurs and Enterprises in Poland," *Journal of Small Business Management* (1997): 76–82. Cited in Richard DeMartino and Robert Barbato, "Motivational Factors of Intending Female and Male Entrepreneurs."

    [United States] M.A. Fasci and J. Valdez, "Performance Contrast of Male- and Female-Owned Small Accounting Practices," *Journal of Small Business Management* (July 1999): 1–7. Cited in Richard DeMartino and Robert Barbato, "Motivational Factors of Intending Female and Male Entrepreneurs," presented at the SBIDA 2002 Conference, San Diego, Feb. 7–9 2002.
19. Among the men, 25% ranked financial rewards as "very important." Arnaud Chevalier, "Motivation, Expectations and the Gender Pay Gap for UK Graduates." Paper presented at the Royal Economic Society Annual Conference, Warwick, England, April 7–9, 2003.
20. Ibid. The data set is for young UK graduates who have been in the labor market for 42 months max.
21. [Western European and Asia-Pacific women] Catalyst, "Leaders in a Global Economy."

    [Australians] The 2003 survey is of 12,000 Australians. See Christine Jackman, "Mums Say No to Equality," *The Australian,* March 11, 2003.
22. U.S. Census Bureau's Survey of Income and Program Participation (SIPP), 2001 panel, business module. Of men business owners, 29% run their business out of their home, compared with 55% of women business owners.
23. Betsy Morris, "Executive Women Confront Mid-Life Crisis," *Fortune,* September 18, 1995, 65. Yankelovich Partners was hired by *Fortune* to survey 300 career women, ages 35 to 49. About 94% were managers or executives. Nearly half had salaries of more than $60,000.
24. Ibid., 68 and 74.
25. Ibid.
26. Ibid.
27. Amy Bach, "Nolo Contendere," *New York Magazine,* December 11, 1995, 51–52. This article originated from a study funded by the W. M. Keck Foundation.
28. Carl Hoffmann and John Shelton Reed, "Sex Discrimination?—The XYZ Affair," *The Public*

Interest (Winter 1981): 21–39. Employees surveyed at this point in time are the ones who would be most likely at the height of their career at the turn of the century. Hoffmann Research Associates (HRA) is the research company. The Fortune 500 company gave permission for publication of results on the condition of anonymity; hence, it was called the XYZ Corporation when HRA published the results summarized here.

29. Radcliffe Public Policy Center, *Life's Work: Generational Attitudes Toward Work and Life Integration* (Cambridge, MA: Radcliffe Public Policy Center, 2000).

30. Catalyst, "Leaders in a Global Economy." Thirty percent of Asia-Pacific men and women executives feel work and children are of equal priority; 65% prioritize work; 5% prioritize children.

31. Only about 11% of Asia-Pacific men executives have no children, compared with 69% of the women executives. Catalyst, "Leaders in a Global Economy."

32. Ibid. Worldwide, 11% of the men executives surveyed had a spouse who worked full-time, compared with 74% of the women, i.e., almost 7 times as likely. Catalyst is a women's advocacy group that conducts research to encourage women's advancement.

33. Kris Maher, "Landing a Job in a Bad Market," *Wall Street Journal*, July 8, 2003, D1 and D2.

34. Phone interview with Cathey Cotten, founder/managing principal of MetaSearch Inc. (a tech-recruiting firm), by Sophia Ruiz and Warren Farrell, February 27, 1998.

35. Kris Maher, "Landing a Job in a Bad Market," *Wall Street Journal*, July 8, 2003, D1 and D2.

36. Joyce P. Jacobsen, *Occupational Sex Segregation and the Tipping Phenomenon: The Contrary Case of Court Reporting*, p. 2. Paper presented at the annual meeting of the Allied Social Sciences Association, June, 1997. Dr. Jacobsen is an economist at Wesleyan University in Connecticut.

37. T.J. Benedetti, L.M. Baldwin, C.H.A. Andrilla, and L.G. Hart, "The Productivity of Washington State's Obstetrician-Gynecologist Workforce: Does Gender Make a Difference?" *Obstetrics and Gynecology* 103, no. 3 (March 2004): 499–505.

38. James P. Gander, "Gender-Based Faculty-Pay Differences in Academe: A Reduced-Form Approach," *Journal of Labor Research* 18, no. 3 (Summer 1997): 451–461. For similar findings among faculty at Canadian universities, see M.R. Nakhaie, *Canadian Review of Sociology and Anthropology-Revue Canadienne De Sociologie Et D Anthropologie* 39, no. 2 (May 2002): 151–179.

39. Kate O'Beirne, "An Army of Jessicas," *National Review*, May 19, 2003, 40.

40. Ibid.

CONCLUSION TO PART I: Twenty-five Ways to Increase Your Pay

1. U.S. Department of Labor, Bureau of Labor Statistics, Office of Employment Projections. Table III-1, "Occupational Employment and Job Openings Data, 2002–12, and Worker Characteristics, 2002." Download from: http://www.bls.gov/emp/optd/optd003.pdf. Table from America's Career Info Net (www.acinet.org), a subsite of www.careeronestop.org.

CHAPTER 7   What Women Contribute to the Workplace

1. [teachers] National Education Association, *Status of the American Public School Teacher, 2000–2001* (Washington, DC: NEA Research, 2003), 55.

   [*Web of Inclusion*] Sally Helgesen, *The Web of Inclusion* (New York: Doubleday, 1995).

   [*Female Advantage*] Sally Helgesen, *The Female Advantage* (New York: Doubleday, 1990).

2. [Armed Services] U.S. Department of Defense, Directorate for Information Operations and Reports, as of May 15, 2004, from http://www.dior.whs.mil/mmid/casualty/castop.htm. Women accounted for 13 of 556 hostile deaths.

   [coal mines] Rena Singer, "S. African Women Gain Ground Below Surface," *USA Today*, May 17, 2002.

[cabdrivers] In addition to the owners' agreement, homicide figures were provided by Guy Toscano, economist, the Office of Safety, Health, and Working Conditions, U.S. Department of Labor. In 1995, 68 male and 1 female cabdrivers were victims of homicide.

3. Lynn Rosener, Educational Software Designer and Usability Specialist for The Learning Company in Fremont, California; and Susan Morse, "Why Girls Don't Like Computer Games," *AAUW Outlook* (Winter 1995): 16–19.

4. Lyn Kathlene, "Alternative Views of Crime: Legislative Policymaking in Gendered Terms," *The Journal of Politics* 57, no. 3 (August 1995): 696–723.

5. Michele Swers, "Understanding the Policy Impact of Electing Women: Evidence from Research on Congress and State Legislatures," *Political Science and Politics* 34 (2001): 217–220.

6. Susan E. Tiffet, "Board Gains," *Working Women* (February 1994): 38, as cited in Judy B. Rosener, *America's Competitive Secret: Utilizing Women as a Management Strategy* (New York: Oxford University Press, 1995), 135.

CHAPTER 8   Why Women and Men Approach Work So Differently, Yet So Similarly

1. U.S. Department of the Treasury, Internal Revenue Service, Statistics of Income Division. Unpublished Table E2-1, "Number of Male-Operated Sole Proprietorships by Six Broad Industry Categories, 1985–2000"; Table E2-3, "Business Net Income of Male-Operated Sole Proprietorships by Six Broad Industry Categories, 1985–2000"; Table E3-1, "Number of Female-Operated Sole Proprietorships by Six Broad Industry Categories, 1985–2000"; and Table E3-3, "Business Net Income of Female-Operated Sole Proprietorships by Six Broad Industry Categories, 1985–2000." Data provided by Dr. Ying Lowry, an economist at the Small Business Administration. In 2000, an estimated 12.2 million men-owned businesses had combined net incomes of $163.9 billion or $13,460 on average. An estimated 7.4 million women-owned businesses had combined net incomes of $48.7 billion, or $6,566 on average.

2. The Rochester Institute of Technology studied 261 women and men business owners. Cited in Jim Hopkins, *USA Today,* May 18, 2003.

3. U.S. Bureau of the Census, Survey of Income and Program Participation (SIPP), 2001 Panel, wave 2. The data was for individuals who were majority or sole owners of a business.

4. Hopkins, *USA Today,* May 18, 2003.

5. U.S. Census Bureau, "Characteristics of Business by Gender," April 24, 1997, revision of *1994 Survey of Employer Businesses by Gender Ownership.* The employee figures are from the statistical analysis to question 3: 12% of men-owned firms reported that all their employees were part-time, as did 24.5% of women-owned firms. Data available only on the Internet at http://www.census.gov/csd/gen/.

6. Hopkins, "Mars vs. Venus Extends to Entrepreneurs, Too."

7. Rochester Institute of Technology study of 261 women and men business owners. Cited in Hopkins, *USA Today,* May 18, 2003.

8. Susan Coleman, "Access to Capital: A Comparison of Men- and Women-Owned Small Businesses," *Frontiers of Entrepreneurship Research,* 1998.

9. This dynamic is best explained in Warren Farrell, *The Myth of Male Power* (New York: Berkley, 1993), especially Chapters 2 and 3.

10. David Buss, *The Evolution of Desire: Strategies of Human Mating,* 2nd ed. (New York: Basic Books, 2003).

11. U.S. Bureau of Labor Statistics, Table 2, *Census of Fatal Occupational Injuries, 2002* (Washington, DC: U.S. BLS, 2003).

12. Tamar Lewin, "Men Whose Wives' Work Earn Less, Studies Show," *New York Times,* October

12, 1994, 1. The study by Frieda Reitman of Pace University and Joy Schneer of Rider University examined 231 men.

13. For an analysis of many of the studies on the division of labor among dual-career couples, see Warren Farrell, *Women Can't Hear What Men Don't Say* (New York: Tarcher/Putnam/Penguin, 1999), Chapter 5.

14. U.S. Department of the Treasury, Internal Revenue Service, Statistics of Income Division. Unpublished Tables E2-1, E2-3, E3-1, and E3-3.

CHAPTER 9   The Myths That Prevent Women from Knowing Why Men Earn More

1. Democratic National Convention, July 1984.
2. During the third presidential debate, October 13, 2004.
3. [man earned] "Proclamation of 'National Pay Inequity Awareness Day,'" April 11, 1996, by President William J. Clinton.

     [vogue] Barbara Hagenbaugh, "Women's Pay Suffers Setback," *USA Today,* August 27, 2004. This headlined the 75.5% figure as "new news" even though it was from 2003 and the first and second quarter of 2004 data had been available since April and July 2004, respectively.

     [2004] U.S. Department of Labor, Bureau of Labor Statistics News Release, "Usual Weekly Earnings of Wage and Salary Workers: Second Quarter 2004," July 20, 2004. Full-time workers who are women earned 80.1% of what their male counterparts earned. In the first quarter of 2004, the figure was 79.7% (U.S. Department of Labor, Bureau of Labor Statistics News Release, "Usual Weekly Earnings of Wage and Salary Workers: First Quarter 2004," April 16, 2004).

4. I received such a shirt from the AAUW via a catalog order on June 5, 1991.
5. Carol Klieman, *Chicago Tribune,* reprinted as "Closing Wage Gap for Women May Depend on a Little Research," *San Diego Union-Tribune,* September 29, 1997.
6. Barbara Reynolds, *Ms.* magazine. Cited in Klieman, "Closing Wage Gap for Women May Depend on a Little Research."
7. Tamar Lewin, "For Some Two-Paycheck Families, The Economics Don't Add Up," *New York Times,* April 21, 1991, E-18.
8. Sally Helgesen, *The Female Advantage: Women's Ways of Leadership* (New York: Doubleday Currency, 1990).

     [*Megatrends*] Patricia Aburdene and John Naisbitt, *Megatrends for Women* (New York: Fawcett Columbine, 1992), 100–101.

     [interactive style] Judy B. Rosener, *America's Competitive Secret: Utilizing Women as a Management Strategy* (New York: Oxford University Press, 1995).

     [ambiguity] Dafna Eylon, "Gender Differences and Empowerment: Initial Findings," University of Richmond conference paper, presented at Washington, DC, the Eastern Academy of Management, 1996.

9. Aburdene and Naisbitt, *Megatrends for Women.*
10. The Gallup Organization, Table 21, *Gender and Society: Status and Stereotypes, an International Gallup Poll Report,* March 1996.
11. Ibid.
12. The Gallup Organization, May 10, 2002. Among men, 29% prefer men bosses and 13% prefer women bosses. The question asked was, "If you were taking a new job and had your choice of a boss, would you prefer to work for a man or a woman?"
13. Robert Michels, *Political Parties: A Sociological Study of the Oligarchical Tendencies of Modern Democracy* (New York: Hearst's International Library Co., 1915), translated by Eden and Cedar Paul. Original work was written in German and published in 1911.
14. For a complete description of more than 50 areas in which men tend to contribute to the home,

and the deficiencies of housework studies, see Warren Farrell, *Women Can't Hear What Men Don't Say* (New York: Tarcher/Putnam/Penguin, 1999), Chapter Five, especially pp. 100–106.

15. See Note 9.
16. Australian Nurses Federation Survey, as reported in Australia's *The Age,* February 26, 2004, A3, and 10–11.

CHAPTER 10 Discrimination Against Women

1. Eight tables in a Census Bureau report released in 2003 on child care arrangements were organized by characteristics of the mother; none by characteristics of the father. See U.S. Bureau of the Census, *Who's Minding the Kids? Child Care Arrangements; Spring 1999* (Washington, DC: U.S. Census Bureau, 2003), available at www.census.gov/population/www/socdemo/child/ppl-168.html, accessed August 20, 2004.
2. Karen MacPherson, "Half of Working Moms Leave Preschoolers with Relatives," syndicated by the Pittsburgh Post-Gazette in *The Journal,* January 21, 1998, A2.
3. Ibid. The article draws from U.S. Census Bureau data released in 1996, indicating that dads were most numerous among the relatives, followed by grandparents, and then siblings, aunts, and uncles.
4. A search on Google (as of August 11, 2004) reveals 57 pages came up for "women networking," but not a single entry for "men networking." (Go to Google and type in site: .gov "women networking" and hit search; then hit back, and type "men networking" and hit search). Among the programs are a "Women's Networking Breakfast" sponsored by the Minority Business Development Agency (www.mbda.gov/?action=calendar_popup&section_id=1&site_id=1&event_id=2667), an SBA (Small Business Administration) program called WNET ("Women's Networking Roundtable", www.sba.gov/test/wbc/docs/roundtable_list.html), a women's networking tea at NASA's Goddard Flight Center (http://www.gsfc.nasa.gov/goddardnews/20030509/ann.html), and a women's networking breakfast at a convention for energy-industry professionals sponsored by the Department of Energy (www.energy2002.ee.doe.gov/WomensBreakfast.htm).
5. The Gallup Organization, "Gender and Society: Status and Stereotypes, an International Gallup Poll Report," March 1996. Table 21 lists the results for the question, "If you were taking a new job and had your choice of a boss (supervisor), would you prefer to work for a man or a woman?" The poll was of 22 countries, representing 53% of the world's population. The 22 countries are: Canada, Chile, China, Columbia, El Salvador, Estonia, France, Germany, Honduras, Hungary, Iceland, India, Japan, Latvia, Lithuania, Mexico, Panama, Spain, Taiwan, Thailand, United Kingdom, and United States.
6. Ibid.
7. The survey was conducted by Catalyst, a New York–based organization focusing on women's career issues, which surveyed 461 women executives at Fortune 1000 companies. See Stuart Silverstein, "Differing Views of the Executive Glass Ceiling," *Los Angeles Times,* February 28, 1996, D-1 and D-13.
8. A 1990 Supreme Court battle between Johnson Controls, Inc., and the United Auto Workers dealt with this issue. See Peter T. Kilborn, "Who Decides Who Works At Jobs Imperiling Fetuses?" *New York Times,* September 2, 1990, front page.
9. Women comprise 48% of executive, administrative, and managerial positions. U.S. Department of Labor, Bureau of Labor Statistics. *Highlights of Women's Earnings, 2002* (Washington, DC: U.S. Department of Labor, 2003), 10.
10. Korn/Ferry International and UCLA Anderson Graduate School of Management, Table 51, and Table 52, *Decade of the Executive Woman: Survey of Women in Senior Management Positions in the Fortune 1000 Industrial and 500 Service Companies* (Los Angeles: Korn/Ferry International, 1993), 37.

11. Time, May 13, 1996.

12. U.S. Department of Labor, Bureau of Labor Statistics, *Current Population Survey,* March 2003. The average worker working 40 hours per week earns $634; the average worker working 45 hours per week earns $913.

CHAPTER 11   Discrimination in Favor of Women: Why Women Are Now Often Paid More Than Men for the Same Work

1. Based on raw data from the U.S. Census Bureau's Survey of Income and Program Participation, 2001 Panel, wave 2.

2. Mark Sieling, *Monthly Labor Review,* June 1984, 32. His source is the Bureau of Labor Statistics, *1981 Survey of Professional, Administrative, Technical, and Clerical Pay (PATC survey).*

3. Laurie A. Morgan, "Glass-Ceiling Effect or Cohort Effect? A Longitudinal Study of the Gender Earnings Gap for Engineers, 1982 to 1989," *American Sociological Review* 63 (August 1998): 479–493.

4. Lawrence C. Baker, "Differences in Earnings Between Male and Female Physicians," *The New England Journal of Medicine* 334, no. 15 (April 11, 1996): 960–964.

5. U.S. Bureau of Labor Statistics, Table A-26, "Usual Weekly Earnings of Employed Full-Time Wage and Salary Workers by Detailed Occupation and Sex, Annual Averages 2003" (unpublished table).

6. Interview with Heinz Holba, president of L. A. Models, on July 29, 1997, by Betty Mazzetti Hatch, founder of La Belle Agency (which discovered Kathy Ireland, etc.), upon my request.

7. Korn/Ferry International and UCLA Anderson Graduate School of Management, *Decade of the Executive Woman: Survey of Women in Senior Management Positions in the Fortune 1000 Industrial and 500 Service Companies* (Los Angeles: Korn/Ferry International, 1993); 48. Table 86, "Age."

8. Ibid.

9. Ibid., 22.

10. Ibid., 50. Table 94.

11. See Jacqueline Simenauer and David Carroll, *Singles: The New Americans* (New York: Simon & Schuster, 1982), 15. For cross-cultural data documenting this pattern in 37 cultures, see David M. Buss, *The Evolution of Desire: Strategies of Human Mating* (New York: Basic Books, 1994).

12. The economic theory that comes closest to this is Public Choice Economics, for which James Buchanan won the Nobel Prize in economics in 1986. He showed how bureaucracies can become destructive by making decisions that benefit individuals at the expense of the public. The Nobel Committee cited his book *Liberty, Market, and State: Political Economy in the 1980's* (New York: New York University Press, 1985).

13. America's Commitment: Women 2000. A Five-Year Review of Federal Programs Benefiting Women. See http://secretary.state.gov/www/picw/2000commitment/educ_train.html.

14. Ibid., Section B. "Education and Training. The Social Security Administration's career counselors have counseled 1,800 of its employees between 1992 and 2000.

15. Ibid.

16. A search on Google (August 11, 2004) reveals 57 pages for "women networking," but not a single entry for "men networking."

17. Angela Neustatter, "Should Men Work with Children?" *The Independent* (*London*), May 9, 1993, 20.

18. Ibid.

19. The e-mail was to NPR host Marty Nemko from Patrick Hart on June 20, 2004. Nemko's show is on the workplace. I adapted the e-mail slightly to shorten it.

20. U.S. Department of Health and Human Services, Administration on Children, Youth, and

Families, *Child Maltreatment 1997: Reports From the States to the National Child Abuse and Neglect Data System* (Washington, DC: G.P.O., 1999).

21. Link to study at http://www.ask.hrsa.gov/StateProfiles.cfm.
22. Richard Drogin, "Statistical Analysis of Gender Patterns in Wal-Mart Workforce," February 2003, 21. Table 14.
23. Ibid.
24. Ibid.
25. Ann Zimmerman, "Judge Certifies Wal-Mart Suit As Class Action," *Wall Street Journal,* June 23, 2004.
26. Young America Foundation, *Comedy and Tragedy: College Course Descriptions and What They Tell Us About Higher Education Today, 1998–1999* (Herndon, VA: YAF, 1998). The exception is Princeton, which offers more courses in economics than women's studies.
27. See Thomas Sowell, *Civil Rights: Rhetoric or Reality* (New York: Perennial, 1985).
28. Bonnie Zimmerman, president, National Women's Studies Association, gave me these estimates in an interview on February 11, 1999.
29. See Warren Farrell, *Women Can't Hear What Men Don't Say* (New York: Berkley, 1999) for complete documentation of more than 50 of these studies.
30. Carl Hamilton, "Protest Raises Questions about Gender Bias: Domestic Violence Staff Walks Out on Video Showing Abuse of Men," *Cecil Whig* [Maryland], May 16, 2003.
31. Ibid.
32. For extensive documentation of these findings, see *Women Can't Hear What Men Don't Say* (New York: Tarcher/Putnam/Penguin, 1999), Chapter 6, 123–165, and the Appendix, 323–330.
33. Interview by Warren Farrell, February 28, 2003.
34. Ibid., March 13, 1998.
35. Ibid., Feb. 25, 1998.
36. Catalyst, "Women in Leadership: Comparing European and U.S. Women Executives," (New York: Catalyst), 2002. Forty percent of U.S. and 21% of European women still do have mentors.
37. Ibid.

CHAPTER 12   The Genetic Celebrity Pay Gap

1. Credit to Jean Kilbourne, author of *Can't Buy My Love: How Advertising Changes the Way We Think and Feel* (New York.: Simon and Schuster, 2000). See also Nancy Friday, *The Power of Beauty* (New York: Harper Collins, 1996) and my *Why Men Are the Way They Are* (New York: Putnam-Berkely, 1987) Chapter 2.
2. Interview with Heinz Holba, president of L. A. Models, on July 29, 1997, by Betty Mazzetti Hatch, founder of La Belle Agency (which discovered Kathy Ireland, etc.), upon my request.
3. Jeff E. Biddle and Daniel S. Hamermesh, "Beauty, Productivity, and Discrimination: Lawyers' Looks and Lucre," *Journal of Labor Economics* 16, no. 1 (January 1998): 172–201.
4. "Blond Ambition: Leggy Lawyer Poses, Profits," *ABA Journal* 82 (January 1996): 12.
5. Among less-educated women, the "marrying up" percentage is even higher; and among top men executives (e.g., at the Young Presidents' Organization [YPO] in 2003), 100% of the men and all but one woman said "Yes," they expected the husband-to-be would earn more.
6. 2001 data (latest available as of 2004) from U.S. Bureau of the Census, Historical Income Tables, "Families," Table F-15. "Work Experience of Husband and Wife-Married-Couple Families, with Husband Working by Presence of Children Under 18 Years Old and Median and Mean Income: 1976 to 2001"; Table F-16. It is reported 8.1 million or 24% of working wives outearn their working husbands (there are 33.7 million working husbands). However, another 3.2 million wives work whose husbands do not (usually, but not always, the husband is retired, disabled, or a full-time student) and 11.5 million husbands work whose wives do not.

This means 11.3 million wives out of 48 million married couples with at least one partner working outearn their husbands, or 23.4% of wives outearn their husbands and 76.6% of husbands outearn their wives.

7. This is a question I have posed to my audiences between about 1980 and 2004.
8. Krishnan Guruswamy, Associated Press, "Surviving Kin Often Get to Rule," *Washington Times,* October 29, 1994. Chandrika Kumaratunga, herself the daughter of two prime ministers, was married to actor-politician Vijaya Kumaratunga. The other woman candidate, Sarima Dissanayake, had experience only in local government. Khaleda Zia was married to President Zia ur-Rahman.
9. Ibid.
10. Ibid.
11. Ibid. Indira Gandhi's father was Jawaharlal Nehru.
12. United States Congress, *Biographical Directory of the United States Congress: 1774–Present.* This was the pattern prior to the 1981 election of Paula Hawkins from Florida. Since then, women have been elected primarily via their own efforts, though often with the support of their husband's fortunes, as with Diane Feinstein. As of 2004, 8 of 33 women who have served in the Senate succeeded their deceased husbands.

CHAPTER 13   Two Nagging Questions . . .

1. Barbara F. Reskin and Patricia A. Roos, *Job Queues, Gender Queues: Explaining Women's Inroads into Male Occupations* (Philadelphia: Temple University Press, 1990).
2. Myra H. Strober and Carolyn L. Arnold, "The Dynamics of Occupational Segregation Among Bank Tellers," as cited in *Gender in the Workplace* Clair Brown and Joseph A. Pechman, eds. (Washington, DC: Brookings Institute, 1987): 107–148.
3. See, for example, Donald J. Treiman and Heidi I. Hartmann, *Women, Work, and Wages: Equal Pay for Jobs of Equal Value* (Washington, DC: National Academies Press, 1981), the results of a study endorsed by the U.S. Equal Employment Opportunities Commission, and which has been dubbed the "Bible" of the comparative worth movement.
4. June Ellenoff O'Neill, "Comparable Worth," *The Concise Encyclopedia of Economics,* 2002.
5. Mark R. Killingsworth, "Comparable Worth and Pay Equity: Recent Developments in the United States," *Canadian Public Policy* 28, Special Supplement I (2002): S171–186.
6. Judith A. McDonald and Robert J. Thornton, "Private-Sector Experience with Pay Equity in Ontario," *Canadian Public Policy* 24, no. 2 (June 1998): 185–208.
7. See June Ellenoff O'Neill, "Comparable Worth," *The Concise Encyclopedia of Economics,* 2002, http://www.econlib.org/library/Enc/ComparableWorth.html, accessed June 29, 2004. Killingsworth, "Comparable Worth and Pay Equity." McDonald and Thornton, "Private-Sector Experience with Pay Equity in Ontario." All discuss the effects of comparative worth policies.
8. Ibid.
9. [Bill Pullman earnings] Lynn Brenner, "What People Earn," *Parade,* June 22, 1997, 5.

CHAPTER 14   Conclusion: Toward a New Vision of Men and Women

1. Richard Drogin, "Statistical Analysis of Gender Patterns in Wal-Mart Workforce," February 2003, 21. Table 14.
2. Jack C. Smith, James A. Mercy, and Judith M. Conn, "Marital Status and the Risk of Suicide," *American Journal of Public Health* 78, no. 1 (January 1988): 79, Figure 3.
3. Warren Farrell, *Why Men Are the Way They Are* (New York: Berkley, 1988).

Index